Capital and the Cotton Industry
in the Industrial Revolution

CAPITAL AND THE COTTON INDUSTRY

IN THE INDUSTRIAL REVOLUTION

By Seymour Shapiro

Cornell University Press

ITHACA, NEW YORK

Copyright © 1967 by Cornell University

First published 1967

Library of Congress Catalog Card Number: 67–23066

PRINTED IN THE UNITED STATES OF AMERICA
BY KINGSPORT PRESS, INC.

Foreword

THE death of Seymour Shapiro on April 8, 1967, at the age of thirty-nine, has cut short what promised to be an unusually productive career. The present work, while still in manuscript, had won him recognition. He was also the author, in collaboration with Raymond De Roover, of a paper on European banking in the eighteenth century, presented at the Third International Economic History Conference. At the time of his death he was completing a study of British trade begun by the late Judith Williams.

Professor Shapiro graduated from Brooklyn College and was awarded his M.A. degree by Princeton University and his Ph.D. by Columbia University. He had taught at Brooklyn College and, when he died, was Associate Professor of History at the University of Massachusetts–Boston. In the fall of 1967, he was to have joined the Department of History and Western European Studies at Indiana University.

Professor Shapiro had finished the final checking of the manuscript for *Capital and the Cotton Industry in the Industrial Revolution* shortly before his death, and had returned it to the Press to be set into type. As his friends, we gladly take up the task of reading proof. We have tried to make sure that this book is as he would have wished it.

ROBERT M. BERDAHL
MORDECAI MELNITSKY

Boston
June 1967

Acknowledgments

THIS study could not have been completed without the generous help I received from a number of scholars and a host of librarians. I take this opportunity to thank all those who contributed to this work.

I owe my greatest debt—a debt I can never hope to repay—to Professor Robert K. Webb of the Columbia University History Department. I am grateful for his unstinting help at every stage in the progress of this work and for his kindness, encouragement, and tireless patience.

The study was read in its entirety by Professors Herman Ausubel and Shepard B. Clough of the Columbia University History Department and Professors Arthur R. Burns, Charles Issawi, and Stanislaw H. Wellisz of the Columbia University Economics Department. I am obliged to them for their comments, from which I benefited greatly.

Early versions of parts of this work were presented to the Seminar on Advanced Countries of the Economic Research Centers of Columbia University. I wish to thank the members of the Seminar, and Professors Goran Ohlin, Carter Goodrich, and Julius Rubin in particular, for their stimulating comments. I am especially grateful to Professor Ohlin, who not only read a considerable part of this study but also was good enough to lend me the results of his unpublished researches on population.

The burden of reading parts of the final manuscript version of this book was graciously assumed by Professor Robert M. Berdahl,

ACKNOWLEDGMENTS

Mr. Mordecai Melnitsky, Professor Roger W. Prouty, and Miss Martha Tolpin, my colleagues at the University of Massachusetts at Boston; I am grateful to them for having done so.

I have benefited greatly from the advice on statistical methods I received from Professor Melvin Hausner of the Courant Institute of Mathematical Sciences of New York University. In this connection, I also wish to thank Professor Wellisz, who saved me from the embarrassment of committing a statistical blunder. Needless to say, I alone am responsible for any persistence in error.

I am grateful to Miss Barbara Corliss, Miss Carol Feraco, Miss Rita Frank, Miss Leslie Holson, and Miss Martha Lee for skillfully typing the manuscript of this work.

Finally, I wish to thank those whose contributions to this study are entirely intangible: Professor Hans Rosenberg, formerly of the Brooklyn College History Department, who first aroused my interest in economic history, and Professors Frederic C. Lane of The Johns Hopkins University History Department and Jacob Viner of the Princeton University Economics Department, who deepened that interest. I also wish to express my thanks to Professor Norman F. Cantor of the Brandeis University History Department for his personal encouragement and kindness. The greatest of my intangible debts is to my family.

SEYMOUR SHAPIRO

Boston
February 1967

Contents

Tables

Capital and the Cotton Industry
in the Industrial Revolution

Introduction

THE platitude that significant historical questions are raised by contemporary developments is probably more nearly applicable to economic history, in which problems arise from the preoccupations of both historians and economists, than to any other branch of history.[1] Recently, one of the major concerns of economists and

---

[1] A few instances, chosen almost at random, will serve to illustrate the point. In 1953, D. C. Coleman read a paper that appeared in revised form as an excellent article and was reprinted in the Economic History Society's *Essays in Economic History* ("Industrial Growth and Industrial Revolutions," *Economica*, N.S., XXXIII [1956], as reprinted in E. M. Carus-Wilson, ed., *Essays in Economic History; Reprints Edited for the Economic History Society,* III [London, 1962], 334–352 and 334, n. 4). The article bears several marks of having been suggested by Norbert Weiner's works on cybernetics and by a correspondence in *The Times* and articles in *The Listener* and *The Manchester Guardian.* Similarly, in 1962, just before Britain's attempt to gain admission to the Common Market failed, an article appeared in the *Economic History Review* that included the following: "The prospects for trade based on privilege and non-economic influences were becoming gloomy indeed during the last quarter of the eighteenth century. All this time, at England's doorstep there lived a population of 200,000,000 Europeans (as compared with 3,000,000 Americans across the Atlantic). They were England's traditional customers, and until recently her only ones. Yet it was only the old woollen industry that seriously carried on—as it had always done—the 'hard sell' on the continent; the new industries cut their teeth on easier, privileged markets, mostly far away. The privileges could not be held forever" (Ralph Davis, "English Foreign Trade, 1700–1774," *Economic History Review,* 2nd ser., XV [1962], 298). The article was probably written while British entry was under public discussion and the statement resembles the arguments put forward by those favoring British entry into the Common Market.

economic historians has been to identify the determinants of secular economic growth and development.[2]

If economic development is taken to mean industrialization, then a consideration of the circumstances of past successful industrializations must naturally follow. If the term is intended to refer specifically to the industrialization of a backward nation under conditions that preclude foreign help, or make it uncertain or undesirable, the Industrial Revolution has special interest—it can be regarded as the prototype of other industrializations.[3] The current interest in the development of backward nations, however, must not obscure the difference between industrialization and an industrial revolution.

Economic or technological revolutions have taken several forms. There have been instances of revolutions that have trans-

---

[2] In 1953, Jacob Viner observed that there were two remarkable things about the literature of economic development—the immensity of its output during the past decade, and its paucity during the previous decade (as referred to in W. K. Hancock, "Essays in Bibliography and Criticism, XXVII: The Under-Developed Economies," *Economic History Review*, 2nd ser., VI [1954], 310). In 1960, K. E. Berrill published an article stemming from a discontent with "current theoretical models of economic growth which have become increasingly elegant while remaining hopelessly unrealistic. This is a discontent which most economic historians share but surprisingly few of them have used their specialist knowledge to produce more realistic approaches to the development" ("International Trade and the Rate of Economic Growth," *Economic History Review*, 2nd ser., XII [1960], 351). This quotation is not intended to help to set off another "empty boxes" controversy, but only to indicate the lesser concern of economic historians with the problem.

[3] If success is measured in terms of economic welfare, however, it is by no means obvious that industrialization is the only form that successful economic growth or development can take (Jacob Viner, *International Trade and Economic Development* [Glencoe, Ill., 1952], pp. 60–62). In the early 1940's, "the income per farm family in the highest income county in Iowa was thirty-nine times the income per farm family in the lowest income county in Kentucky. It is clear that it could not have been agriculture alone which was responsible for the poverty in Kentucky and that agriculture was not a barrier to prosperity in Iowa" (*ibid.*, p. 65). Viner points out that this figure is exactly the same as that found by Colin Clark to be the ratio between the per capita incomes of China and the United States.

formed the productive process in a single industry or part of a single industry by the introduction of an innovation of limited application. There have been economic revolutions that have transformed a single large sector of an economy. Finally, there have been a number of instances in which an entire economy has been transformed.[4]

The Industrial Revolution in England is the earliest example of the revolutionary transformation of an entire economy. To understand such a revolution, it is necessary to "go beyond the curves of industrial growth and beyond mere mechanization to the vital conjuncture of changes in which population growth, large-scale and extensive industrial investment, and the remarkably pervasive effects of the application of science to industry are amongst the most important in producing the rapidly cumulative process of industrialization."[5] This type of revolution is an important step toward the creation of a modern industrial society. It impinges upon almost every sphere of human endeavor. Indeed, it even alters the landscape.

The Industrial Revolution must be given a *locus,* must be placed not only geographically but also in time. It is necessary, however, to "scrap 1760 as D day and 1832 as V-E day."[6] The period associated with the Industrial Revolution in Britain is

---

[4] The classification used here is derived from Coleman, "Industrial Growth," pp. 334–352, esp. pp. 334–335. A discussion of a number of "Industrial Revolutions" before 1760 and after 1830 can be found in *ibid.* and in G. N. Clark, *The Idea of the Industrial Revolution: David Murray Foundation Lecture* ("Glasgow University Publications," no. 95; Glasgow, 1953). A discussion of a much earlier economic revolution can be found in C. M. Cipolla, *The Economic History of World Population* (London, 1962), esp. pp. 18–24. For an example of a technological revolution through limited innovations see E. M. Carus-Wilson, "An Industrial Revolution of the Thirteenth Century," *Essays,* ed. Carus-Wilson, I (1954), 41–60. Examples of broad economic revolutions are to be found in the histories of the U.S.A., Germany, and Japan.

[5] Coleman, "Industrial Growth," p. 350.

[6] Herbert Heaton, "Criteria of Periodization in Economic History," *Journal of Economic History,* XV (1955), 271.

loosely defined here as starting about 1750, 1760, or 1780 and ending around 1830 or 1850. The definition is functional and varies according to the requirements of the analysis. When, in this discussion, the continuity of development is heavily stressed, the century 1750–1850 is implied because it underscores the arbitrariness of the choice.[7] Where the argument stresses rates of industrial growth, the period here considered is usually 1780–1830. The year 1780 is suggested by a radical rise in the rates of increase in the volume of industrial output during the decade 1780–1789. Since the new high level of increase in industrial output was sustained until well past the middle of the nineteenth century, it is not possible to choose a terminal year that would yield a period even roughly compatible with most other definitions of the Industrial Revolution (see Chapter I). The choice of 1830 is an arbitrary one from the point of view of output growth, but not from the vantage point of some of the possible industrial capital cost indicators (see Chapter II). When other writers' uses of the term Industrial Revolution are being considered, the period implied is 1760–1830, the classical age of the Industrial Revolution. Using these dates makes available the vast literature on the subject and facilitates the comparison of this study with others. The classical dates have the advantage of not stressing the growth of industrial output to the exclusion of other factors like the growth of population (see Chapter I). It is worth emphasizing that this book is concerned with a continuing process rather than a clearly defined period.

---

[7] On the continuity of development, "a Scot says that 'sudden catastrophic change is inconsistent with the slow gradual process of economic evolution.' A Frenchman insists that 'on the vast stage of economic history no sudden shift of scene takes place.' An Englishman adds, 'There is no hiatus in economic development, but always a constant tide of progress and change, in which the new is blended almost imperceptibly with the old.' And an American who has made a special study of inventions concludes that 'invention is not an occasional or rare kind of mental activity, but a continuous feature of the behavior of all the higher organisms,' a continuing process since antiquity rather than a disconnected series of episodes attributable to a few men of genius" (*ibid.*, p. 267).

The geographic limits of the Industrial Revolution in Britain are a less complex matter. Ireland remained largely outside the process of industrialization and unaffected by the Industrial Revolution. This study is therefore limited to England, Wales, and Scotland, for the most part.

Within these limits of time and place, the present study is an attempt to analyze the structure, development, and functioning of the capital markets during the Industrial Revolution. It examines the capital problems that appeared during the Industrial Revolution, their causes, their effects, and their solution. In order to be able to allow for the effects of innovation on the demand for capital, the study is limited to a single industry, the cotton industry. The choice has disadvantages as well as advantages; the industry was atypical in some ways. But most of the industry's atypical qualities do not detract from its usefulness here.[8] The transformation of the cotton industry was an early, obvious manifestation of the Industrial Revolution. Its rate of growth was extremely high (see Chapter VI). The industry was in the vanguard of the Industrial Revolution—in Heaton's phrase: "the hare among the tortoises."

The advantages seem to far outweigh the disadvantages. The industry has been studied intensively, and its principal features have been clearly established for the periods before, during, and after the Industrial Revolution.[9] The history of its technological

---

[8] For what may be an interesting exception see E. A. Wrigley, "The Supply of Raw Materials in the Industrial Revolution," *Economic History Review*, 2nd ser., XV (1962), 6 and 12–14. Wrigley argues that "the most important change in raw material provision which took place was the substitution of inorganic for organic sources of supply, of mineral for vegetable or animal raw materials. This was a *sine qua non* of sustained industrial growth on a large scale, for when industrial growth is based upon vegetable and animal raw materials present success can usually be obtained only at the cost of future difficulties" (p. 1). To this rule the cotton industry was an exception.

[9] The literature is enormous. The starting point for any consideration of the history of the cotton industry before 1780 must still be Alfred P. Wadsworth and Julia de Lacy Mann, *The Cotton Trade and Industrial Lancashire, 1600–1780* (Manchester, 1931). For the period of the Industrial Revolution it

development, in particular, is well known and presents few problems.[10] Its transformation pointed the way to some later market developments in the sense that, after its very earliest days, the industry produced for mass consumption and an international market.[11] The revolutionary transformation of the cotton industry started in what then was the largest free-trade area in the world,[12] and the industry soon acquired an important place in the world market.[13]

The spinning branch of the industry has been emphasized throughout this work, since it was the industry's most important completely revolutionized segment; even as late as 1834, there were two hand looms for every power loom in Britain, and one-quarter of the power looms were water-driven rather than steam-powered.[14]

The study of the Industrial Revolution in Britain helps to

---

must be: G. W. Daniels, *The Early English Cotton Industry* (Manchester, 1920) ; George Unwin, Arthur Hulme, and George Taylor, *Samuel Oldknow and the Arkwrights* (Manchester, 1924) ; R. S. Fitton and A. P. Wadsworth, *The Strutts and the Arkwrights, 1758–1830: A Study of the Early Factory System* (Manchester, 1958) , and the relevant portions of P. Mantoux, *The Industrial Revolution in the Eighteenth Century: An Outline of the Beginnings of the Modern Factory System in England,* trans. Marjorie Vernon (2nd ed. rev.; London, 1927) . For the period following 1830, the starting point is S. J. Chapman, *The Lancashire Cotton Industry* (Manchester, 1904) , and the relevant portions of J. H. Clapham, *An Economic History of Modern Britain* (Cambridge, 1939 [Vol. I], 1932 [Vol. II], 1938 [Vol. III]) .

[10] For the earliest phases of the technological development of the industry see Wadsworth and Mann, *Cotton Trade.* For a detailed description of the development of machinery to 1800, see A. P. Usher, *A History of Mechanical Inventions* (rev. ed.; Boston, 1959) , pp. 258–304.

[11] T. S. Ashton, "Introduction," in Elizabeth Boody Schumpeter, *English Overseas Trade Statistics, 1697–1808* (Oxford, 1960) ; S. B. Saul, *Studies in British Overseas Trade, 1870–1914* (Liverpool, 1960) , ch. 1.

[12] Berrill, "International Trade," p. 358.

[13] Saul, *Studies,* ch. 1.

[14] E. Baines, *A History of the Cotton Manufacture in Great Britain* (London, 1835) , pp. 235–239. In addition, there is much more statistical data about the spinning branch of the industry than about the industry as a whole (see Appendix 12 below) .

discredit the profit inflation theory as an explanation of accelerated capital formation in the late eighteenth century, as a historical generalization, as a guide to economic-development policy for backward nations, and as an element in some theories of economic growth (see Appendix 1). The failure of the theory, however, does not imply that price movements were unimportant.

Considered in conjunction with the growth of population, the movement of prices takes on a new importance.[15] The central fact that emerges from a study of this movement in the late eighteenth century is the more rapid rise of agricultural than industrial prices. As in the Price Revolution, the slower rise in the prices of industrial products was probably a result of pressures generated by population growth. The increase in population probably increased the demand for food and brought into production marginal land with higher costs of production. Industrial prices seem to have risen more slowly than agricultural prices because the supply-and-demand price-elasticities for agricultural products were lower than those for industrial goods.

Population growth probably went through three distinct stages in the eighteenth century: abnormally slow growth before 1750, recovery to a normal rate of growth between 1750 and 1780, and revolutionary growth after 1780. These stages seem to correspond to phases in secular price trends. Price declines only occurred before 1760; there was a strong upward trend in prices during the stages of recovery and revolutionary increase in the rates of population growth. The course of population growth and the cumulative effects of this growth probably help to explain the differential increases in the prices of agricultural and industrial products. This explanation, in turn, suggests the possibility that the latter part of the eighteenth century witnessed the emergence of price pressures in the industrial sector of the economy as a result of increases in the cost of the agricultural inputs of industry.

For the cotton industry, using an imported raw material, the

---

[15] The discussion that follows is based on Chapter I.

price of which was probably not affected by the same pressures, and exporting a significant part of its output, the general differential price movements were probably of less importance than they were for other industries.[16] The coincidence between the spectacular growth of the industry's output in 1780–1789 and rising prices of some factors of production does not invalidate this conclusion. The widespread introduction of the factory system probably was a response to price pressures, but the cotton industry was one of the relatively few industries drawing its raw materials from abroad and exporting a significant part of its output. These considerations, along with the rising productivity resulting from the host of technological innovations in the cotton industry during the second half of the eighteenth century, help to explain the inducements that the industry could offer to entrepreneurs and potential financiers.

Rising costs of industry's agricultural inputs were not the only source of price pressure. Money wages (and perhaps real wages) also rose in industrial areas during the latter part of the eighteenth century. At the same time, the prices of industrial producers' goods rose more rapidly than the prices of industrial consumers' goods.

Taken together, these price trends indicate the existence of strong upward pressures on the prices of the items that entered into the costs of industrial production. One plausible way of looking at the innovations and investments associated with the Industrial Revolution would be to regard them as part of the process whereby these price pressures were prevented from developing into real cost increases. Thus, in some industries laborsaving innovations, for example, prevented wage increases from turning into increases in the labor cost per unit of industrial output.

To some extent the Industrial Revolution probably helped to contribute to these price pressures. It probably helped, for example, to increase the demand for labor in industrial regions and

---

[16] The discussion that follows is based on Chapters I and VI.

thereby contributed to the increase in wages in these regions. Assessment of the Industrial Revolution's contribution to the price pressures depends in part on the causes assigned to population growth, since population growth seems to have affected the pattern of price movements. The causes of eighteenth-century population growth have not yet been definitively established.

The revolutionary population growth of the late eighteenth century could be due to an increase in fertility resulting from earlier marriage or household formation, which in turn could be the result of the increased demand for labor and rising wages brought about by the process of industrialization. If so, then it would be possible to assert that the Industrial Revolution, by contributing to the increase in population, contributed to the divergence between agricultural and industrial prices and thereby to the price pressures in industry. If, on the other hand, population growth was the product of a falling death rate due to greater medical knowledge, increasing application of this knowledge, improvements in personal hygiene and public sanitation, and the like, then it would be difficult to maintain that the Industrial Revolution produced some of the price pressures under consideration. The possibility of a reciprocal relationship between the process of revolutionary industrialization, on the one hand, and the price pressures that may have helped to induce the adoption of innovations and investment in innovation, on the other hand, must not be overlooked.

The transition to the new high rate of growth in industrial production, which is characteristic of an industrial revolution, occurred in two stages.[17] In the 1780's, the new rate was attained in consumers' goods output and, in the 1790's, in producers' goods output. Once attained, the new level of growth was maintained for at least three generations. The increases in the volume and value of industrial production were not wiped out by the concurrent increases in population during any of the periods associated

---

[17] The discussion that follows is based on Chapter I.

with the Industrial Revolution. On the other hand, it must be noted that the rates of increase in the volume and value of industrial output almost always exceeded the increases in population before and after, as well as during, the Industrial Revolution. Even during the one decade between 1700 and 1900 when population fell, the volume of production rose. Since the value of output fell faster than population during this decade, it provided the only exception to the rule that output grew faster than population. These trends in production and population suggest that the period of revolutionary industrialization followed a period of fairly successful industrial development. They also help to explain the lag of producers' goods output behind consumers' goods output at the end of the eighteenth century.

The impressive secular growth in output presupposes a demand for investment in industry and the possibility of offering inducements to the investor.[18] The usury laws, however, set institutional limits to these inducements. Given the fact that the Industrial Revolution coincided with, and perhaps even helped to produce, an era of high interest rates, the legal limits on the rates and the attempts to enforce them were of some importance.

An important effect of the usury laws and the efforts to enforce them was their different impact on various types of borrowers. Although the government was not bound by the usury laws in its long-term or short-term borrowing, all other borrowers were. The attempts made to enforce the 5 per cent maximum rate were not equally effective in all sectors of the economy. The laws probably kept the rate of interest on bills of exchange at or near the legal limit of about 5 per cent, but the cotton manufacturer had no difficulty in obtaining up to 15 or 20 per cent on his book debts and probably had no difficulty in paying the same rate on book debts owed by him. Because of the elaborate legal technicalities surrounding the borrowing of money by the mortgaging of land, the usury laws were probably most easily enforced against the

---

[18] The discussion that follows is based on Chapter II.

landowner, thus tending to divert long-term funds from agriculture.

There seems to have been a definite diversion of landowners' capital out of agriculture during the late eighteenth and early nineteenth centuries. This was probably due in part to the difficulty of evading the usury laws in agriculture—a difficulty that became critical in the late eighteenth century when "the" rate of interest pushed against the ceiling set by the laws and even exceeded it. The diversion was also probably partly due to the tendency of some landlords to regard investment in agriculture as a defensive measure undertaken during agricultural depressions in order to protect their rent rolls and the long-term productive powers of their lands by inducing their better tenants to remain. During agricultural booms like the one during the late eighteenth and early nineteenth centuries, the burden of investment seems to have been thrown onto the shoulders of the tenants. Although the English landlord rarely invested directly in the cotton industry, he sometimes built or converted buildings for rental to the entrepreneur. He might go as far in the direction of specializing his investment as installing a source of power and devices for transmitting this power, but he rarely, if ever, went beyond that. A further and perhaps more important consequence of this diversion of capital may have been the relief of some of the pressure being exerted on the millowner by other competitors for capital, notably the government.

The usury laws also probably tended to encourage the reinvestment of industrial profits by limiting the yield on some alternative investments.

Significant as they were, the importance of the usury laws and of interest rates in general should not be exaggerated. Because so much of the long-term investment in the cotton industry was personal in nature, interest rates played only a limited role in regulating the flow of long-term investment. The difficulties encountered by the entrepreneur in search of long-term capital were due to the specific nature of savings rather than to any absolute shortage of capital. In this, as in other respects, the long-term capital market was less highly developed than was the short-term market. The eighteenth-century investor was not highly sensitive to the yields on his investments.

The manufacturer needed both short-term and long-term capital. He rarely got either from foreign sources. While he needed perhaps twice as much long-term as short-term capital, he found that he had a much more efficient mechanism available for the mobilization of the latter than for obtaining access to the former.

His first resort in his search for short-term capital was likely to be the developing network of formal and quasi-formal banking institutions.[19] Within the banking "system," almost the entire burden of distributing short-term capital to the cotton industry fell on the country banks. The Bank of England had other interests. The London banks were too distant except for firms that had special reasons for seeking them out. As soon as the savings banks became significant, their investments were restricted by law to government securities. Except in Scotland, the joint-stock banks developed too late to be of any importance during the early stages of the Industrial Revolution.

The country banks, however, could not have performed their function of distribution without the aid of some subsidiary institution. The London banks, the bill brokers, and the bill dealers helped to channel the supplies of short-term capital available in agricultural areas to the capital-short cotton-textile-producing areas. Once these funds reached the country banks, they were usually distributed to the cotton manufacturers through the discount of bills of exchange. Discounting involved lending; the discounter was a lender, not a purchaser.

The operation of the mechanism of transfer during the Industrial Revolution depended on a number of characteristics of the British economy. The demand for short-term capital was highly

---

[19] The discussion that follows is based on Chapter III.

periodic in both agriculture and the cotton industry. Agricultural production was highly seasonal by its very nature. The demand for yarn and cloth was also seasonal, but the cotton industry was not subject to the very severe crises of production (and hence of demand for capital) that were a normal part of agriculture. The industry was subject, however, to periodic interruption of production. The weather might suddenly make roads impassable or freeze the water needed to turn the water wheels. The fact that industry and agriculture were out of phase helps to account for the periodic appearance of transferable surpluses of short-term capital in agricultural regions and the periodic demand for them in industrial areas. Since rediscounting in London was an essential feature of the transfer mechanism, it was necessary that there be a difference between the London and provincial rates of interest. Both of these characteristics of the economy tended to be modified during the Industrial Revolution. Innovation in industrial technique probably tended to smooth out the productive process in industry and thereby to reduce the periodic divergence between agricultural and industrial demands for short-term capital. The reduction of the frictions that had prevented the easy flow of short-term capital in the provinces probably produced the gradual convergence of London and provincial rates of interest. Nevertheless, these characteristics of the economy persisted.

Having tapped the reservoirs of short-term capital controlled by the banks, the cotton manufacturer was still far from having exhausted the available supply or his ingenuity.[20] One of the characteristic features of the supply of short-term capital in the cotton industry was the variety of sources from which it came. The cotton broker, the shopkeeper, the laborer, and even the government were all laid under contribution. The role of the broker was a relatively simple one—he was financing a customer. But at first glance, the appearance of the laborer and the shopkeeper as suppliers of short-term capital seems rather surprising.

---

[20] The discussion that follows is based on Chapter IV.

The long-pay, carried over from the putting-out system, made the worker an involuntary supplier of short-term capital. Although the long-pay had a secondary utility as a disciplinary device, its persistence was probably due to the means-of-payment problem. The appalling state of the currency turned the manufacturer into a quasi-banker in the sense that he was an issuer of acknowledgments of indebtedness that passed current; it also turned the local shopkeeper into a quasi-banker in the sense that he became a dealer in debts.

The means-of-payment problem was to some extent a reflection of the low priority accorded to the needs of laborers and factory owners in the eighteenth century. The shortage of the means of payment did not extend to those used for the large payments; it was limited to those necessary for small payments like wages. It is not surprising to find a society marked by class distinctions with a long-lived, though inconvenient, dual means-of-payment structure. It can be conjectured that the reform of the currency after the Napoleonic Wars was a relatively early victory of Benthamite principles.

The manufacturer attempted to solve the currency problem in a number of ways. He could, and did, increase the velocity of circulation of the available currency by paying half of his workmen in the morning, sending them off to pay their debts and make purchases, and after reacquiring the coins from the shopkeepers, paying the rest of his workers. He could, and did, economize on the means of payment by adopting the long-pay and by introducing a system of truck payments, though the latter device did not, in all probability, improve his overall capital position. Alternatively, he could and did pay his workers—particularly in Lancashire —with small bills of exchange that had come into his possession, and he thus increased his supply of means for making small payments by using an instrument that had originally been created for making relatively large payments. Since the bill had to be discounted with a shopkeeper, the shopkeeper was drawn into the position of financing the consumption of the worker and thereby indirectly financing the manufacturer, while at the same time helping to solve the manufacturer's means-of-payment problem.

The manufacturer also paid his hands by means of promises to pay. These took a variety of forms. They could be shopnotes, simple promissory notes, or tokens. These too could be, and were, discounted by shopkeepers or were accepted by the community as a whole. Hence these acknowledgments of indebtedness also served as a basis for the indirect financing of the manufacturer's production.

In a few crises the government reluctantly supplied the manufacturer with short-term capital by lending him exchequer bills, and on at least one occasion the government was aided by the Bank of England, which purchased some bills in order to support the market. Although this type of action on the part of either the government or the Bank was quite rare, one aspect of government policy did, in all probability, aid the manufacturer in obtaining short-term capital. The receivers of public revenues were permitted to invest their receipts between the time they received them and the time that they had to account for them. Some of this money was probably used to discount bills of exchange. Thus public monies could be used to supplement the manufacturer's supply of short-term capital.

The manufacturer's search for long-term capital presented different problems for solution.[21] The structure and functioning of British banking institutions relegated them to a role of relative insignificance in the long-term capital market. The Scottish banks, the English joint-stock banks, and the Welsh joint-stock banks were exceptions to the rule. The English and Welsh joint-stock banks, however, did not make their appearance until the mid-twenties; hence they were of very little importance during most of the period associated with the Industrial Revolution.

The relative backwardness of the long-term capital market, with the concomitant emphasis on localization of investment and

---

[21] The discussion that follows is based on Chapter V.

personal contact as a prerequisite for much long-term industrial investment, made personal savings an extremely important element in the capital supply of the entrepreneur. These considerations limited the available supply of long-term loans as well as the supply of participating capital. Personal savings were mobilized by the partnership, one of the oldest and certainly the most personal type of business organization.

The entrepreneurs, who invested their personal savings, were drawn from a very large portion of the British social spectrum and hence were able to tap many different pools of long-term capital. This fact, in conjunction with the wide variety of sources from which the cotton industry drew its *short-term* capital, may help to account for the sustained growth of the industry during the Industrial Revolution. The supply of capital was not dependent on the fortunes of any single group or single type of institution outside the industry. This growth was also sustained by the heavy reinvestment of profits in spite of the lack of agreement on what profits were.

The rate of reinvestment probably depended in part on personal and social considerations—for example, the extent to which capital accumulation was a road to social distinction. It also depended on economic factors like the relative profitability of the cotton industry or the need to invest in order to stave off disaster by making a previous investment profitable.[22]

The last point is worth stressing. Investment can be regarded as a response to opportunity. It can also be regarded as a response to adverse pressure, an attempt to hold a position that had already been stormed. Agricultural investment by landlords during the depressions of the second quarter of the eighteenth century and the third decade of the nineteenth century seems to have been of this sort. Adversity also had its uses in the cotton industry in the 1820's and 1830's, when depression in the spinning branch of the industry seems to have helped to induce a large volume of invest-

---

[22] The discussion that follows is based on Chapter VI.

ment by spinners in power-loom weaving. The object of this investment seems to have been to combat the cost-price squeeze in spinning by creating integrated spinning-weaving firms.

The statistical evidence regarding the cotton industry seems to show the same upward price pressures that were noted in industry as a whole in the late eighteenth century. Innovation and investment in innovation can be regarded as means used to combat these upward price pressures. In the realm of investment, the plowing back of profits seems to have been crucial. The size of the profits from which reinvestment came was probably a result of rising productivity and of production in large quantities for a large national and international market.

Part I

Background

Chapter I

Some Statistics of the Industrial Revolution

LITTLE if any statistical data are available on aggregate profits and investment in the eighteenth century or even for part of the nineteenth century.[1] The situation is somewhat better as regards production, price, and wage data. Since there is disagreement

---

[1] Profit statements are rare for the eighteenth century and even for the first half of the nineteenth century. Actual rates of profit would be difficult to determine without a very careful study of individual firm records, and such a study would run into serious accounting problems. Thus, for example, there would be a problem of accounting conventions. In the 1830's, cost statements of cotton mills showed a depreciation allowance of 7.5% for replacement of machinery and 2.5% for maintenance of steam engines and buildings. Fifty years later these allowances were the same (M. Blaug, "The Productivity of Capital in the Lancashire Cotton Industry during the Nineteenth Century," *Economic History Review*, 2nd ser., XIII [1961], 361). This was evidently an accounting convention that did not change. It seems unlikely that actual depreciation remained constant. This convention would produce a serious problem of interpretation for anyone attempting to determine the rate of profit. Conceivably a similar problem exists for the study of eighteenth-century profit rates. A further difficulty stems from the lack of agreement in the eighteenth century and at least the first half of the nineteenth century about the definition of profit. This lack of agreement is seen both in business practice and in economic theory. On practice see Chapter IV below; on theory see G. S. L. Tucker, *Progress and Profits in British Economic Thought, 1650–1850* (Cambridge, 1960), esp. ch. 5. A further difficulty arises when one shifts from a discussion of the rate of profit of a single firm to a discussion of the rate of profit of an entire economy or a sector of an economy (see Alfred Marshall, *Principles of Economics: An Introductory Volume* [8th ed.; New York, 1949], pp. 620–621).

about the interpretation of eighteenth-century wage data, much of this discussion will focus on the rates of change in production, prices, and wages.[2]

The calculation and analysis of the rates of increase in industrial production during the eighteenth and nineteenth centuries make it possible to determine the timing, size, and nature of the change in output associated with the Industrial Revolution. Tables 1 and 2 show the rates of growth of the physical volume of industrial production in the United Kingdom from 1710 to 1899.[3]

The 1780's and 1790's mark turning points in the growth of the economy's output. This observation does not mean that the larg-

---

[2] Much of the disagreement over wage data is essentially part of the disagreement about real wages and the standard of living during the Industrial Revolution.

A number of difficulties exist that are peculiar to any attempt to use aggregate statistical data to study the Industrial Revolution. By the start of the eighteenth century, most statistics on England and Wales were combined, and "England" often means England and Wales (see T. S. Ashton, "Introduction," in Elizabeth Boody Schumpeter, *English Overseas Trade Statistics, 1697–1808* [Oxford, 1960]). Although he discusses foreign trade statistics, for the most part, Ashton's discussion has wider application because other statistics are derived from foreign trade figures. This is particularly true of production indexes. For the eighteenth century, most of the available statistics cover England and Wales, and very little statistical information is available for Scotland and Ireland; on the other hand, most nineteenth-century statistics cover England, Wales, Scotland, and Ireland, and it is often next to impossible to arrive at separate figures for England and Wales. For this reason, strictly comparable statistics that bridge the eighteenth and nineteenth centuries frequently cannot be obtained. In a few instances, however, an index covering England and Wales in the eighteenth century is comparable to a similar index covering the United Kingdom in the nineteenth century. The reasons for assuming comparability will always be stated when this kind of comparison is made (see the Introduction to the Appendixes below).

[3] These rates are given as the percentage increase in the index of the average annual physical volume of production in a decade over the index of the average annual physical volume of production in the previous decade. Unless otherwise stated, all other rates of growth, rates of change, rates of increase, and their opposites have been calculated in an analogous way.

Table 1. Growth of the volume of total industrial production,
United Kingdom, 1710–1899

| Years | % increases in average annual physical volume | | Rank of each increase * | |
	A Including building	B Excluding building	C Rank of A	D Rank of B
1710–1719	14	13	14	16
1720–1729	12	13	15	15
1730–1739	3	4	19	18
1740–1749	8	4	17	19
1750–1759	11	15	16	13
1760–1769	7	5	18	17
1770–1779	14	14	13	14
1780–1789	29	29	9	8
1790–1799	40	39	1	3
1800–1809	34	36	7	6
1810–1819	23	23	10	10
1820–1829	36	39	5	4
1830–1839	39	46	2	1
1840–1849	37	38	4	5
1850–1859	39	39	3	2
1860–1869	36	28	6	9
1870–1879	31	32	8	7
1880–1889	18	22	12	11
1890–1899	20	17	11	12

* Ranks run from 1, largest increase, to 19, smallest.

Source: Based on Appendix 2. For the sources and methods of computation of Table 1 see the Appendix. The ranks in columns *C* and *D* were determined from the more precise figures in the Appendix.

est rates of increase in production occurred in those decades; they did not. The significance of the last two decades of the eighteenth century lies in the transition to a new higher level of sustained growth of the volume of industrial output.

Three of the indexes, the index of the physical volume of total industrial production (including building), the index of the physical volume of total industrial production (excluding building) (see Appendix 2), and the index of the physical volume of

Table 2. Growth of the volume of industrial consumers' and producers' goods output, United Kingdom, 1710–1899

Years	% increases in average annual physical volume		Rank of each increase *	
	A Producers' goods	*B* Consumers' goods	*C* Rank of *A*	*D* Rank of *B*
1710–1719	14	11	16	16
1720–1729	18	11	12	15
1730–1739	4	4	18	18
1740–1749	0	5	19	17
1750–1759	23	17	10	11
1760–1769	16	4	14	19
1770–1779	15	14	15	13
1780–1789	10	34	17	5
1790–1799	30	38	9	3
1800–1809	32	39	7	2
1810–1819	22	23	11	9
1820–1829	42	37	5	4
1830–1839	50	45	3	1
1840–1849	60	28	1	8
1850–1859	56	30	2	7
1860–1869	48	16	4	12
1870–1879	37	30	6	6
1880–1889	31	14	8	14
1890–1899	18	17	13	10

* Ranks run from 1, the largest increase, to 19, the smallest.

Source: Based on Appendix 3. For the sources and the methods of computation of Table 2 see the Appendix. The ranks in columns *C* and *D* were determined from the more precise figures in the Appendix.

industrial consumers' goods production, behave alike. The behavior of the index of the physical volume of industrial producers' goods production (see Appendix 3) differs significantly from the others.

Between the periods 1710–1719 and 1770–1779, the increase in the volume of total industrial output (including building) fluctuated between a low of 3 per cent and a high of 14 per cent. The 29 per cent increase in 1780–1789 was more than twice as large as the previous high of 14 per cent in 1770–1779. From 1780–1789 through 1890–1899, the rate of growth never fell as low as the peak rate before 1780–1789.

Because of the difficulties of measuring the volume of eighteenth-century building, the index of the physical volume of total industrial production (excluding building) is probably more accurate than the one that includes building. Nevertheless, both indexes behave alike. From 1710–1719 through 1770–1779, the rate of growth in the volume of industrial output (excluding building) fluctuated between 4 per cent and 15 per cent. The 29 per cent increase in 1780–1789 was more than twice the 1770–1779 increase and nearly twice the peak rate before 1780–1789. Between 1780–1789 and 1890–1899, the rate of growth never fell as low as this pre–1780–1789 peak.

The changes in the volume of output of industrial consumers' goods differ only slightly from the changes in industrial output (including and excluding building). From 1710–1719 through 1770–1779, the increase in consumers' goods production fluctuated between 4 per cent and 17 per cent. The 1780–1789 increase of 34 per cent is two and one-half times as large as that of 1770–1779 and twice the peak before 1780–1789.

Although the rates of growth of industrial production never fell below their pre–1780–1789 peaks after 1770–1779, the rate of increase in industrial consumers' goods output did fall slightly below its pre–1780–1789 peak twice between 1780–1789 and 1890–1899. In 1860–1869, the difference was 0.8 per cent; in 1880–1889, it was 3.4 per cent. Since cotton yarn and goods formed a substantial part of industrial consumers' goods output, the first fall can be traced directly to the "Cotton Famine." The second can probably be traced to the impact of the Great Depression and perhaps also to some overweighting of textiles in the consumers' goods index.[4]

---

[4] On the Cotton Famine see J. H. Clapham, *An Economic History of Modern Britain*, II (Cambridge, 1932), 80, 220–225, 384, and 434; and W. O. Henderson, *The Lancashire Cotton Famine, 1861–1865* ("Publications of the

The pattern of growth in the output of industrial producers' goods does not conform closely to the patterns for total industrial production and industrial consumers' goods production. From 1710–1719 through 1770–1779, the rate of increase in industrial producers' goods output fluctuated between 0 and 23 per cent. This range of fluctuation is larger than any of the others and indicates a higher degree of secular instability in producers' goods output than in the other categories of production.[5]

The pattern of growth in the output of producers' goods is unique in having a turning point in 1790–1799 rather than in 1780–1789. The 10 per cent growth of production in 1780–1789 ranked seventeenth in a series of nineteen increases; the simultaneous increases in the other kinds of industrial output ranked ninth, eighth, and fifth. On the other hand, the 1790–1799 increase of 30 per cent (with a rank of 9) is comparable to the 1780–1789 increases in the other types of production (29 per cent, 29 per cent, and 34 per cent) .

The 1790–1799 rate of growth in producers' goods output was 3 times that of the preceding decade and 1.3 times as large as the highest rate before 1790–1799. During the eleven decades from 1790 to 1899, the increase in the volume of industrial producers' goods production fell below the pre–1790–1799 level only twice, in 1810–1819 and 1890–1899. In the first of these decades the increase was 1 per cent less and in the second 5 per cent less than the peak rate before 1790–1799 (see Table 2) .

University of Manchester, Economic History Series," no. 9; Manchester, 1934) . On the Great Depression see H. L. Beales, "The 'Great Depression' in Industry and Trade," *Essays in Economic History: Reprints Edited for the Economic History Society,* ed. E. M. Carus-Wilson, I (London, 1954) , 406–415; W. W. Rostow, *The British Economy of the Nineteenth Century* (Oxford, 1948) , pp. 58–89 and 145–160. Criticism of the overweighting of textiles was voiced in Arthur D. Gayer, W. W. Rostow, and Anna Jacobson Schwartz, *The Growth and Fluctuation of the British Economy, 1790–1850* (Oxford, 1953) , II, 691–692. Also see Appendix 3 below.

[5] The other ranges are as follows: total industrial production (including building) , 3% to 14%; total industrial production (excluding building) , 4% to 15%; industrial consumers' goods production, 4% to 17%.

The 1780's and 1790's clearly mark a turning point in the development of British industry. In the eighties, the rates of growth of the volume of industrial production jumped to a new high level—a level that, except for a moderate dip in 1810–1819, was sustained for at least a century. The industrial consumers' goods sector led the way in the 1780's; the industrial producers' goods sector followed in the next decade. Since the industrial producers' goods sector was smaller than the industrial consumers' goods sector, the movements in the rates of growth of total industrial production more closely resemble the latter than the former.[6]

The lag of the turning point for the growth of industrial producers' goods output behind that for consumers' goods is significant. It suggests that the transition to the high level of industrial growth after 1780 was aided by the existence of excess or underutilized capacity that could be adapted to production of industrial consumers' goods. This assumption is consistent with other evidence. In the 1780's and 1790's, there were instances in which cotton mills, printworks, bleach works, dye works, and other industrial enterprises were set up in existing corn mills or other mills that were rented or purchased.[7] Attics or other rooms of

[6] There was a definite tendency in the eighteenth and nineteenth centuries for the consumers' goods industries to produce a declining percentage of the total industrial output of the United Kingdom, as indicated by the following estimates.

Value of the production of the consumers-goods industries as a percentage of the value of total industrial output: 1740, 84%; 1783, 71%; 1812, 69%; 1851, 60%; 1881, 53%; 1907, 42% (Walther G. Hoffmann, *British Industry, 1700–1950* [Oxford, 1955], p. 22, table 3).

[7] J. Graham, "The Chemistry of Calico Printing from 1790 to 1835 and the History of Printworks in the Manchester District from 1760 to 1846," MS book, n.d. (from internal evidence 1847 or 1848), Manchester Central Library, pp. 429 and *passim;* McConnel and Kennedy to A. Lane, Jan. 22, 1796, McConnel and Kennedy MSS, Letter Books, Lewis Library of Commerce, University of Manchester; Indenture between Sir Harbord Harbord . . . and Daniel Burton. . . , Jan. 1, 1784, Burton Deeds, no. 3, Manchester Central Library; George Unwin, Arthur Hulme, and George Taylor, *Samuel Oldknow and the Arkwrights* (Manchester, 1924), pp. 118 and 121.

existing houses or other buildings were often used in the early years of the Industrial Revolution in the cotton industry, particularly when hand or horse power was used to drive the machinery.[8] By 1790, much of this excess capacity may have been absorbed. Industrial production not only continued to increase in the 1790's but actually increased at a higher rate (see Table 2).

Changes in the value of the output of industrial consumers' and producers' goods were similar to changes in the volume of output, at least for the period for which it is possible to calculate both values and volumes. Table 3 presents an estimate of the changes

Table 3. Growth of the value and volume of industrial consumers' and producers' goods output, United Kingdom, 1710–1819 *

Years	% increases in average annual value		% increases in average annual volume	
	A Consumers' goods	B Producers' goods	C Consumers' goods	D Producers' goods
1710–1719	13	9	11	14
1720–1729	3	14	11	18
1730–1739	−4	−2	4	4
1740–1749	9	5	5	0
1750–1759	21	22	17	23
1760–1769	10	31	4	16
1770–1779	25	15	14	15
1780–1789	43	22	34	10
1790–1799	61	42	38	30
1800–1809	88		39	32
1810–1819	32		23	22

* This comparison is equivalent to one between price and output changes.

Source: Based on Appendixes 4, 5, 7, and 8. For the sources and methods of calculation of Table 3 see the Appendixes.

in the value of industrial consumers' and producers' goods output.

[8] John Kennedy, "Brief Notice of My Early Recollections," *Miscellaneous Papers on Subjects Connected With the Manufactures of Lancashire* (Manchester, 1849), p. 4.

From 1710–1719 through 1770–1779, the rates of change in the index of the value of industrial consumers' goods production (see Appendix 7) fluctuated between −4 per cent and 25 per cent. From 25 per cent in 1770–1779, the increase in value jumped to 43 per cent in 1780–1789. The 1780–1789 percentage increase in value is 1.7 times the increase for 1770–1779; the percentage increase in volume for 1780–1789 is 2.4 times the increase for 1770–1779. The transition in the 1780's to a high level of increase in industrial consumers' goods output was, therefore, more radical when measured in terms of volume than value. Unfortunately, it is not possible to estimate the value of consumers' goods production beyond 1810–1819, because the only suitable index of consumers' goods prices ends at 1823. Nevertheless, it is clear that the new higher level of increases in the value of industrial consumers' goods output was sustained for at least the three decades from 1780–1789 through 1800–1809.

Although the increase in the value of consumers' goods production for 1810–1819 fell below the 1780–1789 level to 32 per cent, it still was above the pre–1780–1789 peak of 25 per cent. This fall in the rate of increase is not peculiar to the value of consumers' goods production; the increase in the volume of consumers' goods production jumped from 14 per cent in 1770–1779 to 34 per cent in the following decade, stayed above that level for two more decades, and then fell to 23 per cent in 1810–1819. Except for 1720–1729, the increases in the values and volumes of industrial consumers' goods output rose and fell together during the ten decades for which the movements can be determined (see Table 3).

For the volume of industrial producers' goods output, 1790–1799 was the decade of transition to a new higher level of sustained growth. The evidence for a climb to a higher level of sustained growth in the value of industrial producers' goods production is less clear-cut. Because the only suitable index of producers' goods prices (see Appendix 5) ends at 1801, it is impossible to carry the estimates of the value of producers' goods output beyond 1790–1799. Hence it is impossible to determine with certainty if the rise in the rate of increase in the value of production from 22 per cent in 1780–1789 to 42 per cent in 1790–1799 signaled a take-off to a new level of sustained growth paralleling the concurrent movement in the volume of production. It seems likely that for several decades, except for 1810–1819, the rate of increase in the value of industrial producers' goods output continued at or above the level reached in 1790–1799, but this cannot be proved. The rates of increase in the several indexes of the volume of production were relatively high from 1820–1829 to 1850–1859. During these decades, a fall in the rate of increase in the value of producers' goods output to a level below that of 1790–1799 would have required a catastrophic drop in the prices of producers' goods—a drop that evidently did not occur.[9]

There were some general differences between the behavior of the indexes of the volume of producers' and consumers' goods output and the indexes of the value of producers' and consumers' goods output. Neither volume index fell, while both value indexes fell in 1730–1739. The decreases in the value indexes were the result of price falls. In addition, the decline in the rate of growth of the volume of industrial producers' goods output from 15 per cent in 1770–1779 to 10 per cent in 1780–1789, which ran counter to the trend in each of the other three categories of industrial production, did not have a counterpart in the concurrent in-

---

[9] In the absence of an index of producers' goods prices, it is necessary to fall back on the available indexes of the general level of prices. Two of these indexes are reproduced and graphically compared in E. Victor Morgan, *The Study of Prices and the Value of Money* (Historical Association pamphlets, no. 53; London, 1950), pp. 25–26 and chart 2 opposite p. 25. These indexes, the Silberling index of wholesale prices, 1780–1850, as reproduced from Norman J. Silberling, "British Prices and Business Cycles, 1780–1850," *Review of Economic Statistics*, V (1923), 219–262, and the Jevons and Sauerbeck indexes as linked by Sir Walter Layton and George Crowther *An Introduction to the Study of Prices* (London, 1938), pp. 235–237, show falling prices during much of the first half of the nineteenth century, but the decline in prices does not seem to be large enough to offset the rise in the volume of production (see Appendix 6 below).

creases in the value of the output of industrial producers' goods, which went from 15 per cent in 1770–1779 to 22 per cent in 1780–1789 (see Table 3).

It seems almost certain, therefore, that 1780–1789 marks the transition to a higher rate of growth in the value, as well as the volume, of the output of industrial consumers' goods. It seems likely, though not certain, that 1790–1799 marks the transition to a new higher rate of growth in the value, as well as the volume, of the output of industrial producers' goods. Finally, it is extremely likely that ideal indexes of the value and volume of total industrial output (including and excluding building) of the United Kingdom or England and Wales in the eighteenth century would all show a turning point in the 1780's, because such indexes would be heavily weighted with consumers' goods.

Estimates of the changes in the per capita industrial output of either the United Kingdom or England and Wales would undoubtedly constitute a better measure of industrial growth than the changes in the aggregate volumes and values of the various types of industrial production. Unfortunately, it is not possible to construct formal per capita output indexes for the United Kingdom or for England and Wales. Nevertheless, a comparison between the rates of growth of the population of England and Wales and the industrial output of the United Kingdom would have considerable validity.[10] Tables 4, 5, and 6 make it possible to

---

[10] Since it is not possible to construct a good index of the population of the United Kingdom in the eighteenth century, it is therefore impossible to construct an index of the per capita industrial output of the United Kingdom. There is a good series of estimates of the population of England and Wales in the eighteenth century (see Appendixes 9 and 10). The best population estimates for Ireland are constructed by a substantially different method and are probably less accurate. See the following works of K. H. Connell: *The Population of Ireland, 1750–1845* (Oxford, 1950); "Land and Population in Ireland, 1780–1845," *Economic History Review*, 2nd ser., II (1950), 278–289; and "The Population of Ireland in the 18th Century," *Economic History Review*, 1st ser., XVI (1946), 111–124. In the book, Connell accepted the census figures for 1821, 1831, and 1841 and constructed estimates for various years from 1687 to 1791, but he cautioned that all these figures

compare the rates of increase in the population of England and Wales with the rates of growth of the industrial production of the United Kingdom in the eighteenth century.

The rate of increase in the volume of total industrial production (including building) never fell below the rate of population growth during the eighteenth or nineteenth centuries. The rate of increase in the volume of total industrial output (excluding building) fell below the rate of population growth in only one decade, 1760–1769, and in that instance an expansion in the volume of building served to keep the rate of increase of the total volume of industrial production above the rate of population growth (see Table 4). The low level of increase in total industrial production (excluding building) coincided with what has been called "the biggest building boom of the century." [11]

Except for this decade, the rate of increase in the volume of

---

"and especially those for the century before 1780, may remain seriously inaccurate" (*Population of Ireland*, p. 25). For Scotland, the situation is even worse; there is no suitable continuous series for the eighteenth century. In the absence of an index of the industrial production of England and Wales, it is not even possible to construct an index of the per capita industrial output of England and Wales.

Although it is not possible to construct a formal index of per capita industrial production, a comparison between changes in the population of England and Wales and increases in the industrial output of the United Kingdom is useful. This procedure may seem risky, but there is an extenuating circumstance. The same shortage of Irish and Scottish statistical data that makes it impossible to construct good United Kingdom population estimates resulted in a useful distortion of the various indexes of the industrial production of the United Kingdom. For the eighteenth century, these indexes are based on statistics that actually refer in large measure to England and Wales, although the indexes purport to cover the entire United Kingdom (see the discussion of sources in Hoffmann, *British Industry*, pp. 227–304, and the discussion and notes in Appendix 2 below). This circumstance makes the proposed comparison a valid one for the eighteenth century without necessarily accepting or rejecting the assumption that an index of the industrial output of England and Wales is also an exact index of the industrial production of the United Kingdom.

[11] T. S. Ashton, *Economic Fluctuations in England, 1700–1800* (Oxford, 1959), p. 98.

Table 4. Growth of population in England and Wales and of the volume of total industrial production, United Kingdom, 1710–1899

Years	A % increases in average annual population *	% increases in average annual physical volume of total industrial production	
		B Including building	C Excluding building
1710–1719	2.0	14	13
1720–1729	0.0	12	13
1730–1739	−0.4	3	4
1740–1749	1.9	8	4
1750–1759	5.1	11	15
1760–1769	6.8	7	5
1770–1779	6.7	14	14
1780–1789	7.3	29	29
1790–1799	9.4	40	39
1800–1809	12.0	34	36
1810–1819	14.8	23	23
1820–1829	18.1	36	39
1830–1839	12.7	39	46
1840–1849	13.4	37	38
1850–1859	11.8	39	39
1860–1869	12.4	36	28
1870–1879	13.6	31	32
1880–1889	13.3	18	22
1890–1899	11.8	20	17

* Population is treated throughout in the same way as volumes and values of output in order to obtain comparable percentage-increase figures.

Source: Based on Appendixes 2, 9, and 10. For the sources and methods of calculation of Table 4 see the Appendixes.

industrial consumers' goods output remained above the rate of population growth from 1710–1719 through 1810–1819 (see Table 5). This is not surprising, since the constituents of the index of the physical volume of total industrial production (excluding building) resemble the components of the index of the physical volume of industrial consumers' goods production (see Appendixes 2 and 3).

From 1710–1719 through 1810–1819, there was only one decade in which the rate of increase in the volume of producers' goods output was less than the rate of population growth. The exception, 1740–1749, may have been due to the severe depression in construction between 1739 and 1750, which was probably caused by a tightening of credit, and the dearth of food in the early

Table 5. Growth of population in England and Wales and of the volume and value of industrial consumers' goods production, United Kingdom, 1710–1819

| Years | A % increases in average annual population * | Consumers' goods production | |
		B Physical volume	C Value
1710–1719	2.0	11	13
1720–1729	0.0	11	3
1730–1739	−0.4	4	−4
1740–1749	1.9	5	9
1750–1759	5.1	17	21
1760–1769	6.8	4	10
1770–1779	6.7	14	25
1780–1789	7.3	34	43
1790–1799	9.4	38	61
1800–1809	12.0	39	88
1810–1819	14.8	23	32

* In order to obtain comparable percentage-increase figures, population is treated in the same way as values and volumes of output.

Source: Based on Appendixes 3, 4, 7, 9, and 10. For the sources and methods of calculation of Table 5 see the Appendixes.

forties.[12] It seems more likely, however, that the failure of the volume of industrial producers' goods output to rise in 1740–1749 was due to the cumulative effects of the population stagnation of 1720–1729 and the slight population decline of 1730–1739. The population trend probably affected the demand for consumers'

---

[12] Ashton, *Economic Fluctuations*, p. 95. According to John Summerson, "The war period of 1743–8 seems to have witnessed building activity at its lowest ebb" (*Georgian London* [London, 1945], p. 94).

goods more quickly than the demand for producers' goods. The trend did not result in an actual fall in the volume of output of consumers' goods, but the rate of increase in output, which had been 11 per cent in 1710–1719, changed very little in 1720–1729, the decade of population stagnation, and fell to 4 per cent in 1730–1739, the decade of population decline. Producers' goods output followed a similar course with a lag of about a decade.

Table 6. Growth of population in England and Wales and of the volume and value of industrial producers' goods production, United Kingdom, 1710–1819

Years	*A* % increases in average annual population *	% increases in average annual producers' goods production	
		B Physical volume	*C* Value
1710–1719	2.0	14	9
1720–1729	0.0	18	14
1730–1739	−0.4	4	−2
1740–1749	1.9	0	5
1750–1759	5.1	23	22
1760–1769	6.8	16	31
1770–1779	6.7	15	15
1780–1789	7.3	10	22
1790–1799	9.4	30	42
1800–1809	12.0	32	
1810–1819	14.8	22	

* In order to obtain comparable percentage-increase figures, population is treated in the same way as values and volumes of output.

Source: Based on Appendixes 3, 5, 8, 9, and 10. For the sources and methods of calculation of Table 6 see the Appendixes.

The rate of increase, which had been 14 per cent in 1710–1719, rose to 18 per cent in 1720–1729, the decade of stagnation in population growth, fell to 4 per cent in 1730–1739, the decade of population decline, and fell again to 0 per cent in 1740–1749, the decade in which the rate of population growth very nearly returned to its prestagnation level. The failure of the rate of increase in the output of industrial producers' goods to respond in 1740–1749 to the reappearance of population growth and a small increase in the rate of growth of consumers' goods output can be traced, perhaps, to the delayed impact of stagnation and decline in population on the rate of household formation and hence on the demand for housing (see Table 6).

The 0.4 per cent fall in population in 1730–1739 was accompanied by the only decrease in the value of industrial consumers' goods production between 1710 and 1819 and the only decrease in the value of producers' goods output between 1710 and 1799. Since the volumes of production rose, the decreases in value must have been the result of price movements (see Tables 5 and 6). A price drop is a plausible result of a decline in population and may conceivably explain the decrease in the value of output.

Neither the 1780's, which marked the critical turning point in total industrial production (including and excluding building) and industrial consumers' goods production, nor the 1790's, which were a turning point in the output of industrial producers' goods, were of similar direct importance in the history of population. The former decade was the last of three successive decades that each exhibited a population growth of about 7 per cent. The rate of growth rose by 2.1 per cent in the next decade, but each of the decades from 1800–1809 through 1820–1829 saw the rate of increase rise by more than 2.1 per cent (see Tables 4, 5, and 6). That population grew at an increasing rate from 1770 to 1829 may be significant, but there is no evidence that the eighties or nineties exhibited an unusual leap in the rate of growth. This does not imply that population growth failed to affect the rate of increase in output, nor does it imply that population growth did not help determine the decade in which industrial output moved to a new high level of increase. It implies, rather, that population growth made itself felt through a series of successive increases that did not exhibit a marked discontinuity when the rates of increase in industrial output did.

The establishment and analysis of price movements presents

problems comparable to those encountered in the study of industrial output. Tables 7, 8, and 9 present the best available price data.[13] Table 7 presents the price indexes for the eighteenth and nineteenth centuries. Since there are no suitable indexes of United Kingdom prices in the eighteenth century or of English prices in the nineteenth century, two different sets of indexes have been used.[14] One describes the movement of the prices of English

---

[13] Hamilton's price index cannot be used (Earl J. Hamilton, "Profit Inflation and the Industrial Revolution, 1751–1800," *Quarterly Journal of Economics*, LVI [1942], 258). The index is presented graphically, but the figures can be retrieved by consulting the various individual price series in W. Beveridge *et al., Prices and Wages in England from the Twelfth to the Nineteenth Century*, Vol. I (London, 1939). An analysis of the index indicates that there are crucial differences in the movements of its components that may contradict the profit inflation theory. Between 1750 and 1800, the agricultural products in the index rose more in price than did the overall index; the prices of processed agricultural products rose more than those of unprocessed agricultural products. At the same time the prices of industrial products rose less than the index and less than those of either kind of agricultural product. Finally, most of the overall price increase occurred between 1790 and 1800. On the basis of this index it is possible to argue that price inflation produced cost inflation rather than profit inflation (David Felix, "Profit Inflation and Industrial Growth: The Historical Record and Contemporary Analogies," *Quarterly Journal of Economics*, LXX [1956], 455–457). In choosing 1800 as a terminal date, Felix probably exaggerates the extent to which the rise in agricultural prices exceeded the rise in industrial prices. He recognizes it as a bad choice, but did not realize just how bad it was. For 1800 was a year of very bad harvests following a year of bad harvests. Agricultural prices soared. In January 1799, potatoes had sold in Lancashire at 5½d. a score; in January 1801, the price was 1s. 8d. In 1798, a bushel of wheat cost 6s. 9d. at Windsor; in 1799, 11s. 7d.; in 1800, 16s. In 1798, a loaf of bread cost 8d. in London; in 1799, the same loaf cost 13d.; and in 1800, it cost 17½d. (Ashton, *Economic Fluctuations*, pp. 25–26 and 181). There is no doubt that agricultural and industrial goods were subject to different rates of inflation, but not to the extent suggested by comparing prices in 1750 and 1800.

[14] The inconvenience in using two sets of price indexes has one beneficial aspect. Price indexes that cover very long periods are subject to criticism precisely because they cover long periods. Breaking the two-century period into two roughly equal parts anticipates this criticism, although it will not satisfy the purist.

Table 7. Indexes of average annual prices, 1700–1899

Years	English consumers' goods		C English producers' goods	D General level of prices U.K.
	A Including cereals	B Excluding cereals		
1700–1709	60	67	74	
1710–1719	64	70	70	
1720–1729	60	65	67	
1730–1739	54	60	64	
1740–1749	57	63	67	
1750–1759	59	62	66	
1760–1769	62	65	74	
1770–1779	68	69	74	
1780–1789	73	75	82	
1790–1799	85	86	90	86
1800–1809	116	110		106
1810–1819	124	122		95
1820–1829				73
1830–1839				66
1840–1849				60
1850–1859				60
1860–1869				64
1870–1879				63
1880–1889				50
1890–1899				43

Base: A, B, and C—Oct. 1795–Oct. 1800 = 100; D—1796–1800 = 100.

Source: Based on Appendixes 4, 5, and 6. For the sources and methods of calculation see the Appendixes.

consumers' goods (including and excluding cereals) from 1700 to 1819 and the movement of the prices of English producers' goods from 1700 to 1799; the other describes the movement of the general level of United Kingdom prices from 1800–1899. Table 8 presents the percentage increases in the price indexes. Table 9 summarizes the results of a series of calculations based on the indexes.

One characteristic of secular price movements in the eighteenth century is obvious from a glance at the price tables. All the

Table 8. Percentage increases in average annual prices, 1710–1899

Years	English consumers' goods		C English producers' goods	D General level of prices U.K.
	A Including cereals	B Excluding cereals		
1710–1719	7	5	−5	
1720–1729	−7	−7	−4	
1730–1739	−9	−8	−4	
1740–1749	6	5	5	
1750–1759	2	−2	−1	
1760–1769	6	5	11	
1770–1779	10	8	0	
1780–1789	6	8	13	
1790–1799	17	15	10	
1800–1809	37	28		24
1810–1819	7	11		−11
1820–1829				−24
1830–1839				−10
1840–1849				− 9
1850–1859				0
1860–1869				7
1870–1879				− 1
1880–1889				−22
1890–1899				−13

Source: Based on Appendixes 4, 5, and 6. For the sources and methods of calculation see the Appendixes.

declines in English prices occur before 1760–1769. From 1710–1719 through 1810–1819 the Index of the Average Annual Price of English Consumers' Goods fell only in 1720–1729 and 1730–1739; the Index of the Average Annual Price of English Consumers' Goods (Excluding Cereals) fell in the same decades and in 1750–1759 as well. From 1710–1719 through 1790–1799 the Index of the Average Annual Price of English Producers' Goods fell for these decades and in 1710–1719. The latter part of the eighteenth century is clearly a period of inflation (see Tables 7 and 8).

Hamilton's explanation notwithstanding, the price inflation

Table 9. Indexes of the average annual English price level for consumers'
and producers' goods, 1700–1799

| Years | Consumers' goods | | C Producers' goods |
	A Including cereals	B Excluding cereals	
1700–1749	100	100	100
1750–1799	118	110	113
1700–1759	100	100	100
1760–1799	122	114	118
1700–1779	100	100	100
1780–1799	131	124	124
1720–1759	100	100	100
1760–1799	125	118	121
1760–1779	100	100	100
1780–1799	122	120	116

Base: Indicated in each section of the table.

Source: Based on Appendixes 4 and 5. For the sources and methods of calculation
see the Appendixes.

was not related to an increase in the money supply resulting from
an influx of specie, since there was no net specie gain in the second
half of the eighteenth century.[15] Two better alternative explanations of the long-term inflation have been advanced. T. S. Ashton
has traced the inflation to a tendency for the supply of money to
outrun demand.[16] H. J. Habakkuk has suggested that "the general
tendency of prices to rise after 1760 seems to be associated primarily with an increased demand for primary products generated
largely by population growth." [17] Both explanations are consistent

---

[15] Elizabeth Boody [Schumpeter], "English Prices and Public Finance,
1660–1822," *Review of Economic Statistics*, XX (1938), 27–31.

[16] *An Economic History of England: The 18th Century* (London, 1955), p.
198.

[17] "Essays in Bibliography and Criticism, XXXII: The Eighteenth Century," *Economic History Review*, 2nd ser., VIII (1956), 437.

with the price movements and are not necessarily inconsistent with each other.

The price data below suggests that Habakkuk's analysis is the more accurate one. Although specie imports played no role in the price rise, this does not mean that the supply of money was of no consequence. The efforts to increase the money supply made by the monetary authority, by the banking institutions, and by the creation of private money (see Chapters III and IV) suggest that the upward pressure on prices, generated by population growth, had to be validated by an increase in the supply of money. Population pressure can be regarded as having "caused" the price rise, but an increase in the supply of money—an increase to which the monetary authorities and the banking institutions were not fully equal—can be regarded as a necessary enabling factor.

Three possible turning points suggest themselves for the purpose of a closer analysis of long-term price movements in the eighteenth century: 1750, 1760, and 1780.

If change is recognized but continuity of development is stressed, the arbitrary choice of 1750 seems best. A comparison between the price levels in the first and second halves of the eighteenth century indicates that the level of prices was higher in the second half, but not much higher. If the average of each of the three indexes is taken as 100 for 1700–1749, the comparable figures for 1750–1799 are 118 for consumers' goods (including cereals), 110 for consumers' goods (excluding cereals), and 113 for producers' goods (see Table 9).

If the conventional view of the Industrial Revolution is adopted, then 1760 seems like the best turning point. When 1700–1759 is taken as 100, the comparable figures for 1760–1799 are 122 for consumers' goods (including cereals), 114 for consumers' goods (excluding cereals), and 118 for producers' goods.

If one identifies the beginning of the Industrial Revolution with the movement of the rate of growth in industrial output to a new higher level in 1780–1799 and takes 1700–1779 as 100, the index numbers for 1780–1799 are 131 for consumers' goods (in-

41

cluding cereals) and 124 for consumers' goods (excluding cereals) and producers' goods (see Table 9).

These comparisons suggest a number of conclusions that are independent of the turning point selected. In all the comparisons, the price level of each of the three categories of goods is higher for the last part of the century than it is for the first. The price level of consumers' goods (including cereals) always rose more in the later period than the price levels of either of the other two classes of goods, indicating that the strongest inflationary force in the early phase of the Industrial Revolution was the rising price of cereals. This upward price pressure was felt in spite of the increasing volume of wheat output, the increasing productivity per acre of wheat lands and the transformation of England into a net importer of wheat in the 1760's.[18]

The latter part of the eighteenth century also witnessed a larger increase in the price level of producers' than of consumers' goods (exclusive of cereals). This difference in increases, though small, suggests the possibility that the early decades of the Industrial Revolution were characterized by a small but definite cost inflation that—other things being equal—would have tended to deflate rather than inflate profits. Indeed, the crucial decade 1780–1789 saw the largest percentage increase in the average annual price of producers' goods in the eighteenth century. This 13 per cent increase was more than twice as large as the rise in the price of consumers' goods (including cereals) and more than one and one-half times the rise in the price of consumers' goods (exclusive of cereals) (see Table 8).

The divergence between bread prices and wheat prices in the second half of the eighteenth century, which can be seen in Table

---

[18] On the increasing volume of wheat output, see R. M. Hartwell, "The Rising Standard of Living in England, 1800–1850," *Economic History Review,* 2nd ser., XIII (1961), 408. On the increasing productivity of wheat lands, see M. K. Bennett, "British Wheat Yield per Acre for Seven Centuries," *Economic History,* III (1935), 28. Net import and export figures for Great Britain are given in Ashton, *Economic Fluctuations,* p. 183, statistical table 3; the figures include flour.

10, suggests the same conclusion. In 1770–1779 and 1780–1789, wheat prices went from 156 to 159, while bread prices only went from 133 to 134. If the average of the annual wheat and bread prices for 1740–1749 is taken as 100, bread prices rose to only 167, while wheat prices went to 181. Adulteration is sometimes used to explain away this kind of comparison. Although there is no doubt that adulteration was practiced, there seems to be no indication

Table 10. Average wheat and bread prices and price relatives, 1735–1799

Years	A Wheat prices, Windsor *	B Price relative of A	C Bread prices, London †	D Price relative of C
1735–1739	59.5	113	5.40	103
1740–1749	52.7	100	5.25	100
1750–1759	62.9	119	5.90	112
1760–1769	70.6	134	6.38	122
1770–1779	82.4	156	6.98	133
1780–1789	84.0	159	7.05	134
1790–1799	95.2	181	8.75	167

* In *d.* per bushel.
† In *d.* per quartern loaf.
Base: B and D—1740–1749 = 100.
Source: Computed from T. S. Ashton, *Economic Fluctuations in England: 1700–1800* (Oxford, 1959), p. 181, statistical table 1.

that it was more widespread in the nineties than it had been in the forties.[19]

The limits imposed on the discussion by the termination of one of the price series at 1801 must be accepted.[20] It is possible, however, to refuse to regard the entire eighteenth century as the unit of discussion. Hence another type of comparison suggests itself, one in which the period from the proposed turning point to the end of the century is compared to a period of equal duration

---

[19] See Hartwell, "Rising Standard of Living," pp. 414–415.
[20] The time limit is in keeping with the terms of reference of the profit inflation theory.

before the turning point. If the division is made at 1750, the results are identical to those derived from considering the century as a whole. When the division is made at 1760, the comparison between the price levels for 1720–1759 and 1760–1799 yields results that are essentially the same as those obtained from all the previous comparisons. A significant difference appears only when 1780 is regarded as the turning point.

Taking the level of prices of each of the three categories of goods as 100 in 1760–1779, the level of prices for 1780–1799 can be computed as 122 for consumers' goods (including cereals), 120 for consumers' goods (excluding cereals), and 116 for producers' goods. In one regard, this comparison yields the same results as the others: the largest rise in the level of prices occurs in consumers' goods (including cereals). Cereals still set the pace. But this comparison does differ from all the others in one way: it is the only one in which the prices of producers' goods rose less after the turning point than the prices of consumers' goods (excluding cereals) (see Table 9). This finding does not invalidate the point made above that the period 1780–1799, when compared with all the rest of the eighteenth century, may well have been a period in which the movements of prices tended to deflate profits by slightly increasing the costs of production. The choice of periods is important and some statistics are ambiguous.

The eighteenth century was, on balance, a century of rising prices; the nineteenth, a century of falling prices. Although no good single index of the general level of prices is available for the eighteenth century, it is possible to judge how such an index would behave on the basis of the three price indexes and estimates of the ratio of the value of consumers' goods output to producers' goods output.[21]

During the nine decades from 1710–1719 through 1790–1799, the general level of prices definitely rose in five decades and fell in two. The 5 per cent fall in producers' goods prices in 1710–1719

---

[21] Hoffmann, *British Industry,* p. 22, table 3.

was probably too small to offset the 7 per cent increase in the prices of consumers' goods (including cereals). It also seems likely that the 1 per cent fall in producers' goods prices in 1750–1759 was too small to offset the 2 per cent increase in the prices of consumers' goods (including cereals). Thus the general level of prices probably rose in seven (or possibly six) of the nine decades from 1710–1719 through 1790–1799 and probably fell in two (or possibly three) decades.[22] In the nineteenth century, prices definitely remained unchanged in one decade, rose in two decades, and fell in six (or probably, but not certainly, seven) decades.[23]

Nineteenth-century price movements differed from those of the previous century in another way. Not only did falling prices tend to occur more often in the nineteenth century, but the downward trend tended to last longer and go further than it did in the eighteenth century.

Whatever year is chosen as the focus for the inception of the Industrial Revolution—1750, 1760, or 1780—or as the focus for its end—1830 or 1850—the price pattern is clear. The period associated with the Industrial Revolution started with a rising price level and ended with a falling one. This would tend to support W. A. Lewis' general thesis that rising prices coincide with a period of investment and forced saving and that prices tend to fall as goods start to pour out (see Appendix 1 below). The picture is obscured, however, by monetary considerations.

The price fall occurred after the end of the Napoleonic Wars and roughly coincides with Great Britain's return to the gold standard. The return to gold, in and of itself, would have had a marked deflationary effect, and it is impossible to determine how much of the post-war price fall was due to the change in monetary policy and how much, if any, was due to the mechanism postulated by Lewis.

In recent years there has been very extensive discussion of price

---

[22] *Ibid.*, and Tables 7 and 8 above.

[23] This doubt arises from a discrepancy between the English and U.K. price indexes and is dealt with in Appendix 6.

inflation theory.[24] One of the principal fruits of this debate has been the emergence of the distinction between demand-pull inflation and cost-push inflation. A demand-pull inflation can be defined as "one in which prices are conceived as *pulled* up by an excess of total monetary demand over the limitations that are set on the supply side." A cost-push inflation can be defined as "one in which prices are apparently *pushed* up by direct action of sellers without any prior excess demand. The expanded . . . [money] requirements of business at the increased price levels are generally met out of the elastic resources of . . . [the] flexible credit system." [25] It seems likely that the inflationary phase of the price movements during the period with which the Industrial Revolution is associated was characterized by elements of both types of inflation.

The substantial increases in central government expenditure and indebtedness during the Seven Years' War, the War of American Independence, and the French Revolutionary and Napoleonic Wars exerted a long-term pull on prices.[26] This pull was probably reinforced by the growing security of the English funds, which "enabled them in turn to be used as the basis of a pyramid of other loans within the business community." [27] In 1745, it was possible for the junior partner in the great sugar-factoring firm of Messrs. Lascalles and Maxwell to write, "Those who had great riches in the Publick Funds (which are the bulk of the rich people in the Kingdom) are as poor as those that have none, for they

---

[24] An excellent survey of this literature can be found in M. Bronfenbrenner and F. D. Holzman, "Survey of Inflation Theory," *American Economic Review,* LIII (1963), 593–661.

[25] J. M. Clark, *The Wage Price Problem* (n.p.: Committee for Economic Growth without Inflation, American Bankers Association, 1960), p. 1. Italics in the original.

[26] After some reduction the funded debt in 1830 was between five and six times as large as the entire national debt had been in 1763 (J. R. McCulloch, *A Descriptive and Statistical Account of the British Empire* [4th ed.; London, 1854], II, 435).

[27] A. H. John, "Insurance Investment and the London Money Market of the 18th Century," *Economica,* N.S., XX (1953), 139.

cannot raise money upon any of them." [28] By 1818, David Ricardo, testifying before a select committee on the usury laws, was able to describe an entirely changed situation in which money could easily be raised on the security of the funds and could be raised in nearly complete disregard of the usury laws.[29]

Additional demand-pull on price levels can probably be traced to the operations of local government, and particularly to the administration of the poor laws. From 1776 to 1818–1821, real expenditures on the poor in England increased by 277 per cent. It has been estimated that in 1818–1821 perhaps 20 per cent of the entire population was receiving parish aid.[30] To some extent parish poor payments were financed by involuntary loans made by overseers of the poor in the form of advances to the parish. The advances had to be short-term loans because the overseer had to be reimbursed within the year or lose the legal right to reclaim an advance.[31] The total volume of these loans was probably not very large. In addition, there was at least one occasion on which a local government corporation issued its own paper money and another on which a poor-law authority issued its own notes.[32]

While it is likely that increased government expenditure and indebtedness was the principal source of demand-pull, there were a number of other possible sources of such a pull. The rapid growth and elaboration of a credit-creating banking network without a fully developed central credit-controlling authority probably tended to produce or facilitate the development of de-

---

[28] Quoted in *ibid.*, p. 140.

[29] "Minutes of Evidence taken before the Select Committee on the Usury Laws, April 30, 1818," *Speeches and Evidence* (P. Sraffa and M. H. Dobb, eds., *The Works and Correspondence of David Ricardo*, Vol. V) (Cambridge, 1952), pp. 337–347.

[30] J. T. Krause, "Some Neglected Factors in the English Industrial Revolution," *Journal of Economic History*, XIX (1959), 533.

[31] Sir William Searle Holdsworth, *A History of English Law* (London, 1938), X, 271–272.

[32] L. S. Pressnell, *Country Banking in the Industrial Revolution* (Oxford, 1956), pp. 25 and 174.

mand-pull.[33] This was especially likely to be true at a time when credit was not regulated by interest rates, but was rationed instead (see Chapter III). Innovations in techniques of commercial lending had a similar effect, and during the course of the eighteenth century there emerged an elaborate system for borrowing on the security of tea-, pepper-, and dividend-warrants.[34] The development and extension of the long-pay and the related practice of quasi-banking by shopkeepers and industrialists had a similar effect (see Chapter IV). Taken together, all these developments enormously facilitated excess credit creation.

It is somewhat more difficult to assess the role of cost-push in late eighteenth-century price inflation. Some of the economic factors that are held responsible for recent cost-push inflations [35] are largely absent in the late eighteenth and early nineteenth centuries—notably, oligopoly pricing and strong labor unions. It is true that another factor that might have contributed to cost-push was clearly in evidence; there was undoubtedly some customary and contract pricing in the eighteenth century.[36] Thus, for example, the price paid by Winchester College for a piece of cloth remained unchanged at 120s. from 1612 to 1791.[37] It is impossible, however, to assess the extent to which this price masked changes in quality or quantity and the extent to which this type of pricing prevailed in the economy as a whole.

There does seem to be one identifiable source of cost-push inflation. It is clear that agricultural prices tended to rise more than industrial prices. This phenomenon is probably traceable to population growth at a time when domestic agriculture was

---

[33] Chapter III below and R. De Roover, "New Interpretations of the History of Banking," *Journal of World History*, II, no. 1 (1954), 70 and n. 148.

[34] John, "Insurance Investment," p. 139.

[35] Bronfenbrenner and Holzman, "Survey of Inflation Theory," pp. 613–628.

[36] A. J. Brown, *The Great Inflation, 1939–1951* (London, 1955), ch. 1.

[37] P. Deane and W. A. Cole, *British Economic Growth, 1688–1959* (Cambridge, 1962), p. 13.

largely protected by high transportation costs and tariffs; possibly cost-push inflation was a result of a rise in the price of the agricultural inputs of industry. It is, of course, possible that the resulting cost increase was not passed on to the consumer. It could have been absorbed by the entrepreneur in the form of a reduction in profits or by the laborer in the form of a wage reduction, or it could have been avoided by a reduction in labor costs through an increase in productivity without a reduction in wages. Of these possibilities, the last seems the most plausible. The evidence is only sufficient to suggest that population pressure probably generated cost-push inflationary pressure, which may have been offset in part or *in toto* by reductions in labor costs due to increases in productivity.

The movements of prices and wages can be directly compared by the use of an index of real wages. Since there is no good single index of real wages, it is necessary to use the two indexes prepared by E. W. Gilboy, on which Tables 11 and 12 are based. An examination of the indexes is not decisive for the disputes over the worker's standard of living, welfare, or comfort. Too many uncertainties remain.[38] Nevertheless, the indexes suggest several conclusions.

There was a substantial difference between London and Lancashire wage movements in the eighteenth century. During the first six decades, the differences were comparatively small. In the first two decades, the index of money wages in Lancashire was somewhat below the London index; in 1720–1729, however, the Lancashire index rose above the London index and remained above it for the rest of the period covered by both indexes. The differences between the two was fairly small until 1760–1769, when a substan-

---

[38] For a discussion of these difficulties, see Ashton, *18th Century,* pp. 233–234. The best way to overcome these difficulties seems to be through a consideration of per capita consumption (see T. S. Ashton, "Changes in the Standards of Comfort in Eighteenth Century England," *Proceedings of the British Academy,* XLI (1955), 171–187; and Gayer, Rostow, and Schwartz, *Growth and Fluctuation,* II, 626, table 77, and 949–951 and 957–967.

tial divergence appeared. It continued to grow until at least 1780–1787, when the London index ends and makes further comparison impossible. The London index, which had been 107 in 1700–1709 and 118 in 1750–1759, only reached 123 in 1780–1787, while the Lancashire index went from 97 in 1700–1709 to 129 in

Table 11. Lancashire money and real wages, 1700–1796

Years	A Money wages *	B % increase in A	C Real wages *	D % increase in C
1700–1709	97		99	
1710–1719	106	9	103	4
1720–1729	122	15	123	19
1730–1739	132	8	145	18
1740–1749	132	0	138	−5
1750–1759	129	−2	128	−7
1760–1769	157	22	141	10
1770–1779	198	26	157	11
1780–1787	204	3	156	−1
1780–1789	210	6	160	2
1790–1796	231	10	154	−4

* The wages are for building and road laborers.
Base: 1700 = 100.
Source: Calculated from E. W. Gilboy, "Cost of Living and Real Wages in 18th Century England," *Review of Economic Statistics*, XVIII, no. 3 (1936), 140, table 2. She uses money-wage figures from her own *Wages in 18th Century England* (Cambridge, Mass., 1934) and gets her prices from Elizabeth Boody (Schumpeter), "English Prices and Public Finance, 1660–1822," *Review of Economic Statistics*, XX, no. 1 (1938), 35, table 5.

1750–1759 and reached 204 in 1780–1787. The Lancashire index continued to rise, reaching 231 in 1790–1796, when the index ends.

Each index provides information only about the relative movement of wages in the area to which it pertains. The comparisons gain in significance when the actual wage levels are considered. Early in the eighteenth century, the unskilled laborer was paid 20d. in London and 8d. in Lancashire; at mid-century the wage was 24*d.* in London and 12*d.* in Lancashire; in the 1780's it was still 24*d.* in London, but the wage had risen to 20*d.* in Lancashire.[39]

Similar movements occur in the indexes of real wages. The index of real wages in London, which had been 117 in 1750–1759, fell to 94 in 1780–1787, while the Lancashire index rose from 128

Table 12. London money and real wages, 1700–1787

Years	A Money wages	B % increase in A	C Real wages	D % increase in C
1700–1709	107		108	
1710–1719	109	2	106	−2
1720–1729	110	1	110	4
1730–1739	115	5	129	17
1740–1749	117	2	123	−5
1750–1759	118	1	117	−5
1760–1769	120	2	109	−7
1770–1779	120	0	95	−13
1780–1787	123	3	94	−1

Base: 1700 = 100.

Source: See Table 11 for sources. The London wages are the wages of bricklayers, masons, and other laborers and craftsmen in the building trades. The alternative to Gilboy's London index is R. S. Tucker, "Real Wages of Artisans in London, 1729–1935," *Journal of the American Statistical Society,* XXXI (1936), 73–85. Tucker's indexes are much less satisfactory (see Gilboy's criticism in "Cost of Living," pp. 139–141).

to 156. By 1790–1796, however, the Lancashire index had fallen slightly to 154.

The divergent movements suggest the gradual leveling up of provincial wages. Industrializing areas like Lancashire evidently set the pace in the race to reach the level of wages paid in the metropolis.[40] As one might expect, money wages increased faster

[39] Elizabeth W. Gilboy, *Wages in 18th Century England* (Cambridge, Mass., 1934), pp. 254–292, app. 2.

[40] *Ibid.* Ashton conjectured that Lancashire wages were above London wages by 1800 (Ashton, *18th Century,* p. 232). E. W. Gilboy noted three areas

than real wages in eighteenth-century Lancashire; between 1700–1709 and 1780–1787, the former rose from 97 to 204 and the latter from 99 to 156. The leveling-up process can be regarded as an indication of a growing integration of the labor market, but regional differences persisted within England and among England, Scotland, and Ireland.[41]

The war years 1793–1815, were evidently marked by rising money wages, retail prices that rose faster than money wages, and, therefore, falling real wages. From 1815 to 1847, money wages fell, but retail prices fell faster and helped to produce a slight rise in real wages.[42] However, some of this data is ambiguous.[43] In the

---

with a definite rise in real wages in the eighteenth century: Lancashire and the North and West Riding of Yorkshire. Lancashire and the West Riding were industrial areas; the North Riding was agricultural ("Wages in Eighteenth Century England," *Journal of Economic and Business History*, II [1930], 621).

[41] Calico Printers' Committee, *Report of the Calico Printers' Committee on Wages: Resolutions of the Meeting and List of Prices* (Manchester, 1831), pp. 4–5, gives figures for journeyman wages in England, Scotland, and Ireland. The assertion was made that Scottish wages were 40% to 50% lower than wages in the Manchester area and that Irish wages were even lower. Although the estimates are not the work of disinterested men, they are plausible. Regional wage differences are not surprising, and they can be traced for the eighteenth century in E. W. Gilboy's works, which have been referred to above, and for the nineteenth century in Arthur Lyon Bowley, *Wages in the United Kingdom in the Nineteenth Century* (Cambridge, 1899), and "The Statistics of Wages in the United Kingdom during the Last Hundred Years," *Journal of the Royal Statistical Society*, LXII (1899), 140–151; and in George Henry Wood, *The History of Wages in the Cotton Trade* (London, 1910), and "Real Wages and the Standard of Comfort since 1850," *Journal of the Royal Statistical Society*, LXXIII (1909), 91–103.

[42] Gayer, Rostow, and Schwartz, *Growth and Fluctuation*, II, 626.

[43] *Ibid.*, and table 77. The description given above depends largely on Tucker's indexes of London artisans' money and real wages and cost of living. A discussion of these indexes can be found in *ibid.*, pp. 819–821, 829–833, and 955–957. Tucker's real-wage index is seriously deficient because it is calculated from a cost-of-living index that includes money wages as a significant element. He included money wages as an indirect index of rent because he assumed that the fluctuation in money wages conformed to changes in rents. This seems to be a poor statistical practice (Elizabeth W. Gilboy, "The Cost of Living and Real Wages in 18th Century England," *Review of Economic*

second half of the nineteenth century, money and real wages and the standard of comfort clearly rose substantially after various fluctuations, but the statistics are not comparable to the earlier figures.[44]

A number of tentative conclusions about the Industrial Revolution emerge from the statistical analysis. The 1780's and 1790's mark the transition from a relatively low rate of increase in industrial output to a new high rate of increase that was sustained for over a century.[45] Industrial consumers' goods output led the way in the 1780's and was joined in the following decade by producers' goods output. The lag may have been due to the existence of excess or underutilized industrial capacity that was not absorbed until the 1790's. Perhaps, the existence of this excess capacity can ultimately be traced to the first half of the eighteenth century, which saw an expansion of the domestic market for industrial products that was more rapid than the expansion of overseas trade.[46]

With the possible exception of 1760–1769, the volume of total industrial output probably grew faster than population throughout the eighteenth and nineteenth centuries. Throughout the

---

Statistics, XVIII, no. 3 [Aug. 1936], 139–141). In addition, there are significant differences among Tuckers index of money wages of London artisans, Bowley's index of agricultural money wages, and Kondratieff's index of money wages in the textile industry. The various indexes are compared in Gayer, Rostow, and Schwartz, *Growth and Fluctuation*, II, 626, table 77.

[44] Wood, "Real Wages," 91–103. On balance, the movements in the indexes of real wages provide little support for the profit inflation theory. The postulated lag of wages behind prices should have resulted in a secular fall of real wages in the industrializing areas during the second half of the eighteenth century. There is no evidence of such a fall in the Lancashire index. Also see Appendix 1 below.

[45] The attempt made by P. Deane and W. A. Cole to establish the period 1745–1760 as the period of transition has not proved to be successful (*British Economic Growth*). See the criticisms made by J. R. T. Hughes in his "Measuring British Economic Growth," *Journal of Economic History*, XXIV (1964), 60–82.

[46] A. H. John, "Aspects of English Economic Growth in the First Half of the Eighteenth Century," *Essays*, ed. Carus-Wilson, II (1962), 370.

eighteenth century, the value of total industrial production grew faster than population and, in the one decade in which population fell, it fell further.

Judged by the standards of preindustrial modern England, let us say 1500–1750, the growth of population in the eighteenth century seems to have gone through three distinct phases. In the first of these phases, 1700–1750, the rate of growth seems to have been abnormally low. In the second, 1750–1780, the rate of growth apparently recovered to the normal rate for 1500–1750. In the third phase, 1780–1800, the rate of growth seems to have reached a revolutionary new high level.[47] This pattern of growth and the cumulative effect of the growth probably had an important impact on prices.

All the declines in the eighteenth-century price series considered here occurred in the decades before 1760 and roughly coincide with the period of abnormally low population growth. In the last four decades of the century, a period of recovery and unusual expansion in the rate of population growth, there are no decades of price decline. The fact that in the second half of the century cereal prices increased more rapidly than the prices of consumers' goods in general suggests that the population increase played a significant role in the price increases.

The price data also suggest that the latter part of the eighteenth century witnessed the emergence of price pressures in the industrial sector. Money wages (and perhaps real wages) rose in industrial areas. The prices of industrial producers' goods rose more rapidly than the prices of industrial consumers' goods. If, as seems possible, the increases in cereal prices were representative of the change in the prices of other domestic agricultural products, the prices of the agricultural inputs of industry probably rose more than the prices of industrial products.

Since output attained, and was sustained at, a new high level in the latter part of the eighteenth century, it is possible to regard

---

[47] G. S. L. Tucker, "English Pre-Industrial Population Trends," *Economic History Review*, 2nd ser., XVI (1963), 205–218.

the innovations and investments associated with the Industrial Revolution as a mechanism that prevented these particular price pressures from being translated into cost pressures.

These price movements may also have had a regulatory effect on investment. There is evidence that stagnant or falling agricultural prices in England in the eighteenth century and early nineteenth century tended to induce agricultural investment by landowners and that high or rising prices (particularly if they coincided with high interest rates—see Chapter II) tended to discourage it. The first half of the eighteenth century seems to fit the first, and the latter part of the century the second, pattern of development.[48] The movements of prices may, therefore, have helped to divert capital away from agriculture in the second half of the eighteenth century. Even if this capital was not diverted directly into the industrial sector of the economy, it may have got there by an indirect route, or the diversion may have served simply to reduce the pressure on the available capital by reducing the demand for capital by another sector of the economy.

Against this background, it is now possible to consider the institutional framework and institutional changes that affected capital accumulation during the late eighteenth and early nineteenth centuries.

---

[48] G. E. Mingay, "The Agricultural Depression, 1730–1750,"*Essays* ed. Carus-Wilson, II 309–326.

55

Chapter II

Interest Rates and the Usury Law

LIKE his modern counterpart, the eighteenth- or nineteenth-century capitalist recognized the existence of at least two different types of capital. A participant in the capital market of the Industrial Revolution might think in terms of "temporary" or "permanent" loans; an industrialist, in terms of his "circulating" or "fixed" capital. The distinction was based on the different periods during which the capital was available to the entrepreneur.[1]

This distinction becomes clear if one compares the situation of a spinner who is about to start a new enterprise or construct a new mill to that of an established yarn manufacturer. The first spinner must purchase land, buy or build a mill, and buy or make machinery. The returns on this long-term capital outlay will accrue slowly. Indeed, at first, there will be no returns at all, and the spinner may even be foregoing an alternative income-producing investment. Another characteristic result of a long-term investment in a mill is its adverse effect on the spinner's liquidity position. It is not easy to "cash in" a cotton mill. The market for mills is comparatively small and specialized; cotton mills, like slide trombones, are not equally profitable in all hands. In addition, it may well become more difficult to "cash in" a cotton mill just at the moment in the business cycle when the spinner's need for cash is greatest.

---

[1] Great Britain, House of Commons, Evidence of Lewis Loyd, *Report from the Select Committee on Manufactures, Commerce and Shipping (Reports,* 1833 [690]), Vol. VI, pt. 1, qq. 453–454. Lewis Loyd was a partner in Jones, Loyd and Company, bankers at Manchester and London.

The established yarn manufacturer, in possession of a mill in actual operation, has somewhat different problems. He is concerned with filling orders. To do so he must have the use of short-term capital with which to pay wages and purchase raw materials. The returns on this short-term capital outlay will accrue to him relatively quickly, since the selling price of the yarn will include, among other costs, the whole of the raw materials and labor costs. These short-term capital outlays will not have nearly so bad an effect on the yarn manufacturer's liquidity position as will the long-term outlays.

There are various reasons for this difference. Because the spinner's business consists in filling a succession of orders for which he is paid in a relatively short time, he can at any given moment count on having some of his short-term outlays returned to him in one day, one week, or one month—all in the reasonably foreseeable future. If conditions take a turn for the worse, or if he anticipates a turn for the worse, he can reduce his short-term outlays to the point where he simply empties his productive pipeline, or he can completely stop his short-term outlays. In any of these cases all, or most, of his short-term outlays will be returned to him in a relatively brief time. It may even be possible for him to borrow against this prospective steady return flow of short-term capital or to "cash in" his supplies of raw materials and partly finished goods by selling them. Since the short-term outlays are likely to be smaller than his long-term outlays, it might be very much easier to realize the former.

One type of capital could be substituted for the other. A firm could conceivably meet its short-term needs out of capital available to it on a long-term basis, or it might attempt to meet its long-term requirements by careful management of its short-term capital supply. Most firms attempted to avoid the first of these solutions, since one of the consequences of the Industrial Revolution was the creation of a premium on long-term capital by making investment in transportation, machinery, and factories profitable. The desire to avoid substituting long-term for short-term capital was probably intensified by the emergence of the state as an extremely important competitor for both.[2]

The creation of the 3 per cent consolidated stock in 1757 marks a milestone in the history of the national debt. Early in the eighteenth century, the rate of the perpetual annuities was about 7 per cent. During the next half-century, the rate fell steadily while the governments in power easily crushed the "'15" and the "'45"—the only two major organized insurrections that sought to destroy them. The creation of the consols set the seal on this new-found—if imperfect—stability. As A. J. Youngson pointed out, "this reduction was not the consequence of a fall in the marginal efficiency of capital, but was caused—at least in part—by the transfer of government bonds from that category of security which carries with it risks of non-repayment of principal to that which carries no such risks." [3]

In 1763, toward the end of the Seven Years War, the entire national debt, funded and unfunded, stood at about £139,000,000; in 1830, following a period of postwar debt reduc-

---

[2] There are clear indications that the yield on government securities directly affected the availability of capital in industry. In 1757, Elizabeth Strutt informed her husband, Jedidiah, that she would not be able to procure an expected loan from the Rev. Dr. Benson, because the fall of the price of the government's 3 per cent annuities would have involved the Rev. Doctor in a capital loss if he were to sell his holdings in order to make the loan (Elizabeth Strutt to Jedidiah Strutt, May 3, 1757, as quoted in T. S. Ashton, *An Economic History of England: The 18th Century* [London, 1955], pp. 28–29). In 1786, Samuel Oldknow was told that he might be able to borrow some money from "some persons who are now selling out of the funds" (S. and W. Salte to Samuel Oldknow, Oct. 23, 1786, as quoted in George Unwin, Arthur Hulme, and George Taylor, *Samuel Oldknow and the Arkwrights* [Manchester, 1924], p. 77). At a later date an anonymous writer stated that "the universal opinion of capitalists in favor of an improvement in the funds, which appears likely to be realized, tended to deprive commerce of every kind of support further than actual necessity has required" (*Manchester Magazine*, II, no. 5 [May 1816], 238–239).

[3] *Possibilities of Economic Progress* (Cambridge, 1959), p. 109.

tion, the funded debt alone amounted to £771,000,000.[4] Needless to say, most of the increase was due to the wars of the late eighteenth and early nineteenth centuries. The sharp wartime declines in the prices of long-term government securities had a tendency to "freeze in" investors.[5] By making it difficult for an entrepreneur to obtain long-term capital, these declines naturally tended to make him even more reluctant to substitute long-term capital for short-term.

The capital needs of cotton-factory firms were sufficiently large to tempt most entrepreneurs to utilize as much capital as possible. The temptation was particularly strong for those who were—for the moment—producing a unique or nearly unique product at a high profit. Additional funds, if they were forthcoming, were likely, at least at first, to be short-term rather than long-term capital. Samuel Oldknow, the great muslin manufacturer, thought at one point in his spectacular career that he could make good use of five times as much capital as he had access to. The heavy load of debt that was ultimately to force him out of the cotton industry originated in a series of short-term advances that the Arkwrights ultimately funded into a long-term debt.[6]

The market for short-term capital was much more highly developed during the Industrial Revolution than was the long-term market.[7] Other things being equal, access to short-term capital was likely to be easier than access to long-term capital. In 1806, Sam-

---

[4] J. R. McCulloch, *A Descriptive and Statistical Account of the British Empire* (4th ed.; London, 1854), II, 435. For the terminology of the national debt see C. R. Fay, *English Economic History: Mainly since 1700* (2nd ed.; Cambridge, 1948), pp. 65–66.

[5] D. M. Joslin, "London Bankers in Wartime, 1739–1784," *Studies in the Industrial Revolution: Essays Presented to T. S. Ashton*, ed. L. S. Pressnell (London, 1960), p. 176.

[6] Draft of a letter by Samuel Oldknow to S. and W. Salte, April 22, 1783, quoted in Unwin, Hulme, and Taylor, *Samuel Oldknow*, p. 10, and *passim*.

[7] M. M. Postan, "Recent Trends in the Accumulation of Capital," *Economic History Review*, 1st ser., VI (1935), 6–7; and A. H. John, "Insurance Investment and the London Money Market of the 18th Century," *Economica*, N.S., XX (1953), 143.

uel Hibbert-Ware complained that "the mythology of the ancients denominated certain periods of the world, the age of gold, the age of silver, and the age of iron, and it has not been unaptly remarked that the present one may be fairly stiled [sic] the *age of papers.*" He wrote that "in this market, the cheapness of credit is become almost proverbial, and there are certain *slanderers* hesitating not to say, if a *man of straw* were placed upon the 'change, credit would be offered him by the good people of Manchester." [8] While the use of short-term credit to supplement a firm's capital was very widespread, the ability to dispense with such practices was regarded by entrepreneurs like Robert Owen and McConnel and Kennedy as a criterion of the stability of a firm.[9]

The substitution of short-term for long-term capital could produce considerable difficulties for the manufacturers. It could very easily result in disaster if the firm overextended itself or was caught in a general credit contraction. While short-term capital seems to have been readily available under ordinary circumstances in the form of short-run credits or a short-term bank loan, for example, the flow of such capital could be, and sometimes was, cut off in times of crisis. During the crisis that began in the autumn of 1792, Samuel Oldknow was being pressed for the repayment of a loan made to him by his bankers, Smith, Payne and Smith.[10] Some time between January and June of 1799, Heywood Brothers and Company made a formal loan to McConnel and Kennedy, the only such loan the spinners were to receive from their bankers between 1795 and 1825. On the nineteenth of Octo-

---

[8] *Remarks on the Facility of Obtaining Commercial Credit* (Manchester, 1806), pp. 19 and 51. Italics in the original.

[9] Robert Owen, *The Life of Robert Owen by Himself* (New York, 1920), pp. 16–17 and 25; J. Watson, Jr., to McConnel and Kennedy, May 27, 1802, McConnel and Kennedy MSS, Letters Received, Lewis Library of Commerce, University of Manchester.

[10] Unwin, Hulme, and Taylor, *Samuel Oldknow*, pp. 155–156. The timing of the start of the crisis is confirmed by Arthur D. Gayer, W. W. Rostow, and Anna Jacobson Schwartz, *The Growth and Fluctuation of the British Economy, 1790–1850* (Oxford, 1953), I, 348.

ber, with the crisis of 1799 under way, the bankers were pressing McConnel and Kennedy, who probably had used the money for an expansion of their factory, for payment. By the end of the year, the loan, which probably had taken the form of an overdraft, had been liquidated.[11]

A considerable portion of the capital required in the cotton industry between 1760 and 1830 was supplied on a short-term basis, which, to contemporaries, meant for a period of six months or less. Any loan made for a longer period was regarded as a "pemanent loan." [12] Short-term lending was made possible by the existence and further development of a short-term capital market that was better integrated and better organized than the long-term market. The development of the long-term capital market did not catch up with that of the short-term market until after the middle of the nineteenth century.[13] This relative weakness of

---

[11] Heywood Brothers and Company to McConnel and Kennedy, Oct. 19, 1799, McConnel and Kennedy MSS, Letters Received; and L. S. Pressnell, *Country Banking in the Industrial Revolution* (Oxford, 1956), p. 336. Gayer, Rostow, and Schwartz do not list 1799 as a crisis year, although they take note that Thorpe did (*Growth and Fluctuation*, I, 357). The crisis condition may have been peculiar to the cotton industry or may have been purely in the minds of the cotton manufacturers. Spinners feared high cotton prices and August 1799 saw the highest cotton prices paid between 1790 and 1850 (Gayer, Rostow, and Schwartz, *Growth and Fluctuation*, I, 71, n. 4). There is considerable evidence of this fear of high cotton prices. McConnel and Kennedy informed Robert Kennedy that "it is always a bad trade for the spinners when cotton is high and at present the majority of them are complaining heavily" (McConnel and Kennedy to Robert Kennedy, Glasgow, April 4, 1805, McConnel and Kennedy MSS, Letter Books). Robert Owen informed Jeremy Bentham that "cotton spinning is the best trade when the raw material is low" (Letter of Robert Owen to Jeremy Bentham, Oct. 25, 1818, Bentham Papers, Vol. IX [Additional MSS, no. 33545], f. 338, British Museum). Kirkman Finlay, who was both merchant and spinner, in 1833 remembered 1799 as a year in which the cotton industry "got a severe blow" (Evidence of Kirkman Finlay, *Report from the Select Committee on Manufactures, Commerce and Shipping* [1833], q. 740).

[12] Evidence of Lewis Loyd, *Report from the Select Committee on Manufactures, Commerce and Shipping* (1833), qq. 453–454.

[13] Postan, "Recent Trends," pp. 5–7.

the long-term capital market is also characteristic of many modern underdeveloped countries. The reasons may be similar: high productivity of capital in mercantile activities and a related high general liquidity preference.[14]

Little, if any, of the short-term capital seems to have come from abroad.[15] Foreign investment in Great Britain prior to 1760 was probably largely restricted to long-term investments, like government securities and Bank of England stock. Even in this restricted sphere, there was a net efflux of capital between 1760 and 1830. Contrary to the opinions of some contemporaries, Dutch investors in British government securities were selling out from the seventies onward, and by 1816 most of these securities were held by British subjects.[16] There was an absolute as well as a relative decline in these Dutch holdings.[17] The same trend is reflected in the ownership of Bank of England stock. Foreign holdings of Bank stock had once been quite substantial, but by 1811 foreign proprietors of the Bank of England formed only one-tenth of the whole number of stockholders, and by 1835 they were negligible in number.[18] Great Britain, it is true, received a windfall after 1789, when some French refugee capital was hurriedly transmitted to London via Hamburg because of the fear of possible expropriation, and this capital may have played a significant part in the

---

[14] M. R. Solomon, "The Structure of the Market in Undeveloped Economies," *Quarterly Journal of Economics*, LXII (1948), 535–537.

[15] Albert H. Imlah, "British Balance of Payments and the Export of Capital, 1816–1913," *Economic History Review*, 2nd ser., V (1952), 226–228, 234–235, and 227, n. 1; Ashton, *18th Century*, pp. 127–128.

[16] For a contemporary opinion see "Mercator," *A Letter to the Inhabitants of Manchester on the Exportation of Cotton Twist* (Manchester, April 28, 1800), p. 9, n. For the Dutch retreat see Ashton, *18th Century*, p. 127. For British holdings see Arthur Hope-Jones, *Income Tax in the Napoleonic Wars* (Cambridge, 1939), p. 112.

[17] A. Carter, "Dutch Foreign Investment, 1738–1800," *Economica*, N.S., XX (1953), 322–40, and "Note on a 'Note on Yardsticks,'" *Economic History Review*, 2nd ser., XII (1960), 440–444.

[18] J. H. Clapham, *The Bank of England: A History, 1694–1914* (Cambridge, 1944), I, 255, and II, 131.

credit expansion of the early nineties. The flight of capital from France to England was, however, only a brief episode that ended with substantial repatriation after the reintroduction of a specie currency in France in 1796.[19] In general, foreign capital seems to have played a small and diminishing role in the British capital market.[20]

Despite the absence of extensive foreign investment of capital on a long-term or a short-term basis, the British economy proved itself well adapted to providing short-term capital for the transformation and expansion of the cotton industry. This capital came from a considerable variety of sources; the banking institutions, the manufacturers, the business community in general, and the laborers in the cotton industry, all contributed to the financing of the changes and expansion associated with the Industrial Revolution.

Some potential sources could not, however, be freely tapped. There is a great deal of truth in M. M. Postan's statement that

by the beginning of the eighteenth century there were enough rich people in the country to finance an economic effort far in excess of the modest activities of the leaders of the Industrial Revolution. It can, indeed, be doubted whether there had ever been a period in English history when the accumulated wealth of landlords and merchants, of religious and educational institutions would have been inadequate for the purpose. What was inadequate was not the quantity of stored-up wealth, but its behavior. The reservoirs of savings were full enough, but conduits to connect them with the wheels of industry were few and meagre.[21]

---

[19] See Ashton, *18th Century,* p. 127.

[20] There is some indication of this in the difficulty of finding foreign proprietors of British cotton factories. I know of only one: a native of Alsace named De Jong who was a partner in a Warrington cotton mill in the twenties (William Otto Henderson, *Britain and Industrial Europe 1750–1870; Studies in British Influence on the Industrial Revolution in Western Europe* (Liverpool, 1954) , p. 28, n. 51.

[21] "Recent Trends," p. 2.

One of the factors affecting the flow of capital was the interest rate, or more precisely, the interest rates. These were legally limited to a maximum of about 5 per cent during the Industrial Revolution. This restriction on the inducements that an entrepreneur could offer for the use of capital applied to both short-term and long-term loans. The usury law passed during the reign of Queen Anne reduced the maximum legal rate of interest from 6 per cent to 5 per cent. The law itself made minor exceptions for the rates on loans on ships and on ship's cargoes. This law remained in effect until it was repealed by stages between 1833 and 1854. The first step in the direction of repeal exempted from the operation of the law bills of exchange with less than three months to run, and this exemption was extended in 1837 to include bills with less than twelve months' currency.[22]

One important borrower, the government, was always exempt from the operation of the usury laws. Government expeditures and taxation, which had been heavy in the second half of the seventeenth century and the first fifteen years of the eighteenth century, were moderate between the death of Queen Anne and the outbreak of the American Revolution.[23] The Revolutionary and Napoleonic Wars, however, sent taxation and government borrowing sharply upward until peace and the postwar conversions somewhat eased the government's capital needs, although the termination of the income tax in 1816 and other tax cuts made reducing the national debt difficult.[24]

----

[22] On the Usury Law and its repeal see P. Sraffa and M. H. Dobb eds., *The Works and Correspondence of David Ricardo*, V (Cambridge, 1952), 335–337, ed. n.; and Sir William Searle Holdsworth, *A History of English Law*, ed. A. L. Goodhart and H. G. Hanbury (7th ed. rev.; London, 1956), XIII, 330.

[23] H. J. Habakkuk, "England," *The European Nobility in the Eighteenth Century: Studies of the Nobilities of the Major European States in the Pre-Reform Era*, ed. A. Goodwin (London, 1953), pp. 9–10; Fay, *English Economic History*, pp. 70–71; for the statistics see McCulloch, *Descriptive and Statistical Account*, II, 435.

[24] On taxation see Hope-Jones, *Income Tax*, pp. 112 and 124–125; on the conversions see Clapham, *Bank of England*, II, 94 and 150; on the difficulty of

Although the usury laws applied to most loan transactions in which the government was not the borrower, these statutes could be and were evaded.[25] It would not be accurate, however, to say that the restrictions were without effect. The evasions were not equally easy to achieve in all types of loans. Ricardo's statement before a parliamentary committee in 1818 that the law was evaded "upon almost occasions" and his assertion on the floor of the House of Commons in 1821 that "the laws had always been inoperative; and during the war indirect means had been found of obtaining seven, eight, ten and fifteen per cent interest" referred only to the financing of stock-exchange transactions or to the use of government securities to finance other transactions.[26]

The usury laws permitted the interest rate to be legally stretched from 5 per cent to 5¼ per cent by allowing a one-quarter of 1 per cent commission for special expenses involved in making a particular loan. Although frequent use was probably made of this loophole, the burden of proving that special expenses

---

reducing the debt see Elie Halévy, *A History of the English People* (2nd ed. rev.; London, 1949–1952), II, 37–40, 119–121, and 297–299.

[25] The maximum rate in Ireland was 6 per cent; in Scotland it was the same as in England and Wales. For a list of methods of evasion see J. B. Smith, "Notes on Usury" (no date, but from internal evidence before 1833), J. B. Smith MSS, MS923.2/S339, f. 7, J. B. Smith Papers. Manchester Central Library. The penalties for evasion, however, were high (Ashton, *18th Century*, p. 28).

[26] Quotations from Great Britain, House of Commons, *Parliamentary Papers, Report from the Select Committee on the Usury Laws, 1818*, 1845 (376/611), Vol. XII, and *Hansard's Parliamentary Debates*, N.S. (1821), both as reprinted in Sraffa, ed., *Works of Ricardo*, V, 337. For Ricardo's description of the use of government stock to evade the usury laws see Sraffa, ed. *Works of Ricardo*, V, 338, 341–342, and 345. Ricardo agreed that the use of government securities gave its holders "a greater facility of raising money than other persons possess" (p. 345). The most important technique used for this purpose was called "continuation." For a definition of this term see Sir Robert H. I. Palgrave, ed., *Dictionary of Political Economy*, ed. H. Higgs (3 vols.; London, 1923–1926), I, 396. In essence, the borrower sold his government securities and at the same time contracted to buy them back at a specified future date at a specified higher price. The difference in prices was the interest.

were in fact involved rested, in a court of law, with the creditor and made it difficult for him to raise the interest rate indefinitely by adding additional expenses to the cost of the loan. Banks could and did add somewhat to the cost of getting a loan by tacking on special charges like postage.[27] In 1828, the *Circular to Bankers* estimated that before 1825 the normal cost to bankers of making advances to their customers was 6½ per cent.[28] In 1830, Sir John Wrottesley, then an M.P. for South Staffordshire, wrote in a memorandum to Sir Robert Peel that manufacturers "by commission and other details (too tedious to particularize) pay 7 per cent interest." [29] Although the usury laws did not in fact keep the cost of borrowing at 5 or even 5¼ per cent, they probably helped to prevent the rate of interest actually paid from being pushed even higher.

On bills of exchange, the interest rate proper was kept at 5 per cent. In 1818, David Ricardo, testifying before a parliamentary committee, said that "discounts are strictly regulated by the laws of usury." [30] The interest rate on bills of exchange was actually kept at 5 per cent because a creditor could lose his right to protest a bill if it was drawn, even by accident, at a higher than legal rate of interest; the illegal discount of a bill could also cost the discounter the right to use the bill as proof of the existence of a debt.[31] In addition to the possible loss of capital, the lender had to consider the legal penalty; this was a fine three times the size of the capital involved, and it was in fact sometimes exacted.[32]

Perhaps the most widespread means of evading the usury laws in the cotton industry sprang from the ability of the parties to a

---

[27] Pressnell, *Country Banking,* pp. 285–286.

[28] L. S. Pressnell, "Public Monies and the Development of English Banking," *Economic History Review,* 2nd ser., V (1953), 386.

[29] Sir John Wrottesley, "Observations on the Change of the System of Banking" (March 1830), Peel Papers, Vol. CCXX [Additional MSS, no. 40,400], f. 145, British Museum.

[30] Sraffa, ed., *Works of Ricardo,* V, 344–345.

[31] Pressnell, *Country Banking,* pp. 286–287.

[32] T. S. Ashton, *Economic Fluctuations in England, 1700–1800* (Oxford, 1959), p. 175, n. 5.

sale of goods to vary their terms.[33] McConnel and Kennedy offered their yarn for sale to merchants and weavers, who usually had a choice of terms in making their payments. The buyer could either pay with a bill having two months to run after a two-month credit period, or he could pay with a two-month bill immediately upon receipt of his goods. If the purchaser decided to forego the credit period, he was allowed to deduct $1\frac{1}{4}$ per cent from the invoice he received.[34] On an annual basis this came to about $7\frac{1}{2}$ per cent. This meant, in effect, that McConnel and Kennedy received about $7\frac{1}{2}$ per cent interest on its book debts.

Evans and Sons, the Derby spinners and bankers, made a similar use of its book credits. In 1807, with trade somewhat depressed, terms for sewing cotton were eight months credit or a $7\frac{1}{2}$ per cent discount, and candlewick terms were six months credit or a $7\frac{1}{2}$ per cent discount. The firm also authorized its agent to raise these discounts to 10 per cent—if the competition warranted it. The rates of interest on the Derby firm's book credits were, therefore, between $11\frac{1}{4}$ and 15 per cent on sewing cotton and between 15 and 20 per cent on candlewicks. These rates seem to have been related to the state of trade. Early in 1809, when trade was recovering, Evans and Company became reluctant to give the extra $2\frac{1}{2}$ per cent discount, and later in the year, when the boom was under way, they became extremely reluctant to do so. Since these changes in terms did not apply to cash customers, they cannot be regarded as price changes; they were, rather, changes in interest rates.[35]

The Strutts stated their terms somewhat differently. In 1827,

---

[33] J. B. Smith places this first on the list of methods of evasion of usury laws ("Notes on Usury," f. 7).

[34] McConnel and Kennedy MSS, Letter Books, *passim*. The deduction was sometimes higher. In 1796, McConnel and Kennedy offered to deduct 2 per cent for a customer in Ireland for foregoing a three-month credit period. In this case the annual rate is 8 per cent (McConnel and Kennedy to Charles Bourne and Company, Dublin, May 25, 1796, McConnel and Kennedy MSS, Letter Books).

[35] L. S. Pressnell, "The Rate of Interest in the Eighteenth Century," *Studies,* ed. Pressnell, pp. 200–201.

they wrote that "we allow 10 p ct for Cash or Bill due in 14 days or 7½ p ct for bill at 3 Mos. from date of Invoice." [36] These terms remained the same as late as 1862.[37] The Strutts' rate of interest was, therefore, about 10 per cent.

The charging of interest rates like those above constituted gross evasions of the usury laws, although they did not constitute breaches of them.

There was one important type of loan on which almost no evasion of the usury laws was possible—mortgage loans. This was probably due to the elaborate legal formalities involved in mortgaging land, which made evasion extremely difficult and made the punishment of violations relatively easy.[38] This obstacle to evasion may have produced some difficulty in mobilizing landed wealth for direct investment in industry during periods when interest rates were high. The difficulty of evading the usury laws did not, of course, preclude the sale of land for the same purpose.[39] Although it does not seem likely that the mortgaging of land would be undertaken to raise short-term capital, it might, perhaps, be used to raise long-term capital.

Although it is almost impossible to avoid using terms like "the" short-term rate of interest or "the" long-term rate of interest, it must be understood that between 1760 and 1830 the phrase "the rate of interest" had considerably less meaning than it was to have, let us say, a century later. There existed during the earlier period many different capital markets—markets that were often partly insulated from each other. Each of these had its own interest rate. In general, provincial rates of interest were higher than

---

[36] W. G. and J. Strutt, Derby, to D. and G. Holy, Sheffield, Aug. 16, 1827, as quoted in R. S. Fitton and A. P. Wadsworth, *The Strutts and the Arkwrights, 1758–1830: A Study of the Early Factory System* (Manchester, 1958), p. 300.

[37] *Ibid.*, p. 300, n. 1; Pressnell, *Country Banking*, p. 286.

[38] There were, of course, noneconomic reasons for the purchase of land and for investment in such land once it was purchased. These reasons were summed up in Malthus' statement that "every day lands are purchased with the fruits of industry and talents. They afford the great prize, the *'otium cum dignitate'* to every species of laudable exertion" (Sraffa, ed., *Works of Ricardo*, II, 222–223).

[39] Postan, "Recent Trends," pp. 4–5 and 7–10.

London rates, but they tended as a rule to move in the same direction as London rates, although there were lags, of course. The parallelism of movements was assured by the commercial and financial dominance of London and the existence of important provincial financial centers linked to London.[40] The links between London and the provinces were growing stronger during the period we are considering. One possible interpretation of the development of British banking during the eighteenth and nineteenth centuries is that it was a movement in the direction of creating a more nearly "frictionless" capital market; the establishment of closer links between London and the provinces can be interpreted as a stage in this development.

A further warning must be issued against assuming a constant relationship between interest rates on short-term and long-term capital. In modern free-enterprise economies, the normal short-term rate of interest is ordinarily lower than the normal long-term rate. The average difference between the two rates can be regarded as being influenced by two sets of factors operating on the short-term rate in opposite directions. The short-term rate, at any given moment, would be higher than it is were it not for the fact that the short-term lender retains—in lieu of some of the interest due him—a greater degree of freedom to maneuver in the capital market. At the same time, the short-term rate is higher than it would be were it not for the extra expense and inconvenience to the short-term borrower resulting from the need to continually review short-term borrowing.[41]

---

[40] Ashton, *Economic Fluctuations*, p. 88; Pressnell, "Rate of Interest," pp. 201–203. For geographical variations in the rates of interest see Ashton, *18th Century*, pp. 26–27. Adam Smith noted a difference in the rates of interest between England and Scotland (*An Inquiry into the Nature and Causes of the Wealth of Nations*, ed. E. A. Seligman [2 vols., 1910 ed.; London, 1947], I, 80). In 1833, Samuel Gurney noted a difference between the discount rates of English and Scottish banks (Evidence of Samuel Gurney, *Report from the Select Committee on Manufactures, Commerce and Shipping*, qq. 373–374). The rate in Scotland was in both cases higher.

[41] D. H. Robertson, *Lectures on Economic Principles* (London, 1959), III, 77.

Although the existence of this gap between rates is well established for the present British capital market,[42] it is far from established for the period under consideration.[43] There is relatively little information on which to base a conclusion.

The yields on East India bonds and the discount on navy bills can be regarded as indicators of the short-term rate of interest; there are, however, serious gaps in both these series. If the yield on Bank of England stock is taken as an indication of the long-term rate of interest and compared with the two indicators of the short-term rate, it appears that there was no constant relationship between the two rates. Between 1776 and 1786, for example, each of these rates was the highest rate at some time or other; during

---

[42] *Ibid.*, p. 78.

[43] The only available series is the one for the rate of discount charged by Overend, Gurney and Company, the great London bill dealers. This series does not start until 1824. A comparison of the Gurney discount rate and the Yield on consols is shown in Table A. Gurney's rate, it must be remembered,

Table A. Consol yields and discount rates, 1824–1830

Year	Yield on consols (%)	Gurney's rate of discount (%)
1824	3.30	3.50
1825	3.54	3.88
1826	3.79	4.50
1827	3.61	3.25
1828	3.54	3.04
1829	3.34	3.38
1830	3.49	2.81

is a London rate for bills and probably for particularly good bills. It does not tell us much about the rate of interest in the provinces, where bills of what might be regarded in London as a much inferior type were discounted. The Gurney rate may be regarded as the minimum rate for certain types of discount. The consol figures are from George Frederick Warren and Frank Ashmore Pearson, *Gold and Prices* (London, 1935), p. 403. Overend, Gurney and Company's discount rate is from W. T. C. King, *History of the London Discount Market* (London, 1936), p. 80.

most of this period one short-term rate—that for the discount on navy bills—was above the long-term rate, and the other was below.[44]

Although little is known about the movement of short-term rates, a great deal is known about long-term rates. The movements of the long-term rate of interest can be seen in the yields of

Table 13. Average yield on government 3% securities by decades, 1731–1900

Years	% yield	Years	% yield
1731–1740	3.0	1821–1830	3.6
1741–1750	3.2	1831–1840	3.4
1751–1760	3.2	1841–1850	3.2
1761–1770	3.6	1851–1860	3.2
1771–1780	3.9	1861–1870	3.3
1781–1790	4.6	1871–1880	3.2
1791–1800	4.6	1881–1890	3.0
1801–1810	4.8	1891–1900	2.7
1811–1820	4.6		

Source: Based on Appendix 12.

Table 14. Average yield by periods, 1731–1900

Years	% yield
1731–1760	3.2
1761–1830	4.2
1831–1900	3.1

Source: Based on Appendix 12.

long-term government securities, which are summarized in Tables 13 and 14 (see Appendix 11 for all yields discussed).

During the seventy years that fall between 1761 and 1830, the

---

[44] Pressnell, "Rate of Interest," pp. 211–214. The article contains graphs based on these rates and yields. In giving evidence before the select committee of 1818, Ricardo indicated that he thought that the yield on exchequer bills was the best criterion of the market rate of interest (Sraffa, ed., *Works of Ricardo,* V, 344–345). Unfortunately only a few scattered exchequer-bill prices are available at present.

average annual yield on these government securities was at, or over, 5 per cent for only eleven years: 1781–1782, 1784, 1797–1799, 1803–1805, 1812, and 1816. All but two of these were war years, and the two that were not, 1784 and 1816, immediately followed a major war. Until the point at which the usury laws came into effect was reached, the rates of interest for loans on mortgages, personal bonds, and bills were probably higher than the yields on government stock.[45] It is, however, difficult to estimate how large the differences between these rates were.

In 1828, when the average rate of interest paid by country-bank customers was said to be between 6 and 7 per cent,[46] the yield on consols averaged around 3½ per cent. The average yield on consols was the same in 1830, when manufacturers were reported to be borrowing at up to 7 per cent.[47] The rates seem to indicate a spread of 2½ to 3½ per cent between the yield on long-term government securities and the higher interest rates paid to country bankers. Although the amount of evidence available is not large, it is probably safe to say that more often than not the short-term rates of interest in the provinces were in fact over the 5 per cent limit fixed by the usury law.

The yield on long-term government securities was exceptionally high between 1761 and 1830. The average yield for these seventy years was 4.2 per cent. This yield must be compared with an average yield of 3.2 per cent for the thirty years from 1731 to 1760, and the even lower yield of 3.1 per cent for the seventy-year period from 1831 to 1900. In no single year between 1761 and 1830 did the average annual yield fall as low as 3.2 per cent; in no single year between 1731 and 1760 or between 1831 and 1900 did the average annual yield rise as high as 4.2 per cent.

It is not necessary to assume the indicated differential of 2½ to 3½ per cent between yield of long-term government securities and country interest rates to believe that the usury laws generated real

---

[45] Ashton, *18th Century*, p. 28.

[46] Pressnell, *Country Banking*, p. 286.

[47] Wrottesley, "Observations," Peel Papers, Vol. CCXX, f. 145.

pressures in the capital markets that were relieved partly by evasion of the law and partly by diversion of capital into endeavors where such evasion would be easier. The existence of a spread between the rates of as little as 1 per cent would have put the average annual rate in the provinces over 5 per cent in thirty-eight of the seventy years between 1761 and 1830.

As has been indicated, however, the usury laws were selectively rather than generally effective. It seems certain that, when the yield on long-term government securities went over 5 per cent, there was a tendency to divert funds from agriculture to these securities.[48] An officer of an insurance company that had invested in mortgages stated, in his testimony in 1818 before the Select Committee on the Usury Laws, that during the Napoleonic Wars, "for a period of, I think, six or seven years, mortgages were not to be obtained; the term 'mortgage' had become almost obsolete." [49] This diversion of funds from agriculture may also have benefited the cotton manufacturer, who was, in practice, only partially subject to the usury laws. It also seems possible that this diversion of funds from agricultural investment may have operated at times when the yield on long-term government securities was below 5 per cent, but in the absence of more data, not much more can be said.

---

[48] Ashton, *18th Century,* pp. 27–28. On the difficulty of obtaining mortgage loans during periods of high interest rates, see Evidence of Samuel Gurney, *Report from the Select Committee on Manufactures, Commerce, and Shipping,* q. 162; Clapham, *Bank of England,* II, 60. The root of the capital difficulties of agriculture may have gone much deeper than the operation of the usury laws. Coke of Norfolk only doubled his rents in the forty years between 1776 and 1816, while reinvesting 11 to 17 per cent of his gross rents in his technically advanced estates. It is possible that the yield on agricultural investment was so low that landowners would have had great difficulty in bidding for capital even in the absence of the usury laws (R. A. C. Parker, "Coke of Norfolk and the Agrarian Revolution," *Economic History Review,* 2nd ser., VIII [1955], 156–166).

[49] *Parliamentary Papers, Report from the Select Committee on the Usury Laws, 1818,* Vol. XII, q. 197, as quoted in Pressnell, "Rate of Interest," p. 184, n. 2.

One factor that tended to counteract the selective effects of the usury laws on investment needs to be mentioned. The investor of the late eighteenth and early nineteenth centuries, whether investing on a short-term or a long-term basis, tended to be somewhat less sensitive to changes in interest rates than his successors.[50] This tendency was reflected in the relative inflexibility of many interest rates and bank charges during the Industrial Revolution, although the process of creating the "purer," yield-sensitive investor was already under way. The rigidity of some of the rates and charges referred to was so great that at times they seem almost like customary rates and fees. Bank rate—the Bank of England's discount rate—remained at 5 per cent for the forty-nine years from 1773 until 1822, when it was reduced to 4 per cent. The rate was changed only twice between 1822 and 1836.[51] In Manchester, at least, bankers' interest payments and interest charges remained for many years the same as Bank rate. The rate of commission on bills provided by Lancashire banks never varied, while the rate of commission charged for providing cash rose from one-quarter of 1 per cent to three-eighths of 1 per cent during the early days of the restriction period and stayed there for about a quarter of a century, after which it returned to the former rate.[52]

Rather than vary their interest rates frequently, bankers rationed the credit they extended. When Samuel Oldknow was establishing his connection with the Derby banking firm of Evans and Sons in 1786, the bankers wrote that they would discount a

---

[50] Postan, "Recent Trends," p. 7.

[51] Clapham, *Bank of England*, II, 85. For tabulations of Bank rate for the years 1694–1822, see *ibid.*, I, 299; for the years 1797–1914, see *ibid.*, II, 429–432. The figures for the years before 1773 are incomplete. Bank rate was not, however, the only way in which the Bank controlled the volume of its discounts. In 1795, for example, it rationed its discounts (*ibid.*, I, 269–270). In 1821, in order to increase its discounting, it raised the currency of the bills it would discount from sixty-five to ninety-five days (*ibid.*, II, 85).

[52] T. S. Ashton, "The Bill of Exchange and Private Banks in Lancashire, 1790–1830," *Papers in English Monetary History*, ed. T. S. Ashton and R. S. Sayers (Oxford, 1953), pp. 46–48.

fixed amount of bills of exchange for him each week at "common interest" and that "on these terms we can generally choose our customers; which is more satisfactory to us than any trifling advantage we would make in time of necessity." [53] At a time when business failures were frequent, when bad debts must have been an important element in banking costs, when high productivity of capital and high hopes for the future must have made the interest rate a relatively poor means of rationing credit, direct rationing of credit was, no doubt, an attractive device.

The use of direct rationing, instead of indirect impersonal rationing on the basis of the borrower's ability to pay, is not surprising in a closely-knit localized society in which connection and influence counted for much and the ability to pay a higher interest rate did not count for everything. One cannot help but wonder if the rate of interest was much of a consideration in the loans made by Richard Arkwright and Thomas Coutts (the banker to the royal family) to Georgiana, Duchess of Devonshire, in order that she might pay her gambling debts.[54]

Outside the banking system, however, there was a tendency for investors to become more sensitive to yields on investments. The general growth and development of the market for government securities and for chartered joint-stock company shares, which continued during the Industrial Revolution, probably facilitated this transformation of the investor. Although this evolution was never absolutely complete at any time, it was probably further advanced in the 1820's than it had been in the 1720's and still further along in the 1860's than it had been a generation earlier.[55]

In a period of high yields on a relatively large and often growing volume of government securities, the operation and at least partial effectiveness of the usury laws meant that the cotton indus-

---

[53] Thomas Evans and Sons to Samuel Oldknow, December 1786, as quoted in Urwin, Hulme, and Taylor, *Samuel Oldknow*, p. 177.

[54] Fitton and Wadsworth, *The Strutts*, pp. 94–96.

[55] Postan, "Recent Trends," pp. 4–5 and 7; John, "Insurance Investment," pp. 142–143.

try was at a disadvantage in its competition for capital on either a short- or a long-term basis. This disadvantage, though it was not so great as the one faced by the agricultural investor, was none the less real, and it must have been deeply felt. The cotton manufacturer was an investor in an industry with rising productivity. He was, therefore, in a position to bid up interest rates. The inflexibility of some of these rates placed him at a disadvantage, or rather prevented him from taking fuller advantage of the rising productivity in the industry.

One would expect the formal institutions in the capital market to be the first resort of a manufacturer who was endeavouring to improve his access to capital. The nucleus of this market was a complex of developing banking institutions. Although these institutions were dynamic in the late eighteenth century and early nineteenth century, they could not be adapted to all—or even most—of the changing capital needs of an economy that was launched on a course of revolutionary transformation. The banks were best suited to supply short-term capital and will be considered in that connection.

Part II

The Markets for Short-Term Capital

Chapter III

The Banks and the Cotton Industry

DURING the Industrial Revolution, the market for short-term capital was best suited to meet the manufacturer's need for "circulating" or "floating" capital, most of which was used to pay wages or buy raw materials.[1] Although it is difficult to estimate the amount of working capital used by the cotton industry, it clearly was smaller than the total amount of fixed capital invested in the industry. In 1832, Samuel Greg, who owned five mills producing about 1.5 per cent of the total yarn and cotton-goods output of the United Kingdom, estimated the ratio of fixed to working capital at two to one. In 1834, it was probably about the same, although some spokesmen for the industry, preoccupied with their attempts to block the passage of factory legislation, fell into an understandable error and estimated it at four or five to one.[2]

Working capital was essential to the industry, but it was needed in smaller amounts than fixed capital. Part of this need was met by the more or less formal institutions in the capital markets; part of it, from sources outside the formal capital markets.

---

[1] "Working capital" would be the current equivalent. "Circulating capital" was used by J. R. McCulloch, for example (*Commercial Dictionary* [London, 1834], p. 443). "Floating capital" was used by A. Baynes (*The Cotton Trade: Two Lectures* [London, 1857]).

[2] See M. Blaug, "The Productivity of Capital in the Lancashire Cotton Industry during the Nineteenth Century," *Economic History Review,* 2nd ser., XIII (1961), 371 (for a discussion of Greg's 1832 estimate) and 372 (Blaug's correction of McCulloch's estimate for 1834). For the contemporary overestimate, see *ibid.,* pp. 374–375; the error resulted from a confusion between the fixed and variable costs and the ratio between fixed and working capital.

The heart of the short-term market was the banking system. By 1830, the most important elements in this system were the Bank of England, the private London banks, the private country banks, the savings banks, and the joint-stock banks. These actually constituted a loosely and partially joined network rather than an integrated "system," although even the moderate integration of the 1830's marked an improvement over the 1760's.

If the banks were the heart of the market, bills of exchange were its life blood. The bill of exchange probably originated as a device to avoid the actual transfer of coin and became a credit instrument by being drawn for a longer period than was necessary for remittance.[3] The practice of discounting bills of exchange is of great antiquity and was well known in England in the later Middle Ages.[4]

The bill of exchange was the product of a sale. It was an order by a seller to a buyer to pay a specified sum to a named third party (or anyone designated by him) on a specified future date. The instrument was drawn by the seller (or creditor) and became legally binding when the buyer (or debtor) accepted it by writing "Accepted" on its face and signing it. The third party had only to endorse it to make the bill transferable to someone else, and an indefinite number of transfers was possible. Any endorser became contingently liable for the debt and each endorser added to the security of the bill.[5] As Adam Smith observed in *The Wealth of Nations*, "though the drawer, acceptor, and the endorsers of the bill should, all of them, be persons of doubtful credit, yet still the shortness of the date gives some security to the owner of the bill. Though all of them may be very likely to become bankrupts, it is a chance if they all become so in so short a time. The house is

---

[3] A. E. Feavearyear, *The Pound Sterling: A History of English Money* (Oxford, 1931), pp. 150–151.

[4] W. T. C. King, *History of the London Discount Market* (London, 1936), pp. 4–5.

[5] *Ibid.*, pp. xvi–xvii; R. G. Hawtrey, *A Century of Bank Rate* (London, 1938), pp. 4–6.

crazy, says a weary traveller to himself, and will not stand very long; but it is a chance if it falls tonight, and I will venture therefore, to sleep in it tonight." [6] Although the instrument made no mention of any interest, the sum specified in the bill was usually the amount for which the goods would have been sold for cash, plus an interest payment.

The bill of exchange had a number of useful characteristics. It usually originated in a real commercial transaction; it was negotiable; it was regarded as legal evidence of the existence of a debt; where such a bill existed, the law provided relatively good facilities for collection; and it increased in security with each endorsement. [7] Because of these characteristics, the recipient of a bill of exchange bearing the name or names of well-known firms—this usually meant London firms—could, if he preferred not to hold the bill to maturity, pay it out. [8] Indeed, a considerable part of the payments and receipts of merchants and manufacturers was in this form. [9] It was probably the high degree of utility of bills of

---

[6] *An Inquiry into the Nature and Causes of the Wealth of Nations,* ed. E. R. A. Seligman (2 vols., 1910 ed.; London, 1947), I, 275.

[7] King, *London Discount Market,* pp. xvi–xvii; Hawtrey, *Century of Bank Rate,* pp. 4–6; Sir William Searle Holdsworth, *A History of English Law,* ed. A. L. Goodhart and H. G. Hanbury XII (London, 1938), 529; J. H. Clapham, *The Bank of England: A History, 1694–1914* (Cambridge, 1944), I, 204, n. 3.

[8] On the importance of London bills, see Hawtrey, *Century of Bank Rate,* p. 7. The request for, and sometimes the insistence on, payment in London bills is a constant refrain in the correspondence of McConnel and Kennedy (McConnel and Kennedy MSS, Letter Books, *passim,* Lewis Library of Commerce, University of Manchester). There seems to have been a premium of just under one-half of 1 per cent on London bills (McConnel and Kennedy to J. Monteith, Sr., May 12, 1801, and McConnel and Kennedy, Feb. 26, 1802, McConnel and Kennedy MSS). In 1808, when the pressure on the means of payment was more severe, the premium went over one-half of 1 per cent (McConnel and Kennedy to Robert McGavin and Company, Nov. 14, 1808, McConnel and Kennedy MSS, Letter Books).

[9] This was particularly true of Lancashire (T. S. Ashton, "The Bill of Exchange and Private Banks in Lancashire, 1790–1830," *Papers in English Monetary History,* ed. T. S. Ashton and R. S. Sayers [Oxford, 1953], pp. 37–49.

exchange for making payments that caused Byles, a lawyer writing in 1829, to refer to them as "these wheels of the vast commercial system."[10]

Although bills of exchange could be, and were, paid out for some of a cotton firm's purchases, they were not suitable for all types of disbursements. They were useless for tax payments, or for payments at a distance to persons who might not be expected to be familiar with the credit of firms engaged in the cotton industry.

Besides holding a bill until it fell due or paying it out, a recipient could discount it. Adam Smith, in 1776, observed that "money is more readily advanced upon them [i.e., bills] than upon any other species of obligation, especially when they are made payable within so short a period as two or three months after their date."[11] This statement seems to have been true throughout the period except in time of acute crisis. The holder of a bill of exchange who wished to discount it did so by endorsing the bill and "selling" it to a "buyer" for an amount less than its face value. The difference between the face value and the amount paid by the buyer was the discount, which was expressed as a per cent per year.

Despite the terminology, the discounting of a bill of exchange was not a simple sale; it was, in fact, a loan secured by the transfer of the bill, with the "seller" retaining a contingent liability for payment. What was involved was an exchange of present money for a larger amount of future money; the discount itself was analogous to interest paid in advance.[12] That the practice of discounting bills of exchange was a device for lending money is further indicated by the fact that country banks, when discounting, sometimes took collateral security.[13] Contemporaries under-

---

[10] Quoted in King, *London Discount Market,* p. 4.

[11] Adam Smith, *Wealth of Nations,* I, 274.

[12] For a discussion of bill-of-exchange discounting as a financial operation see King, *London Discount Market,* p. xvii.

[13] L. S. Pressnell, *Country Banking in the Industrial Revolution* (Oxford, 1956), p. 294.

stood the purchase of bills of exchange at a discount to be loans. Adam Smith wrote that "the payment of the bill when it becomes due replaces to the bank the value of what it has advanced, together with the *interest.*" [14] The widespread English practice of using the bill of exchange as the foundation for short-term loans caused a Frenchman to rhapsodize in 1817 that "England has a lever with which she could pick up the world; that lever is the bill of exchange." [15]

The period 1760 to 1830, taken as a whole, saw a considerable increase in the volume of bills discounted. This rise is reflected in the figures for Bank of England discount income. Although these figures must be used with great caution, they clearly indicate a much higher level of discounts in the economy as a whole between 1760 and 1830 than between 1728 and 1760, the preceding period for which complete information is available. [16]

Banks were an important source of discount funds. At the center of the loose network of English and Welsh banks was the

---

[14] Adam Smith, *Wealth of Nations*, I, 269. My italics.

[15] Riffe, *Projet d'une nouvelle banque publique* (1817), quoted by Paul Leuilliot in "The Industrial Revolution in France," *Journal of Economic History*, XVII (1957), 249.

[16] See Clapham, *Bank of England*, I, 301–302, and II, 433–434, for the figures. From 1728 to the early sixties, Bank income from discounts fluctuated slightly at a low level. In the early sixties, income rose somewhat, and from then to the late nineties, it proceeded to fluctuate rather violently around a level that was perhaps five to ten times as high as the average level for the period from the late twenties to the early sixties. In the late nineties, there began a spectacular climb in discount income that reached a peak of over £900,000 in 1809–1810—a figure that the Bank did not equal until 1914–1915. The decade of spectacular climb was followed by a decade of descent, which was almost as remarkable; however, the low pre-1760 level was not reached during the 1820's or 1830's. Because Bank rate fluctuated before 1773 and after 1822, and because the attitude of the Bank towards its discounting changed, too much weight cannot be placed on these figures. It is, however, safe to say that the entire period 1760–1830, and not just the restriction period, formed an era of exceptionally heavy discounting at the Bank, and perhaps throughout the country. Pressnell gives estimates of the circulation of bills from 1793 onward, but in the absence of earlier figures they are not much help (*Country Banking*, pp. 171–172).

Bank of England, which maintained indirect relations with the banking institutions of Scotland and Ireland.[17] The Bank had originated, in Walter Bagehot's phrase, as "a Whig finance company." [18] Adam Smith described it as "the greatest bank of circulation in Europe." [19] It continued to do what Lord North, in 1781, called "all the money business of the exchequer." [20] To this function it had long since added the various functions that tied it so closely to commerce and that caused David Ricardo to refer to the Bank of England as "that company of merchants." [21] Perhaps "that company of London merchants" would have been somewhat more accurate, since both the ownership of Bank stock and the actual business of the Bank were very heavily concentrated in the capital.[22]

Between 1760 and 1830, the nongovernmental business of the Bank of England was of a very restricted sort. During the period under discussion, except for a very brief interval in the 1820's, the Bank did not lend money on mortgage.[23] Only a few of the long-established large chartered joint-stock companies, like the East India Company, the South Sea Company, and the Hudson's Bay Company, received loans from the Bank of England. These loans were in the form of an agreed continuing overdraft—an arrangement that was in effect an extension of long-term credit, though technically an extension of short-term credit.[24] Except for loans allowing subscribers to government loans to complete their payments, almost no direct formal advances were made to private persons by the Bank of England.[25]

---

[17] Clapham, *Bank of England*, I, 167–169.

[18] *Lombard Street: A Description of the Money Market*, ed. Hartley Withers (London, 1915) , p. 45.

[19] *Wealth of Nations*, I, 283.   [20] Clapham, *Bank of England*, I, 174.

[21] R. S. Sayers, "Ricardo's Views on Monetary Questions," *Papers*, ed. Ashton and Sayers, p. 82.

[22] Clapham, *Bank of England*, I, 205, 288.

[23] *Ibid.*, I, 114 and 203–205; II, 82–84.   [24] *Ibid.*, I, 209–210; II, 37–38.

[25] *Ibid.*, I, 203–204.

Short-term lending was almost synonymous with the discount of inland or foreign bills of exchange and formed a substantial part of the Bank's total business.[26] The Bank's discounting tended to be particularly heavy in wartime. During the wars of the eighteenth century, the deposits of London banks fell as their customers bought government securities. Partly as a result of this fall in deposits, the London banks restricted their discounting. The resulting slack was taken up by the Bank of England.[27]

It is almost certain that the Bank of England did not direct discounting at all for proprietors of cotton factories. In order to discount at the Bank of England prior to 1797, a man had to be in trade, he had to be recommended by a director of the Bank, and most important of all, he had to reside in London.[28] There were few cotton factories in the capital. After 1797, London banks, some of which already had drawing accounts at the Bank, were permitted for the first time to maintain discount accounts at the Bank; country bankers did not normally discount directly with the Bank of England until the establishment of branches starting in 1826.[29] From 1797 onward, therefore, the ability of the cotton entrepreneur to get discounts from the banking system was increased; he might discount with his country banker, who could discount with his London agent, who in turn could rediscount with the Bank of England. After 1826, the process could become simpler and more direct. The cotton-factory proprietor's bank

---

[26] The Bank's income from discounts can be found in *ibid.*, I, 301–302, and II, 433–434. This series covers the years 1728–1729 to 1914–1915 (August to August). The Bank's private loan income can be found in *ibid.*, I, 301–302. There are no figures for the Bank's private loan income for the years 1798–1799 to 1846–1847.

[27] D. M. Joslin, "London Bankers in Wartime, 1739–1784," *Studies in the Industrial Revolution,* ed. L. S. Pressnell (London, 1960), pp. 175–176.

[28] Clapham, *Bank of England,* I, 205–206. In 1797, restrictions were only modified to the extent of permitting London bankers to maintain discount accounts at the Bank.

[29] Pressnell, *Country Banking,* pp. 75–76; Clapham, *Bank of England,* I, 172, and II, 120.

could then, if a branch of the Bank was conveniently located, discount directly with the Bank of England.[30]

Although the Bank had done no ordinary discounting for London bankers before 1797, or for country bankers before 1826, it had carried on a discount business almost from its inception. Most of this discounting was done for merchants; on January 1, 1800, about 6 per cent of the bills held by the Bank originated with bankers, and the rest was divided almost equally between merchants engaged in domestic trade and merchants engaged in foreign trade. A further breakdown of the discounts to traders indicates that a considerable part of them were made to distributors of the raw materials required by cotton factories and to the distributors of the products of these factories.[31] This discounting was of some consequence because merchants played a role in the financing of cotton manufacturers. The Bank of England, in its discounting for merchants, was in a sense financing some of the financiers of the cotton factories.

There is reason to believe that a relative decline of this type of financing took place after 1815, indicated by the decline in the number of clients discounting at the Bank after that year. From the seventies down to 1815, the Bank of England had 1,200 to 1,400 discounting clients; by 1819 the number was down to 943; by 1824 the number had fallen to 545; and, in the half century that followed, the clients always numbered less than 500 and sometimes less than 300.[32] This sharp decline after 1815 probably indicates the rerouting of some of this business through the London banks after 1797, through the bill brokers, and, by the late twenties, through the bill dealers.

It is safe to say that the direct access of cotton proprietors to short-term loans from the Bank of England, by discount or by any other means, was negligible under ordinary conditions. Did the Bank of England function differently in times of crisis? By and

---

[30] King, *London Discount Market*, pp. 54–55 and 57–58.
[31] Clapham, *Bank of England*, I, 206–208.   [32] *Ibid.*, p. 205.

large it did not. Sir Francis Baring's reference to the Bank of England as the *dernier resort* of banks in an emergency is somewhat misleading if it is taken to refer to country banks.[33] There seem to have been only a few cases in which the Bank came directly to the aid of a country bank. During the crisis of 1793, it aided some Liverpool banks, and in 1815, the Newcastle Bank. In both cases discounting was presumably involved.[34]

The Bank also made a few emergency industrial loans. In 1816, it assisted several industrial firms that were not in the cotton industry by discounting for them.[35] During the severe crisis of 1825, the Bank loaned over £500,000 to merchants and manufacturers. This sum was distributed through local committees. The geographical distribution of the loans indicates that some of them went to cotton manufacturers. Over a fifth of the loans were made in Manchester and over a sixth of them in Glasgow. The Bank made the loans with great reluctance, however, believing that the government should have followed its own precedents of 1793 and 1811 and loaned the merchants and manufacturers exchequer bills that they could have sold.[36]

When George Grote, the historian and banker, said in 1832 that, if a man's banker would not discount for him, he could "get to the Bank without that special, permanent, and exclusive connection which he preserves with his own banker, and which cuts him off from all other bankers," he was describing a situation that existed for the cotton manufacturer only after 1826, when the Bank of England began to establish branches.[37] By and large, between 1760 and 1830 the manufacturer, even in time of crisis, discounted with his country banker, who in turn discounted with a London bank. It was for the London banks that the Bank of

---

[33] *Observations on . . . the Bank of England*, p. 22, quoted in J. K. Horsefield, "The Duties of a Banker: II," *Papers*, ed. Ashton and Sayers, p. 33.

[34] Clapham, *Bank of England*, I, 261, and II, 58.   [35] *Ibid.*, II, 59.

[36] *Ibid.*, II, 108–109; Pressnell, *Country Banking*, p. 491.

[37] Clapham, *Bank of England*, II, 96–97.

England existed as a last refuge, at least until 1826. The manufacturer had indirect access to the Bank's short-term funds, but this access was becoming somewhat more direct.

The Bank of England affected the supply of short-term capital available to the cotton-factory owner by its general influence in the capital market, and it was able to do this through the market for short-term and long-term government securities, which formed part of the assets of both London and country banks. It is not likely, however, that the Old Lady of Threadneedle Street consciously followed a consistent policy in this sphere of her operations.[38]

The Bank also exercised some influence on credit through its control of its own note issue, although it did not have a legal monopoly of bank-note issue. Since this type of influence was related to the extent of the currency accorded to Bank of England notes, it varied in efficacy from region to region, being greatest in the London money market, where such notes were used, almost exclusively, for large settlements.[39] Outside London and the home counties, the currency of Bank of England notes was considerably less. They had a fairly high degree of currency in Lancashire compared with other bank notes, though not when compared with other means of payment like bills of exchange.[40] The ability of the Bank to affect credit in the provinces by its control over its own note issue would have been greater if the country banks had customarily kept a large part of their reserves in the form of Bank of England notes—but they did not do so.[41]

The Bank of England, although it occupied the center of the London stage, was not the only institution that made its presence felt in the capital market. The other components of the London capital market were the London private banks, the bill brokers,

---

[38] Pressnell, *Country Banking*, pp. 75–76.

[39] Clapham, *Bank of England*, I, 162–163 and 167.

[40] A Shareholder, *A Letter to the Trading Community of Manchester in Reference to the Principles and Practices of Joint Stock Banks* (Manchester, 1834), p. 4; Ashton, "Bill of Exchange," p. 39.

[41] Pressnell, *Country Banking*, p. 76.

and the bill dealers. Because of the real difference in the manner in which they functioned, the London banks were divided into two groups—the City banks and the West End banks.

The West End banks were essentially banks of deposit for the nobility and gentry. They accepted for deposit the rents paid to landowners, and paid interest upon them. They invested in government securities and mortgages and did no significant discounting until after 1840. They did not regard themselves as commercial bankers, and as late as 1825, many of them had neither drawing nor discount accounts at the Bank of England.[42]

The London banks, of which City banks formed the largest part, grew in numbers between 1760 and 1830. Unlike the country banks, which underwent a more spectacular growth, the greatest increase in the number of City banks occurred before, rather than during, the restriction period. Furthermore, their numerical decrease was not nearly so great after the resumption of payments as was that of the country banks.[43]

The City banks accepted deposits from merchants on which they paid no interest, and acted as the London agents for the country banks, on whose balances they generally did pay interest until 1825. The earning assets of the City banks might include bills of exchange and government securities.[44] The liquidity requirements of these banks were too high to permit them to do any

---

[42] Great Britain, House of Commons, Evidence of Lewis Loyd, *Report from the Select Committee on Manufactures, Commerce and Shipping (Reports,* 1833 [690]) , Vol. VI, pt. 1, q. 459; D. M. Joslin, "London Private Bankers, 1720–1785," *Economic History Review,* 2nd ser., VII (1954) , 167–186; Clapham, *Bank of England,* II, 120. One of these banks, Child and Company, seems to have been particularly adventurous. It loaned money to the Duke of Bridgewater for canal building (A. H. John, "Insurance Investment and the London Money Market of the 18th Century," *Economica,* N.S., XX [May 1953], 157) , and it acted as a London correspondent for Livesey, Hargreaves and Company (Joslin, "London Private Bankers," p. 177) .

[43] Clapham, *Bank of England,* I, 158 and 160–163; II, 120–121; Clapham, *An Economic History of Modern Britain,* I (2nd ed.; Cambridge, 1939) , 264; Joslin, "London Private Bankers," p. 173.

[44] Joslin, "London Private Bankers," pp. 167–186; Pressnell, *Country Banking,* pp. 94, 411, and 414.

lending on mortgage, and they left this field, somewhat condescendingly, to the West End bankers.[45]

Having ceased to be banks of issue by the seventies, the City banks kept a large part of their reserves in Bank of England notes; when the Bank made drawing accounts available to the London banks, they began to hold part of their reserves at Threadneedle Street. By 1825, very few of the City banks were without a drawing account at the Bank of England and many of them had discount accounts as well.[46]

Bankers and traders were not the only customers of the City banks; some cotton manufacturers including Arkwright, Oldknow, the Strutts, and Livesey, Hargreaves and Company had accounts with London banks. All these were large firms, and it is questionable whether a small or even medium-size cotton company had sufficiently wide interests to make a connection with a London bank useful or profitable.

Arkwright was a customer, perhaps at different times, of two City banks. He dealt with Smith, Payne and Smith and with Gibson and Johnson.[47] There were special reasons, not applicable to most other firms in the cotton industry, to explain Arkwright's use of City banks. He was, for a time, the holder of important patents; one of the consequences of this was that, as long as he was able to defend his patents, he was much sought after as a partner by a large number of widely scattered firms.[48] As a result, he was engaged in an unusually large number of enterprises; since they involved him in geographically extensive receipts and payments, a

---

[45] Evidence of Lewis Loyd, *Report from the Select Committee on Manufactures, Commerce and Shipping* (1833), qq. 451–459. Jones, Loyd and Company, of which Lewis Loyd was a partner, was a City bank that had been created by a Manchester bank (Clapham, *Bank of England*, I, 163–164).

[46] Clapham, *Bank of England*, I, 162–163, 167, and 172; II, 120–121.

[47] Leland Hamilton Jenks, *The Migration of British Capital to 1875* (New York, 1927); Pressnell, *Country Banking*, p. 455.

[48] Alfred P. Wadsworth and Julia de Lacy Mann, *The Cotton Trade and Industrial Lancashire, 1600–1780* (Manchester, 1931), pp. 488–503. The London banks could also have collected the license fees on the patents.

London bank was useful to him in centralizing his interests. The utility of Smith, Payne and Smith may have derived less from being a London bank than from the fact that it had branches at both Nottingham and Derby—two places with which the Arkwright enterprises were particularly associated.[49]

The Strutts, who had been associated with Arkwright and held an important patent in their own right, were connected with Gibson and Johnson.[50] When the connection with Arkwright was terminated, two of the mills were retained by the Strutts so that they owned, at the very least, three factories in different places.[51] For the Strutts, as for Arkwright, the most important function of their London bank may have been centralization of remittance.

Samuel Oldknow also banked with Smith, Payne and Smith. For him, as for the Arkwrights, the usefulness of the connection may have resided in the bank's branch in Derby. It seems unlikely that the London bank could have provided him with anything that he could not get from a combination of a local bank and his London outlet, S. and W. Salte.[52]

Livesey, Hargreaves and Company, prior to their famous failure in 1788, had three London bankers. Two of these, Gibson and Johnson and Richard Clarke, were City banks, while the third, Child and Company, was a West End bank.[53] Livesey, Hargreaves and Company was a very large firm of calico printers.[54] By 1788,

---

[49] Pressnell, *Country Banking*, pp. 128–129.   [50] *Ibid.*, p. 455.

[51] R. S. Fitton, "Overseas Trade during the Napoleonic Wars, as Illustrated by the Records of W. G. and J. Strutt," *Economica*, N.S., XX (1953), 53.

[52] Smith, Payne and Smith may not have been a regular connection. The bank was, however, one of the creditors of Oldknow's firm (George Unwin, Arthur Hulme, and George Taylor, *Samuel Oldknow and the Arkwrights* [Manchester, 1924], pp. 155–156). Oldknow had previously banked with Evans and Son of Derby (*ibid.*, p. 177). Salte provided Oldknow with cash (*ibid.*, pp. 176–177).

[53] Joslin, "London Private Bankers," p. 177; Pressnell, *Country Banking*, pp. 91–92.

[54] The Peel interests and Livesey, Hargreaves and Company were both integrated vertical enterprises that combined spinning, manufacturing, finishing, and banking. By 1785, Sir Robert Peel and his partners employed 6,800

however, it was also a banking firm with branches at Blackburn, Mossley, and Preston. In addition to having banking connections in London, the firm also maintained an office there, where an agent performed some banking functions for it. This entire banking mechanism seems to have been used as part of an elaborate illegal scheme to raise short-term capital.[55] The firm or its country agents drew bills of exchange on its London agent banks or on its own London office. These bills were made payable to nonexistent persons and covered fictitious transactions. The bill was endorsed with the name of the nonexistent payee. The firm's country agents or the firm then endorsed the bills and discounted them in London or Lancashire.[56] Livesey, Hargreaves and Company also conveyed some property to Gibson and Johnson for a £5,000 advance after first pledging the same property to Allen's bank in Manchester.[57] Had it not been for the criminal aspects of the firm's operations, it is scarcely likely that anything would have justified it in dealing with a London bank.

For most cotton firms, the inconvenience of banking at any considerable distance from their factories would have been very great. In addition to inconvenience, the ordinary cotton manufacturers would probably incur some loss, because the City banks did not allow interest on balances held with them by nonbanking firms. Another reason why most cotton manufacturers would not be likely to bank in London was the difficulty of making remittances.

---

people. About the same time Livesey, Hargreaves and Company employed between 700 and 1,000 printers and was believed to either support or employ 20,000 people in all. Their cloth was believed to occupy more than twelve miles when bleaching (Wadsworth and Mann, *Cotton Trade*, p. 307) .

[55] J. Graham, "The Chemistry of Calico Printing from 1790 to 1835 and the History of Printworks in the Manchester District from 1760 to 1846," MS book, n.d. (from internal evidence 1847 or 1848), Manchester Central Library, p. 407. Charles O'Brien, *The British Manufacturer's Companion and Calico Printers Assistant* . . . (n. pub., 1795), ch. "Of Colour Making: A Retrospect . . . ," n.p., and n. 11; Wadsworth and Mann, *Cotton Trade,* pp. 307–308; Pressnell, *Country Banking*, pp. 91–92 and 453–455.

[56] *Ibid.*, pp. 91–92 and 174.   [57] *Ibid.*, p. 282.

Among traders in the North, the practice of using checks was not very widely developed.[58] Remittance was made easier by the establishment of Bank of England branches, but this did not begin until 1826. The establishment of these branches, while it facilitated dealings between cotton manufacturers and the City banks, also made it possible for the manufacturer to bypass both the country and City banks and deal directly with the bill brokers and bill dealers.[59]

Although most cotton manufacturers did not deal with the City bankers, these bankers performed one very important function—important not only to the cotton industry but to the economy as a whole. Aided by the bill brokers and bill dealers, they organized the surplus capital of the agricultural areas and arranged for its transfer to industrial areas that were short of capital.

The bill brokers, as their name implied, simply brought the seller and buyer of bills together and collected a commission. A banker in an area that was short of capital would send bills to London and the broker in London would transmit them to a buyer in an agricultural area. Since the broker did not endorse the bills he transmitted, he had no contingent liability for the debts represented. The bill dealer actually bought a bill, became contingently liable by endorsing it, and sold it to a banker in an agricultural area who had a surplus to invest. Instead of using his own capital, the dealer could buy the bill with funds lent to him in London.[60] The bill brokers emerged as specialists in the last

---

[58] Clapham, *Bank of England*, I, 221–223. The American spelling is the older one (J. Milnes Holden, *The History of Negotiable Instruments in English Laws* [London, 1955], pp. 208–209). From 1791 to 1853, there was an *ad valorem* stamp duty on all checks except those drawn to payee or bearer. By discriminating against checks drawn to payee *or order,* the law balanced an economic inducement to use checks drawn to bearer against the greater safety of using checks drawn to order. The net result seems to have been to induce some areas like London to use the cheaper bearer form and others like Lancashire to continue to use the safer bills of exchange (Holden, *Negotiable Instruments,* pp. 219–222).

[59] King, *London Discount Market,* pp. 54–55 and 57–58.

[60] *Ibid.,* pp. xviii, 42, and 67–69.

quarter of the eighteenth century, and the growth of their business was facilitated by the long period of high interest rates ushered in by the Napoleonic Wars, and by the operation of the usury laws.[61] After 1815, they began to do a little direct business with the manufacturers. By making remittance easier, the establishment of Bank of England branches no doubt aided in the expansion of the volume of transactions between bill brokers and manufacturers, but the relative size of this part of the brokers' business probably remained small.[62]

For the most part, the bill brokers dealt with country banks, and the sources and destinations of the funds they used were the same as those of the City bankers. Thomas Richardson, one of the founders of the firm that became Overend, Gurney and Company, stated in 1810 that he received bills "from Lancashire in particular" and sent them to Norfolk, Suffolk, Essex, and Sussex for discount.[63]

The description of the bill broker's operations, given in 1841 by Paul Moon James, a Manchester banker, is also valid for the preceding years:

The money which is in the hands of the great bill-brokers in London is chiefly supplied from the bankers in the agricultural districts; they have a surplus quantity of money raised, perhaps, upon their circulation and they make use of that surplus by obtaining from the bill-brokers commercial bills of exchange, and of very great use it is. The money of the agricultural districts is used in supplying the wants of the manufacturing districts; in that way the bills of the manufacturing districts are converted into money by means of the agricultural districts. . . . Manchester absorbs a great deal of the surplus capital which is raised in Norfolk, or in any large agricultural district, by bills of Manchester going up to the bill-broker in London, who receives money from the issuing banker.[64]

---

[61] T. S. Ashton, *An Economic History of England: The 18th Century* (London, 1955), p. 136.

[62] King, *London Discount Market,* pp. 27, 54–55, and 57–58.

[63] *Ibid.,* p. 9.   [64] As quoted in *ibid.,* p. 99.

Bill dealing may have begun earlier, but it cannot have been of much importance until some time after the late twenties.[65] After the crisis of 1825, a number of changes in the business methods of various British financial institutions and changes in their relations with each other facilitated the development of the great bill-dealing houses. The London banks seem to have been impressed by two things during the crisis of 1825: the very heavy demands made on them by the country banks and the great strain to which they subjected the Bank of England by their rediscounting with it. In order to cut down the draining of their reserves by the country banks, the London banks attempted to discourage large London balances by no longer allowing interest in them. They also started to build up their own reserves in order to make rediscounting with the Bank of England unnecessary.[66] Both these steps involved the London banks in a reduction of income for which they compensated by allowing call loans to bill dealers. These loans were repayable almost instantly. The Bank of England soon followed suit by allowing the bill brokers call loans and discount facilities.[67] The elimination of interest payments to the country bankers on their London balances sent them, in their turn, in search of new avenues of investment that they found either in depositing funds with bill dealers or in the purchasing of bills from the dealers or through the agency of brokers. The full impact of these developments was not felt until after 1830; even in 1848 there were only four bill dealers of any consequence in London, and one of them, Overend, Gurney and Company, may have been almost as large as the other three combined.[68]

It was through this network of banks, bill dealers, and bill brokers that surplus agricultural capital supplies were transferred

---

[65] *Ibid.*, p. 42.   [66] *Ibid.*, p. 37.

[67] *Ibid.*, pp. 62–63 and 68; Clapham, *Bank of England*, II, 135. Bill brokers had previously been prevented from regularly discounting at the Bank, although they had apparently made some attempts to use the Bank (Clapham, *Bank of England*, II, 30–31).

[68] King, *London Discount Market*, pp. 42 and 117.

to capital-hungry industrial areas. In his testimony before a parliamentary committee in 1833, Samuel Gurney was most emphatic about the existence of surplus agricultural capital. As a member of the Norwich banking family and a partner in Overend, Gurney and Company, he was in a much better position to know than most. Questioned about the existence of agricultural surpluses in counties like Norfolk and Suffolk, he stated that "there never was a period in which they had occupation for their surplus money in these districts." He also stated that these surpluses were to be found in both "corn counties" and "cattle counties" and that, when they took the form of deposits in the local banks, they could be traced to "every description of people . . . landlords and tenants . . . and the trading community." [69]

The surplus to which Gurney referred was the result of a recurring temporary excess of funds in agricultural areas, and as such it could only serve as a source of short-term capital. The availability of this supply of short-term capital was the result of seasonal fluctuations in the demand for capital and of the tendency of these fluctuations to occur at different times in different sectors of the economy.

The seasonal nature of agricultural production is obvious.[70] The larger the agricultural sector of an economy, the deeper the impact of the seasonal character of agricultural production is likely to be. For this reason Ashton, after referring to the replacement in 1751 of the Julian by the Gregorian Calendar, stated that

neither 25 March nor 1 January is a satisfactory starting point for the economic historian. In a world in which he was king, the year would begin at Michaelmas, September 29th, when the harvest had been got

---

[69] Evidence of Samuel Gurney, *Report from the Select Committee on Manufactures, Commerce and Shipping* (1833), qq. 90, 96, and 103.

[70] Webster's *New International Dictionary* (2nd ed., unabridged; Springfield, Mass., 1961) starts its first entry under "season" with the following words: "A period in which a special type of agricultural work is normal and a particular type of weather prevails. . . ."

in, when farmers were counting their gains, landlords fixing their rents, servants in husbandry entering on a new annual cycle, and temporary recruits to agriculture settling again to their ordinary occupations.

In agriculture the maximum demand for labor, and hence for short-term capital, occurred during the harvests that fell in the summer and early autumn.[71] In some cases the landowner might supply the farmer with short-term capital; in other cases the farmer would have to look elsewhere, perhaps to the country banks.[72]

The industrial sector of the eighteenth-century British economy displayed a number of different seasonal patterns of output, demand for labor, and demand for short-term capital. Some industries reached their peak demands for short-term capital at about the same time that agriculture did; others did not. A number of industries, which depended on domestic agricultural produce and which in some cases might have found themselves directly competing with agriculture for labor, reduced or discontinued production during the harvest and reached their peak outputs some time after the early autumn. Thus it would be possible for surplus agricultural capital to be transferred to brewers, maltsters, distillers, millers, tanners, soap-boilers, and candle-makers.[73]

---

[71] T. S. Ashton, *Economic Fluctuations in England, 1700–1800* (Oxford, 1959), p. 4. Quote from p. 31.

[72] F. M. L. Thompson, "English Landownership: The Ailesbury Trust, 1832–1856," *Economic History Review*, 2nd ser., XI (1958), 127. The example cited is a late one. In 1839, the trustees of the heavily indebted estates of the Marquess of Ailesbury agreed to permit the calling in of the "running half-year's rent," which it was fairly common practice to allow tenants. The running rent had been in effect a credit equal to six months' rent that the landowner allowed his tenants. The 1839 withdrawal of landlords' capital was disastrous in the long run because it caused a deterioration of the estates by forcing out the better tenants (*ibid.*, p. 132).

[73] Ashton, *Economic Fluctuations*, pp. 6–7. In the case of some of these industries, there were additional reasons why output fell in the summer and rose in the late autumn. The list of industries is not complete and is not intended to be.

It is more difficult to generalize about the demand of other industries for short-term capital. If an industry depended on imported raw materials or access to foreign markets, seasonal variations in conditions at sea and the feasibility of storing the raw materials or the finished product probably affected the timing of maximum output and demand for short-term capital. Optimum sailing and arrival times varied according to destination, but regardless of the destination, winter in European waters was to be avoided.[74] In 1760, Horace Walpole repeated a remark by Sir Cloudesley Shovel that "an admiral would deserve to be broke, who kept ships out after the end of September, and to be shot if after October." [75]

Some industries, including branches of the textile industries, needed large amounts of water if they were to maintain production. Water served these industries as a raw material and, even before the Industrial Revolution, as a source of power. The manufacturers sometimes would be forced to reduce their labor force and their demand for short-term capital during the summer, when the seasonal decline in the water supply set in.[76]

The cotton industry was subject to the same seasonal variations in demand for short-term capital. The demand for short-term capital in the bleaching industry probably reached a peak in the spring and fell during the winter months since short days made bleaching difficult. Calico printing also slumped during the winter, when it was likely to get too cold to wash the cloth.[77] The correspondence of the Manchester spinning firm of McConnel and Kennedy abounds with references to "preparations for the spring trade." [78]

There is considerable significance in the fact that the seasonal

---

[74] *Ibid.*, pp. 10–11.

[75] Letter dated Jan. 14, 1760, as quoted in Ashton, *Economic Fluctuations*, p. 4.

[76] *Ibid.*, pp. 8–9.

[77] Wadsworth and Mann, *Cotton Trade*, pp. 295 n. and 138.

[78] McConnel and Kennedy MSS, Letter Books, *passim*.

agricultural demand for short-term capital often ran counter to the seasonal demand for short-term capital in the cotton industry and in many other industries. It helps to explain the existence of the surpluses of short-term capital in agricultural areas during the eighteenth and nineteenth centuries. Since the contrary movements in demand did not originate in the eighteenth century, it also helps to explain why short-term capital had been easier to obtain than long-term capital for centuries before the onset of the Industrial Revolution.

During the second half of the eighteenth century and the first three decades of the nineteenth century, the mechanism for transferring the short-term agricultural surplus to the capital-hungry industrial areas and back again was considerably improved. It consisted of two parts. At its center was the London money market, which became better adapted to the process of transfer as the institutions of which it was composed became more specialized and as relatively new, highly specialized institutions like the bill-dealing and bill-brokerage houses were evolved. At about the same time there came into being the second part of the mechanism—the country banks.

The development of country banking roughly coincides with the era of the Industrial Revolution. There was probably no more than a handful of provincial banks in England before 1750. These had grown to 150 in 1776 and to 280 in the early nineties, before the crisis of 1793 thinned them out somewhat. The growth was quickly resumed, and by 1800 there were 386 in Great Britain, of which about 330 were in England and Wales. A peak of approximately 800 in England and Wales was reached in the second decade of the century and then a decline set in. By 1832, the number had fallen to about 400 private banks and 25 joint-stock banks.[79]

During the Napoleonic Wars, when "country banks were multiplied in every corner of the kingdom . . . and coined money

---

[79] Clapham, *Bank of England,* I, 160–163, and II, 1–2, 90–91, and 120–121.

without restraint," [80] hundreds of banks stopped payment.[81] The fifteen years after the end of the war also saw several hundred failures—never fewer than three a year.[82] The relationship between the creation of the country banks and the wartime pressure for credit under restriction conditions is indicated by the fact that the peaks in the number of country banks, the number of London banks, and the Bank of England's income from discount were all reached about the same time—in 1809 or 1810.[83]

Faced with a demand from a customer for short-term capital, a country bank would usually provide it in the form of a discount of bills of exchange. In lending, the bank would create a deposit in the borrower's account upon which the borrower would draw. There was a limit to the amount of such lending that a country banker could undertake. He had to keep a cash reserve against his deposits. If a country bank lent too heavily, it would exhaust its reserve, not be able to honor the demands made on its deposits, and fail. If the bank made payments in its own notes, these would be presented for payment by other banks receiving them and, if the issuing bank's reserves were exhausted, the bank would fail as a result of its inability to honor its notes. Hence, however sound the firms applying for discount might be and however safe the bills of exchange presented by them, a country banker, using locally available assets, could not undertake unlimited discounting.[84]

The banker was not without recourse. If his London banker

---

[80] Extract from a Memorandum Addressed to Lord Liverpool on the State of the Country in 1816, Huskisson Papers, Vol. XXVII (Additional. MSS, no. 38760), f. 117, British Museum.

[81] H. Oliver Horne, *A History of Savings Bank* (London, 1947), p. 10.

[82] G. E. Fussell and M. Compton, "Agricultural Adjustment after the Napoleonic Wars," *Economic History,* III (1939), 189.

[83] The Bank of England's peak discount income year was August 1809 to August 1810 (Clapham, *Bank of England,* II, 433). The peak year for the number of country banks is difficult to establish, but it seems to have been 1809–1810 *(ibid.,* II, 2). The peak for London banks was 83 in 1810 (Joslin, "London Private Bankers," p. 173).

[84] The discussion above follows very closely the argument of Hawtrey, *Century of Bank Rate,* pp. 9–10.

would lend him the necessary capital by discounting for him, he would be able to discount more heavily for his own customers. The manufacturer would get his loan, the country banker would increase his profits, and the City banker would also profit. This mechanism could only function if a differential existed between provincial and London discount rates; without the differential there would be little, if any, inducement for the country banker to discount in London. When interest rates were high, when they pressed against the upper limit set by the usury laws, the London and provincial discount rates tended to converge and eliminate the profit for the City bank. It was for this reason that the City banks discouraged discounting for country bankers during the Napoleonic Wars.[85] Some of the slack in the short-term capital market was taken up by the bill brokers—not, however, by evading the usury laws, but rather by helping to organize the discount market.[86]

When interest rates were not too high, the City banks utilized the surpluses of those country banks located in predominantly agricultural areas to provide discounts to the country banks in primarily industrial areas. The City banks were agents for both types of country banks, and these country banks maintained balances with their London agents on which interest was paid until 1825 if the accounts were large enough.[87] The country banks, located in areas where the demand for the discounts was larger than their locally available resources, would keep these balances small. The country banks with surplus funds, that is, the banks located in agricultural areas, also kept balances with their agents, but since they could not find adequate short-term investments close to home, they kept them large in order to earn the interest that was paid on them. During the Napoleonic Wars, even these balances were kept rather small, because the war, in all probability, increased the liquidity requirements of even the agricultural

[85] Pressnell, *Country Banking*, p. 98.
[86] King, *London Discount Market*, p. 14.
[87] Pressnell, *Country Banking*, p. 411.

banks.[88] Interest on these balances ceased after 1825. The very heavy drain of reserves from London during the crisis of 1825, and the low level of postwar interest rates, caused the City banks to begin to eliminate the interest payments they had previously made on country bankers' balances. The London banks wished to discourage large balances in order to prevent a repetition of the drain of 1825.[89]

The existence and functioning of the mechanism for the transformation of agricultural surplus funds into short-term loans to cotton manufacturers depended upon several characteristic features of the economy.

The strategic long-standing position of London as a center of foreign trade, of government, and of population, gave the bill on London the special position that facilitated the concentration of the short-term capital market there. As a center of foreign trade, London generated and received a large volume of foreign bills of exchange; as the seat of government, London received taxes from its agents in the provinces and made payments at a distance; as a center of population, London was a center of consumption and its payments for food alone must have created a very large volume of bills of exchange.[90] For these reasons, London was peculiarly suited to become the center of the transfer mechanism.

London's position in the short-term capital market was assured by a peculiarity of English law that even before the passage of the Bubble Act prohibited banking partnerships with more than six members and thereby discouraged branch banking.[91] Hence, Eng-

---

[88] *Ibid.*, p. 94.

[89] *Ibid.*, p. 414; King, *London Discount Market*, pp. 35–38.

[90] During the eighteenth and nineteenth centuries, London's rate of growth was less than that of a number of important provincial cities, but the relative decline does not affect the argument (R. H. Mottram, "Town Life and London," *Early Victorian England, 1830–1865,* ed. G. M. Young [London, 1934], I, 169) .

[91] Feavearyear, *Pound Sterling,* pp. 154–155. The laws in question were apparently intended to protect the monopoly position of the Bank of England.

lish country banking, when it came into being, was, by and large, unit or localized banking, which meant that the country banks could not readily handle the problem of transfer themselves.[92] The prohibition probably tended to encourage the specialization that was characteristic of the short-term capital market.

Some of the innovations in productive technique that are associated with the Industrial Revolution facilitated the operation of the transfer mechanism. The introduction of chemical bleaching, for example, made the bleacher more nearly independent of the weather. Developments of this sort probably tended to spread the short-term capital requirements of the cotton industry more evenly over the year.[93] In addition, chemical bleaching took much less time. Bleaching required about eight months in the middle of the eighteenth century, four months by the late sixties, and a few days by the late eighties.[94] This type of innovation reduced the demand for short-term capital by increasing its turnover rate.[95] Improvements in road transportation in the late eighteenth century tended to produce the same effect: trade and payments, which previously had almost been brought to a standstill by the onset of winter, were kept in motion.[96]

The country bank was the point at which the cotton manufacturer usually came into contact with the complicated mechanism for the transfer of short-term capital. As a rule he tapped the reservoirs of short-term capital by discounting bills of exchange at his bank.[97] His ability to do so allowed him to economize his

---

[92] King, *London Discount Market*, p. 6.

[93] Paul Mantoux, *The Industrial Revolution in the Eighteenth Century: An Outline of the Beginnings of the Modern Factory System in England,* trans. Marjorie Vernon, (2nd ed. rev.; London, 1927), pp. 250–251.

[94] Wadsworth and Mann, *Cotton Trade*, p. 178, n. 2.

[95] This discussion, of course, only refers to the demand for capital at a given level of output. If the innovation increased the demand for yarn or cloth, it may well have increased the overall demand for short-term capital, but this does not affect the argument.

[96] Joslin, "London Bankers in Wartime," pp. 157–158; L. S. Pressnell, "The Rate of Interest in the Eighteenth Century," *Studies,* ed. Pressnell, p. 182.

[97] Pressnell, *Country Banking*, pp. 335–336.

capital. In 1810, it was stated that the increase in available discount facilities was making it possible for the manufacturers to increase their business through a faster turnover of their capital.[98] Hawtrey has described the way in which this was accomplished:

> If a merchant's purchases and sales were paid for exclusively by the drawing of three months bills, his payments and receipts would be a perfect trace of his purchases and sales three months in arrear. He would at any time be paying for what he bought three months before and receiving payment for what he sold three months before. There would be an excess of payments over receipts equal to the value of goods bought and not yet sold up to three months before. This excess (along with the expenses incurred in his business) might be met out of his own capital. But it would be a widely fluctuating amount, and if his capital was sufficient to cover the maximum excess of payments over receipts, then at times when the excess was below the maximum, he would hold a balance of idle cash. Idle cash is a loss. And this loss could be avoided if the merchant so limited the capital employed in his business that it was just enough when the excess of his payments over his receipts was at a minimum, and relied on getting some of his bills discounted whenever the excess rose above the minimum. In effect, he might be increasing his business and supplementing his capital to the requisite extent by the discounting of bills. . . . [The] capital remaining in the business would be no more than the essential minimum. . . . [The] usual practice would be to provide for the fluctuating excess of payments over receipts beyond the minimum by getting bills discounted before maturity. . . . Like the merchant . . . [the manufacturer] would cover the variable margin in excess of his minimum working capital by getting bills discounted. For the manufacturer the variable margin would include the goods he has produced but not yet delivered and those he has delivered but has not been paid for.[99]

This abstract picture is in need of a little modification. The credit periods were not always equal for the cotton manufacturer

---

[98] King, *London Discount Market,* p. 16.

[99] Hawtrey, *Century of Bank Rate,* pp. 6–7.

as buyer and seller. Although the terms of sale and of purchase varied considerably, the cotton spinner at least seems to have got longer credit for his cotton purchase than he gave on his yarn sales.[100] This difference tended to help him to economize his short-term capital.

The use of the bill of exchange as the foundation for the extension of short-term credit in the cotton industry was facilitated by the ubiquity of the bill in Lancashire. Nowhere was the use of the bill of exchange more highly developed. In Lancashire, probably to a greater degree than elsewhere, the bill of exchange served as a substitute for money.[101]

The problem posed by the relatively inelastic supply of coins during most of the period between 1760 and 1830, was met in most districts outside London and Lancashire by the issue of country-bank notes. In and near London, Bank of England notes served as the usual supplement to the coin supply, especially after the London banks ceased to be banks of issue. In Lancashire, however, the necessary supplementation of the supply of hard cash was achieved by the very widespread practice of circulating bills of exchange. This use of bills helps to account for the failure of a specialized banking firm to appear in Manchester until 1771.[102]

Until the demand for the means of payment and short-term loans became very heavy, the merchants and manufacturers were able to manage on their own. The widespread use of bills of exchange for the purpose of payment also helps to explain why banks of issue were rarer in Lancashire than in any other part of the country. As one anonymous writer put it, "Prior to the crisis of 1825, no town kept clearer of local paper than Manchester; and

---

[100] In 1803, for example, McConnel and Kennedy were selling yarn for a two-month bill after a two month's credit period and paying for cotton with six-month acceptances (McConnel and Kennedy to W. G. and J. Strutt, March 7, 1803, and McConnel and Kennedy to W. Kelly, Feb. 22, 1803, McConnel and Kennedy MSS, Letter Books).

[101] Ashton, "Bill of Exchange," pp. 37–49.

[102] Ashton, *18th Century*, p. 185.

on various occasions before that period, when our old private banks contemplated its issue, the public met to suppress the principal, from a thorough conviction of its evil consequences, both to capitalists and to the working classes; our currency was then Bank of England Paper and Bills of Exchange." [103] As late as 1825, when this use of the bill of exchange had begun to decline, nine-tenths of the business of Lancashire was done in bills and only one-tenth in Bank of England notes and gold.[104] In 1830, only seventy-two of the four hundred and fifty country banks in England and Wales did not issue notes. Of the seventy-two nonissuing banks, eleven were located close to London, where Bank of England notes had a higher degree of currency. Twenty-five of the remaining sixty-one were located in the cotton counties of Lancashire, Cheshire, and Derbyshire, and the remaining thirty-six were widely scattered.[105]

The operation of the transfer mechanism may not have been apparent to the manufacturer, but he recognized the importance of the country banks. In addition to short-term loans, the country bank could provide him with access to the means of payment. Frequently these two needs were met simultaneously.[106]

Until the early twenties, the means-of-payment problem was a continuing source of anxiety to the entrepreneur in the cotton industry. The crux of the matter was the shortage of a suitable medium in which to make wage payments. The very real difficulty of obtaining coins and notes for small payments, and wage payments in particular, brought forth various responses. Some manufacturers attempted to create their own currency (see Chapter IV); others attempted to improve their access to existing currency. The second of these responses could provide the cotton manufacturers with a motive for participating in a banking firm. A cotton manufacturing firm could set up a banking company,

---

[103] A Shareholder, *Letter to the Trading Community*, p. 4.

[104] Ashton, "Bill of Exchange," p. 39.   [105] *Ibid.*, pp. 40–41.

[106] In 1786, Samuel Oldknow received £500 in cash every two weeks from his bankers, Evans and Son of Derby, in return for bills that they presumably discounted (Unwin, Hulme, and Taylor, *Samuel Oldknow*, p. 177).

participate in a banking partnership, or act as an agent for an existing bank. In time, some cotton manufacturers abandoned their other businesses for banking; others carried on both enterprises simultaneously.

The number of cotton manufacturers who became bankers is not known. Their participation probably roughly followed the trend of rise and decline of the number of firms engaged in country banking. Between 1833 and 1843, when the total number of country banks was declining, only twenty-one new private country banks that engaged in banking along with other business were created. Of these, only one was engaged in a branch of the cotton industry.[107]

There are numerous examples of cotton manufacturers who participated in country banking. In Scotland, David Dale, who was soon to be associated with Robert Owen in the famous New Lanark mills, was, along with Robert Scott Moncrieff, an Edinburgh merchant, the Glasgow agent of the Royal Bank of Scotland.[108] In Wales, although John Smalley, who was at one time a partner of Arkwright's and who had been a spinner since 1777, may not himself have become a banker, his successors were members of the banking firm of Douglas and Smalley. S. and J. Knight, who had been spinning in Wales from 1792 onwards, established a Welsh bank around 1823.[109]

There is more evidence for England. The most famous case of a combination of banking and manufacturing enterprises was Livesey, Hargreaves and Company. This firm, which was in existence in the seventies, had been an innovator of some importance in the calico-printing branch of the industry, and had developed a fairly

---

[107] Return of all Banking Firms Who United Other Trades With Their Banking Business From Jan. 1, 1833, to April 1, 1843, n.d., Additional MSS, no. 40547, f. 165, British Museum.

[108] *James Finley and Company Limited: Manufacturers and East India Merchants, 1750–1950* (Glasgow, 1951), pp. 55–56; Henry Hamilton, *The Industrial Revolution in Scotland* (Oxford, 1932), p. 126.

[109] Arthur Herbert Dodd, *The Industrial Revolution in North Wales* (Cardiff, 1933), pp. 286 and 318; Pressnell, *Country Banking*, pp. 20 and 29–31.

complete vertically integrated enterprise based on its original printing business.[110] When the firm failed in 1788 for an estimated £1,500,000, it was operating three banks of issue as well as the cotton-manufacturing business. The failure of Livesey, Hargreaves and Company was not soon forgotten and may have helped to discredit country-bank notes in Lancashire.[111]

While a combination of banking and cotton manufacturing was responsible for the first million-pound failure, the same combination also seems to have made the first cotton multimillionaire. The first Sir Robert Peel was reputed to have been worth over £2,000,000 at his death at the age of eighty in 1830.[112] The four Peel brothers, Robert, William, Edmund, and Lawrence, had been engaged in cotton printing before 1770, when Robert parted company with the others.[113] In 1788, Robert Peel was among the founders of the Manchester bank of Peel, Greaves and Company, which was apparently a partner from 1790 to 1805 in the London bank of Peel, Wilkes, Dickenson and Goodall.[114]

The Arkwright enterprise was also associated with a country bank, though not during the life of its founder. In 1804, an Arkwright joined the existing firm of Toplis and Company.[115] William Strutt of W. G. and J. Strutt was a partner in Thomas Evans and Sons until 1808; his sister Elizabeth was also a partner in the banking firm.[116] Other banking firms in which one or more

---

[110] W. E. A. Axon, *The Annals of Manchester* (London, 1886), p. 113 (Axon apparently made extensive use of Manchester newspapers); Wadsworth and Mann, *Cotton Trade*, pp. 142, n. 2, and 307–308.

[111] Graham MS, p. 407; O'Brien, *British Manufacturer's Companion,* ch. "Of Colormaking: A Retrospect," n.p., nn. 9 and 11; Pressnell, *Country Banking,* pp. 174–175.

[112] Axon, *Annals,* p. 180.

[113] Graham MS, p. 357. All the brothers were successful in the cotton industry (*ibid.,* pp. 345–346, 360–361, 365, 378, 407, 412, and 416).

[114] Pressnell, *Country Banking,* pp. 29 and 111.

[115] R. S. Fitton and A. P. Wadsworth, *The Strutts and the Arkwrights, 1758–1830: A Study of the Early Factory System* (Manchester, 1958), p. 242, n. 4.

[116] *Ibid.,* p. 242.

partners were drawn from the cotton industry were Byron, Sedgwick, Allen and Place; Daintry and Ryle; Dakeyne and Company; Pares and Company; Dumbell and Company; and Cunliffe, Brooks and Company.[117] There were undoubtedly others.

A connection between a bank and a cotton-manufacturing firm could help the manufacturer overcome difficulties in finding means of payment. Within certain limits it was possible for the bank to discriminate against customers in favor of a partner. This was made possible by the inflexibility of discount rates and bank charges. If the demand for discounts became too heavy, the banks, prevented by the usury law from discouraging the demand by raising the discount rate, undoubtedly rationed their discounts. Giving a partner preference in the matter of cash was even easier. Discriminating in favor of a partner was, therefore, possible without any immediate loss in bank income. If the process was carried too far, however, it would drive customers to other banks in search of better accommodation.

Better access to the means of payment was only one of the benefits that a cotton-factory owner could hope to reap from a proprietary connection with a country bank; he could also hope to get loans from it. If the manufacturer was one of several partners, however, the deed of partnership frequently limited the amount that the bank could lend to a partner. A partner's borrowing was often limited in this way to a sum less than, or equal to, his capital in the bank. In some cases, partnership deeds specified that the rate of interest charged would be 1 per cent less than the rate paid by other borrowers.[118] The reason for the limitation is obvious: too close an association between a bank and any single

---

[117] Pressnell, *Country Banking*, pp. 20, 29–31, and 334; Graham MS, p. 357.

[118] Pressnell, *Country Banking*, p. 291. The lower interest rate may have been a real advantage. The bank, however, presumably had better information about a partner's solvency than it had about the solvency of other customers, and it also had an exact knowledge of the partners' equity in the bank, which offered additional security for any loan. The lower rate could be justified on the grounds that much less risk was involved in such a loan.

firm could be disastrous, as in the case of Dumbell and Company, whose failure apparently was partly due to excessive borrowing by John Dumbell and his brother.[119]

The liquidity requirements of a bank generally limited the amount and character of lending to its customers, and the coincidence that a customer was also a partner did not alter this fact. The principal liabilities of a bank were its deposits and bank notes if it issued any—and most did. A country bank would attempt to roughly match its note liabilities with its holdings of cash and quickly realizable assets like London bank balances and government securities. The bank's deposits would be used in discounting, since the paper discounted would be liquidated in a relatively short time or could be rediscounted if the need arose. This left only the capital of the bank for lending by other means.[120] Therefore, a firm that engaged in both banking and manufacturing endangered the liquidity position of its bank if it borrowed from the bank much more than it had invested in it.

There were, no doubt, those who attempted to use banking to increase greatly the capital available to them. A memorandum to Lord Liverpool says of the men who undertook banking during the Napoleonic Wars: "Some of them possess no capital of their own; —others very little; in many instances they were set up not so much to supply the wants of the neighborhood, as of the partners themselves, the convenient instrument of persons with small means, but speculative dispositions for extending far beyond what they were otherwise entitled to expect." [121] Retribu-

---

[119] *Ibid.*

[120] *Ibid.*, pp. 288–289. This attitude toward bank capital as the limiting factor in nondiscount loans is indirectly indicated by the action of joint-stock banks in limiting their loans to the amount of paid-up capital (R. Roberts, "2nd Report of the Board or Committee of Management to the Board of Directors of the Bank of Manchester," Jan. 29, 1838, J. B. Smith MSS, no. 923.2/s339, f. 32, p. 11, Manchester Central Library).

[121] Extract from a Memorandum, Originally Addressed to Lord Liverpool, on the State of the Country in 1816, Huskisson Papers, Vol. XXVII (Additional MSS, no. 38760), f. 117, British Museum. There were other types of

tion, however, could come spectacularly, as it did in the case of Livesey, Hargreaves and Company. On the other hand, Arkwright, Toplis and Company may have been typical of the banks that had a cotton partner and managed to survive. The "Mill Account" was occasionally overdrawn for a moderate amount. These overdrafts were apparently related to the business cycle; they usually occured during periods of crisis. This type of borrowing was not used as a regular means of raising short-term capital.[122] From participation in a banking firm a manufacturer could gain a moderate improvement in his means-of-payment position, but he could only increase his access to short-term capital by running an additional risk in what was at best a fairly dangerous business.

The vast majority of firms in the cotton industry did not undertake full banking functions; they looked to country banks for a considerable part of their short-term capital and means of payment. Since most of the Lancashire banks were not banks of issue, they obtained most of the funds they used for discounting by rediscounting in London or by accepting deposits on which the banks paid interest.

McConnell and Kennedy received 5 per cent interest on their

---

complaints about the country banks. Walsingham Collins, a London merchant, wrote that "the large fortunes those gentlemen [i.e., bankers] made and the high reputation and esteem they were held in by all ranks of people, encourages many merchants and traders of every denomination to take the name of Banker; not, in fact, for the profits they hoped to derive from that business, but to strengthen their credit, and get the public money into their hands, the better to enable them to extend their private business . . . they now keep in employ riders to travel the country and solicit customers to open bill accounts at one half the commission merchants formerly had; by which means merchants are greatly injured and deprived of one of the most desirable branches of trade" (*Address to . . . the Representatives in Parliament for the City of London, with Proposals for the Better Regulation of Bankers and Brokers. . . . Also a Scheme for Establishing a Loan Bank* [London, 1778], pp. 7–8). Most of the functions performed by country banks had been, and still were, carried on by merchants.

[122] Pressnell, *Country Banking*, p. 335.

balance until 1818, when Heywood's bank began to pay them 4 per cent on the first £40,000 and 5 per cent on the rest; with the reduction of Bank rate from 5 to 4 per cent in 1822, Heywood's reduced their interest rate to 4 per cent on the entire balance, and in 1824 they further reduced it to 3 per cent.[123] McConnell and Kennedy's responses to these changes are of interest. After a period of thirteen years during which they had made no addition to their plant, they made one in 1818 and another in 1820, the year in which they also established an account with the British Linen Company, a Scottish joint-stock bank whose interest rate was probably higher. After the further reduction in 1824, they built another addition to their plant, eliminated their account with the British Linen Company, and ran their account with Heywood's down to the lowest point since 1813.[124] The general fall in interest rates was apparently pushing McConnel and Kennedy from the very short position represented by their deposit account to the very long position implied in plant construction. That this was rather against their will is indicated by their brief flirtation with the British Linen Company. It seems that this trend toward heavy investment in the face of falling interest rates was not confined to McConnel and Kennedy, but was general in the twenties.[125]

It is unlikely, however, that the fall in interest rates from 5 per cent in 1818 to 3 per cent in 1824 was the sole determinant of McConnel and Kennedy's plant-expansion program. The rate reduction may have facilitated investment in plant by reducing the

---

[123] Ashton, "Bill of Exchange," pp. 46–47. Until 1818, Heywood's and other country banks did not maintain different rates for deposits and bankers' loans. The rates were the same on both sides of the account. However, the bankers could and did raise their lending rates slightly above the deposit rate by charging commissions. This device was legal even when it raised the actual rate above the 5 per cent limit set by the usury laws (see Chapter II above).

[124] McConnel and Kennedy, Ledgers; also Return to the Commissioners on Employment of Children in Factories, copy dated May 1, 1833, p. 1, in McConnel and Kennedy MSS, Misc. Papers.

[125] R. C. O. Matthews, *A Study in Trade-Cycle History: Economic Fluctuations in Great Britain 1833–1842* (Cambridge, 1954), pp. 130–131.

costs of maintaining inventories and thus freeing some resources for investment in plant. In any case, two of the three plants were completed at or near cyclical peaks in business activity. It seems likely that the decisions to construct these plants—the ones completed in 1818 and 1824—were influenced by well-founded favorable expectations with regard to general business activity. On the other hand, the decision to build the plant completed in 1820 was probably taken at, or very near, a cyclical trough in general business activity.[126] In addition, the cyclical behavior of the cotton industry conforms fairly closely to that of business activity in general for the period 1816 to 1825.[127] Thus the plant construction of 1820 is something of a puzzle. It may have been due to some unknown peculiarity of the firm or to an error of judgement, or it may have been motivated by a desire to cut costs in the face of profit margins that, on an industry-wide basis at least, were probably falling.[128]

Country bankers accepted deposits only as a secondary function. It was to their function as short-term lenders that an anonymous manufacturer referred in 1826 when he stated that "not more clearly can the manufacturing greatness of this country be traced to the discoveries and inventions of Watt, Arkwright and the ingenious men of the last half century, than can be demonstrated the truth that to the system of country banking we are indebted for the full development and the wonderful effects of those inventions." [129]

Two other types of banks should be mentioned: the savings bank and the joint-stock bank. The exact date of the origin of the savings banks is not known. In 1816 there were fewer than eighty

---

[126] Arthur D. Gayer, W. W. Rostow, and Anna Jacobson Schwartz, *The Growth and Fluctuation of the British Economy, 1790–1850* (Oxford, 1953), I, 355–356.

[127] *Ibid.*, I, 153–155 and 196–198.   [128] *Ibid.*, I, 155 and 197, n. 2.

[129] A Manufacturer in the North of England, *A Letter to the Earl of Liverpool . . . Regarding Country Banks and the Currency in the Manufacturing Districts* (London, 1826), 5–6.

of them in England. They grew quickly in number and by 1833 there were 408 of them in England and Wales, with over 400,000 depositors and more than £14,000,000 in deposits.[130] The assets of these banks were not available to the cotton industry; after 1817 they were required by law to invest their funds in government securities.[131] The depositors were probably small tradesmen rather than laborers.[132] The high rate of population growth may have prevented the development of savings banks from producing the reduction of hoarding that might otherwise have been expected.

Except for the Bank of England, joint-stock banks did not exist in England and Wales until after 1826, although they had a longer history in Scotland. The great Scottish chartered joint-stock banks came into existence before 1760 and, like the Bank of England, they enjoyed limited liability. The distinctive feature of banking in Scotland was the unchartered joint-stock bank with unlimited liability.[133] These banks were essentially large partnerships, which were illegal in England and Wales, where a limit of six was placed on the number of partners that might engage in banking.[134] A joint-stock bank, with or without limited liability, often enjoyed a higher ratio of capital to deposits than private country banks that drew their capital from a small number of partners. This higher ratio helped to make the Scottish banks a better source of long-term capital than English and Welsh banks.[135]

Joint-stock banking was introduced in England by an act of 1826 that restricted the Bank of England's monopoly of joint-stock note issues to a radius of sixty-five miles from London. One of the reasons advanced for permitting joint-stock banks' issue was the

---

[130] Clapham, *Economic History*, I, 299–300.
[131] Holdsworth, *History of English Law*, XIII, 334–335.
[132] Clapham, *Economic History*, I, 300.
[133] Hamilton, *Industrial Revolution in Scotland,* pp. 260–279.
[134] Clapham, *Bank of England*, I, 158–160.
[135] Evidence of Lewis Loyd, *Report From the Committee on Manufactures, Commerce and Shipping* (1833) , q. 457.

superior ability of the Scottish joint-stock banks to survive crises—a superiority demonstrated in the crises of 1793 and 1825; another was the belief that the Bank of England had not acted in a completely blameless way during the crisis of 1825. The Bank was prepared to accept the limitation of its monopoly partly because so much of its business was concentrated in and around London and partly because accepting the limitation involved an early and long extension of its somewhat limited monopoly.[136] In the brief interval between 1826 and 1830 at least fourteen joint-stock banks were formed, and although some of these were in Manchester, they need scarcely be considered here; they belonged to the future rather than to the recent past.[137]

---

[136] Clapham, *Bank of England,* I, 262–263; II, 87–88, 102, and 121–130.

[137] Samuel Evelyn Thomas, *The Rise and Growth of Joint-Stock Banking* (London, 1934), I, 656.

Chapter IV

The Means of Payment and the
Diversity of the Sources of Supply

THE characteristic feature of the supply of short-term capital in the cotton industry was the variety of sources from which it came. The cotton manufacturer, the merchant, government, the shop-keeper, and the laborer were all laid under contribution. Indeed, there is a sense in which the community as a whole helped to finance the Industrial Revolution.

Of the various ways in which contributions to the supply of short-term capital were made, the most interesting is entrepreneurial borrowing from the laborer. Two related peculiarities of the British economy of the eighteenth century account for the workers' contribution to the manufacturers' supply of short-term capital: the shortage of the means of payment and the wage system.

The shortage of the means of payment did not extend to large payments, which could be made in gold coin, Bank of England notes, country bank notes, bills of exchange, bank drafts, and several other ways. It was limited to those means that were suitable for wage payments.

Wage payments could be made in gold coins, but the denominations in which gold coins were minted were usually so large that such payments involved great inconvenience. One employer stated that "if the work of two men comes near to a guinea, or of three men two guineas, we give them the gold and they must go together till they can get change." [1]

---

[1] Sir John Craig, *The Mint: A History of the London Mint from* A.D. *287 to 1948* (Cambridge, 1953), p. 247. No source is given for the quotation.

By the seventies, the means-of-payment problem had become so acute in Wilmslow, a textile town, that the employers divided the workers in a mill into a number of groups and paid them at intervals of several hours. As soon as one group was paid, the workers were sent out of the mill to settle their debts and make purchases; then the employer recovered the coins from the shopkeepers and paid the next group of workers.[2]

On December 19, 1806, McConnel and Kennedy wrote that "we are under the disagreeable necessity of stopping our works at the end of the week for want of money even to pay wages."[3] This was a large, successful, fairly conservative firm that, when it struck its balance a few weeks later, had a capital of just under £69,000 and showed a profit of almost £6,400 for its operations in 1806.[4] That their difficulty grew out of a shortage of coin is further indicated by the considerable efforts they made to get silver coins from Ireland.[5] In the same and following years, they, like other cotton-manufacturing firms, purchased copper coins from Matthew Boulton, who was manufacturing them.[6] In 1812, when the shortage again was unusually severe, they sent requests for coins to their agents in Belfast and Glasgow. The Glasgow agent was able to collect and send £220 of silver coin, but the Belfast agent replied that he doubted that there was £5 worth of shillings and sixpences in all Belfast.[7] Conditions were even worse in Ireland than in England. The exchanges were running against both England and Ireland, but the latter had also been drained of specie by

---

[2] Ashton, *An Economic History of England: The 18th Century* (London, 1955), pp. 215–216.

[3] McConnel and Kennedy to John Lang, McConnel and Kennedy MSS, Letter Books, Lewis Library of Commerce, University of Manchester.

[4] McConnel and Kennedy MSS, Ledgers.

[5] McConnel and Kennedy to J. T. How, Belfast, Oct. 4 and 25, 1806, McConnel and Kennedy MSS, Letter Books.

[6] McConnel and Kennedy to Matthew Boulton, Jan. 18, 1808, McConnel and Kennedy MSS, Letter Books. There were many other letters to Boulton on the subject of his coins.

[7] G. W. Daniels, "The Early Records of a Manchester Cotton-Spinning Firm," *Economic Journal*, XXV (1915), 187–188.

an unfavorable exchange with England that was intensified by restriction.[8]

Samuel Oldknow's cash problems were even more acute than McConnel and Kennedy's. They were ultimately to lead to a very complete and elaborate system of truck and paper-money payments, but in 1793 Oldknow and his partner were making frantic efforts to raise cash by entering the retail market.

They fitted up a light cart and sent a young man with it, full of goods, to supply the retailers in every part of the country, and to bring home the specie every Saturday, whatever might be the loss. The expedient succeeded for about three weeks, but had now failed, and he [Peter Ewart, Oldknow's partner] was come to Liverpool to try if by any possible means he could raise a few hundred guineas, to get over another week and keep his people alive. . . . [The Workers] . . . had agreed to wait this young gentleman's return from Liverpool, and what money he was able to raise, they had consented should be laid out in oatmeal, which being boiled up with water, potatoes, and some of the coarser pieces of beef, should be shared out in fair proportions among them; and thus in the cheapest manner provide for their subsistence.[9]

During the crisis of 1793, Oldknow was able to limit his cash payment of wages to about one-tenth of his wage bill.[10]

The Strutts also had trouble in getting enough coins to pay their wages. They got some of their cash from banks; at one time or another they received cash from Thomas Evans and Sons of Derby, Abel Smith and Company of Nottingham, and Smith, Payne and Smith of London. They also were supplied with coin by their London agent. In addition, they economized on cash by

---

[8] F. W. Fetter, "Introduction," *The Irish Pound, 1797–1826: Reprint of the Report of the Committee of 1804 of the British House of Commons on the Condition of the Irish Currency* (Evanston, Ill., 1955), pp. 17–19.

[9] W. C. Henry as quoted in R. S. Fitton and A. P. Wadsworth, *The Strutts and the Arkwrights, 1758–1830: A Study of the Early Factory System* (Manchester, 1958), pp. 240–241.

[10] George Unwin, Arthur Hulme, and George Taylor, *Samuel Oldknow and the Arkwrights* (Manchester, 1924), p. 187.

paying their wages in kind. In the mid-eighties, the Strutts had been making their wage payments almost entirely in cash; less than twenty years later, five-sixths of their wage payments were in rent or truck. It would be a mistake to assume that payments in kind always involved the exploitation of laborers. Between 1807 and 1830, the Strutts sold their workers over half a million gallons of milk at a total profit of 70£.[11]

Why did the supply of coins prove to be so inflexible in eighteenth-century Britain that enormous exertions and ingenious devices were necessary to make possible the payment of wages? As a rule, coins were minted from gold, silver, and copper.[12] When it came to using these coins for wage payments, each of them presented a special problem.

If, as has been indicated, eighteenth-century gold coins were minted in denominations that were too large for wage payments, why was there not an appropriate change in the policy of the mint? There does not seem to have been a shortage of gold in the eighteenth century. The ratio, by weight, of the world output of gold to that of silver seems to have been about one to thirty; it had been about one to thirty-two in the sixteenth century and one to forty-four in the seventeenth century.[13] Compared with that of silver, the minting of gold was heavy throughout most of the eighteenth century and its export relatively small.[14]

---

[11] Fitton and Wadsworth, *The Strutts,* pp. 241–243, 244–246, and 250.

[12] There were occasional experiments with other metals, notably tin (Craig, *The Mint,* pp. 178 and 182) .

[13] Dickson Leavens, *Silver Money* ("Cowles Commission for Research in Economics Monographs," no. 4; Bloomington, Ind., 1939) , p. 3, table 1.

[14] For the output of the Mint, see Craig, *The Mint,* pp. 410–422, App. I. The export of British coin and bullion obtained from British coin was prohibited; hence there are no records of such exports. Exports of foreign coin and bullion were recorded, since their export was legal. These figures are available from 1695 onward (G. N. Clark, *Guide to English Commercial Statistics: 1696–1782* ["Royal Historical Society Guides and Handbooks," no. 1; London, 1938], pp. 35–36) . Oddly enough the imports of foreign coin and bullion were not recorded (*ibid.,* p. 36) . The only available contemporary import figures seem to be a merchant's estimates for the import of gold pieces

There were several ways in which the denominations of gold coins could be reduced without debasement. The face value of the gold coins could be reduced and the coins themselves could either be reduced in size (without changing their fineness) or reduced in fineness (without changing their size).[15] Unfortunately, each of these possible solutions had important drawbacks.

The first possibility, reduction in size, required the minting of coins so small that they would have been easily lost. The magnitude of wages only set the upper limit for the denomination of convenient coins. If the gold coins were to be truly convenient, it would have been necessary to provide an adequate supply of acceptable coins that were of sufficiently low denomination to be suitable for wage earners' disbursements. Small coins also had the disadvantage of losing value through wear more rapidly than large coins made from the same alloy. They had a larger surface area per unit of volume—and hence per unit of value—than large coins. This probably accounts, at least in part, for the fact that gold sovereigns in the early nineteenth century had an average effective life of eighteen years, and half sovereigns of nine to ten years, in spite of the larger allowance made for loss before retirement of the smaller coin.[16] If, as seems possible under eighteenth-century conditions, small coins would tend to have a velocity of circulation that was disproportionately large, the loss of value would be further accelerated by the reduction in size.

Various experiments with small gold coins were attempted in

---

and bullion from Jamaica (Great Britain, House of Lords, *House of Lords Papers*, N.S., VI, 102). The export figures can be found in the following: *House of Lords Papers*, N.S., IV, 91 and 436, V, 334–335, and VI, 107; Great Britain, House of Commons, *Journal of the House of Commons*, XIII, 147–152 and 723, and XVIII, 672 and 682; J. Macgregor, *Commercial Statistics* (London, 1850), IV, 340 and 410.

[15] "Fineness" refers to the purity of bullion. The "carat" was the usual unit of fineness. English gold coins were supposed to be made of 22-carat gold in the eighteenth century—i.e., composed of 22 parts gold to 2 parts of some other metal. Modern monetary usage usually describes the fineness of gold coins in parts of gold per thousand parts.

[16] Craig, *The Mint*, p. 310.

the eighteenth century. In 1718, a quarter-guinea was minted, but only £37,380 were struck and the idea was dropped for fifty years—partly because the coin was too small in size and partly because of the objections of the "moneyers." The organization of the eighteenth-century mint was such that these objections were not a minor matter. In this instance, "the moneyers felt so strongly over the offer of only the customary piece-rates for this more troublesome dwarf that they refused the payment and were never paid at all." [17] In 1762, another experiment with the same coin lasted less than a year. This attempt to produce the quarter-guinea failed for the same reasons as the previous one and because of the realization that the odd value—5s. 3d.—was inconvenient.[18]

In 1758, the Bank of England suggested the issue of a one-third–guinea gold coin to relieve the shortage of silver coins. Some were issued from 1797 to 1811, but even under restriction conditions they were thrown back upon the Bank.[19]

The second possibility, reduction in fineness, would have produced other difficulties. Some alloying of gold is necessary to produce a usable coin, but there were limits beyond which the dilution of gold was undesirable. Pure or nearly pure gold is extremely soft and malleable and therefore subject to loss of value through wear; indeed, excessively fine coins can have their designs obliterated by flow without actual abrasion of the coins.[20] The use of alloys served to reduce loss through abrasion and inconvenience and possible loss through flow. By the early sixteenth century, some English coins were minted from twenty-two-carat gold, and after 1601 practically all gold coins were of that fineness.[21] Reduction in fineness could not go much beyond that point without greatly facilitating counterfeiting. One of the obstacles to counterfeiting was the color of the coin, which was highly distinctive and difficult to imitate by eighteenth-century methods. By the

---

[17] *Ibid.*, p. 219.   [18] *Ibid.*, p. 241.   [19] *Ibid.*, pp. 241 and 260–261.
[20] *Ibid.*, p. 103.   [21] *Ibid.*, p. 131.

eighteenth century, experience had taught that addition of much more than one part in eleven to gold destroyed the unique color of the metal and made imitation easier. It is true that even in the eighteenth century a complex addition might have preserved the color of the coin while reducing its fineness, but it would have vastly increased the difficulty of verifying the fineness of the alloy and hence probably would have been opposed by the mint.[22]

Thus far Britain's failure to solve the wage-payments problem by producing an adequate supply of small gold coins has been considered from the vantage point of the Tower of London, where the mint was located and where many officials of the mint lived. Viewed from a merchant's countinghouse or from Threadneedle Street, the stronghold of Ricardo's "company of merchants," the failure may have appeared in a different light.

Carlo Cipolla has identified four great gold coins—the Byzantine *nomisma,* the Moslem *dinar,* the *fiorino* of Florence, and the *ducato* of Venice—as the "dollars" of the Middle Ages. These coins constituted a sort of "super money" that "could move freely throughout Europe" and that, one or two at a time, "predominated as the international currency and everywhere enjoyed much more prestige, being much more eagerly demanded and much more easily accepted." Most other high-denomination coins were "nothing but a more or less faithful copy of the prevailing one, imitating its weight, its fineness, and often even the design and the inscriptions." The four "dollars" had a number of important common characteristics: "High unitary value, intrinsic stability, support by an economy at the same time strong, sound, and playing a pre-eminent role in the system of international exchanges—these seem to have been the three basic elements of the formula that made the fortunes of the 'dollars of the Middle Ages.' "[23]

The British refusal or inability to solve the wage-payment prob-

---

[22] *Ibid.,* pp. 103 and 269.

[23] Carlo M. Cipolla, *Money, Prices, and Civilization in the Mediterranean World: Fifth to Seventeenth Century* (Princeton, 1956), pp. 13–21 and 24.

lem by reducing the denomination of gold coins in the eighteenth century preserved their "high unitary value" and assured their "intrinsic stability." [24] The gold coins of England were eminently suited to serve as the "dollar" of the eighteenth and nineteenth centuries.

The difficulties presented by the use of silver for the payment of wages were of an entirely different kind from those presented by gold. Silver should have proved much more serviceable than gold, and wages were indeed sometimes paid in silver, but never with any degree of ease. Silver coins were unlimited legal tender until 1774. In that year, they became legal tender by tale to £25 and by weight to any amount.[25] In 1816, they ceased to be legal tender for amounts over 40s.[26]

In 1666, Charles II, with Stuart generosity, had abolished all charges for seigniorage and made the taxpayer shoulder the costs of minting gold and silver coins. One of his reasons for doing so was to "relieve the King of the deficits to which his generous increase of salaries had reduced the seigniorage account." [27] Hence, both gold and silver coins were minted at no cost to the bullion owner and were supposed to have an intrinsic value only a little below that of their face value. The value of silver was low enough to make it possible to produce coins of denominations sufficiently small for wage payments without being too tiny for convenience. Nevertheless, acute shortages of silver coin persisted down to the 1820's.[28]

There were various reasons for the shortages. Until 1770, it was in the interest of the actual coiners of money at the mint to coin gold rather than silver and coins of large rather than small de-

---

[24] By "intrinsic stability," Cipolla means stability of fineness (*ibid.*, p. 23, n. 24, and p. 25, n. 30).

[25] J. Viner, "Clapham on the Bank of England," *The Long View and the Short: Studies in Economic Theory and Policy* (Glencoe, Ill., 1958), p. 272. The statute lapsed in 1783 (R. G. Hawtrey, *The Gold Standard: In Theory and Practice* [5th ed.; London, 1947], p. 69, and R. G. Hawtrey, *Currency and Credit* [4th ed.; London, 1950], p. 294).

[26] Craig, *The Mint*, pp. 284–286.   [27] *Ibid.*, p. 168.   [28] *Ibid.*, p. 311.

nomination. Since it was legal to export bullion and foreign coin, but not British coin, there was a premium of bullion over British coin, and this tended to pull heavy coin out of circulation.[29] As a result, almost no silver bullion was offered to the mint, unless it was driven there by law. Up to the middle of the eighteenth century, it was believed that native mining companies were obliged to offer silver to the mint and they did so, but a lawyer's discovery that they need not do so when the mint price was below the market price ended the practice.[30] The amounts of silver offered to the mint from native or foreign companies had never been large in the eighteenth century, and by 1750 "the very art of coining silver on a large scale had been lost." [31]

The shortage of silver coins was not simply a direct result of a shortage of silver bullion. It is true that a relative world-wide shortage may have developed in the eighteenth century as the ratio of world silver output to gold output, which was forty-four to one in the seventeenth century, went to thirty to one in the eighteenth century.[32] Nevertheless, large quantities of silver entered and left Britain in the eighteenth century and the production of silver plate flourished.[33]

At the root of the problem was the geographical differences in the ratios at which gold and silver exchanged and the patterns of British international trade and British international settlements. In England, silver coin exchanged for gold coin at the rate of about 14.5 to 1 from 1663 to 1717, and 15.2 to 1 from 1717 to 1816.[34] In Europe, only Portugal and Spain usually had higher rates. In the Far East, the rate tended to be much lower—12 to 1 in India, 9 to 1 in Japan,[35] and in some places it occasionally went

---

[29] Ashton, *18th Century*, pp. 168–169.   [30] Craig, *The Mint*, p. 246.
[31] *Ibid.*, p. 248.   [32] Leavens, *Silver Money*, p. 3, table 1.
[33] Craig, *The Mint*, p. 215.
[34] Hawtrey, *Gold Standard*, pp. 67–68. The ratio for the fine silver in coin to the fine gold in coin would have been 15.5 to 1 (by weight) in the early years of the eighteenth century (Ashton, *18th Century*, p. 168 and n. 3).
[35] *Ibid.*, p. 169. These ratios were also for weights of fine metal in coin.

as low as 8 to 1.[36] What this meant in effect was that, for much of Britain's foreign trade, it was profitable to make payments in silver and receive payments in gold.

At the beginning of the eighteenth century, Britain had an overall favorable visible balance of trade. She had an unfavorable visible balance with East India, northern Europe, and the American colonies and a favorable one with western and southern Europe.[37] The effects of the deficit with India on the coinage of silver are suggested by the exports of foreign coin and bullion from England. From 1699 through 1719, £12,840,000 in coin and bullion was exported, of which £8,970,000 went to India.[38] Since India required settlement in silver, it is safe to assume that at least this considerable part of England's coin and bullion exports consisted of silver. Even if silver had not been required for settlement but had been made optional, the profitability of payment in silver would have assured its use.

The drain of silver to the East persisted throughout the century. From 1700 to 1717, the East India Company shipped out 22,500,000 ounces of silver, which would have sufficed for a coinage of £5,730,000. The totals for the next forty years came to about

---

[36] Craig, *The Mint*, p. 215.

[37] S. B. Saul, *Studies in British Overseas Trade, 1870–1914* (Liverpool, 1960), p. 4, table 1. The table is based on Ralph Davis, "English Foreign Trade, 1660–1700," *Economic History Review*, 2nd ser., VII (1954), 151, table 1, and 163–166. Davis' figures for 1699–1701 are taken as representative of the structure of trade at the start of the eighteenth century. The years 1699–1701 are close enough to the year in which the official values were fixed for the figures to be taken as values rather than as representative of volumes. Davis' table suggests the importance of re-exports for the favorable visible balance.

[38] John Oxenford [First Clerk and later Deputy to the Inspector General of Imports and Exports], An Essay Towards Finding the Ballance [*sic*] of Our Whole Trade Annually from Christmas of 1698 to Christmas, 1719, MS in Osenford's hand, n.d. [1723], Colonial Office Records, 390/14, Public Record Office, as reprinted in Clark, *English Commercial Statistics*, pp. 69–149, App. IV (figures on pp. 77–79). The attributions of authorship and date are Clark's (p. 25). Since the years referred to start with Christmas, I have designated the year starting in one year as the following year—e.g., year starting Christmas 1698 is called 1699.

80,000,000 ounces, from which about £20,000,000 in silver coins could have been minted. The average annual exports from 1700 to 1757 would have produced £450,000 of silver coin. During the same period, the largest amount of silver coins produced in a single year came to £149,000. In only three of the fifty-eight years was the output of the mint over £100,000; in only eleven years was it over £10,000; in twelve years it was under £1,000, and in six of these, silver coins were not minted at all.[39]

The English pattern of settlements in the middle of the eighteenth century differed very little from the pattern of fifty years earlier. There was still an unfavorable visible balance with the Far East and the Baltic—both of which were silver-hoarding areas. The Baltic probably tended to have an unfavorable balance with the Far East as well. An unfavorable British balance with her West Indian colonies was settled indirectly through the "slave triangles." Britain had a favorable balance with each of the other major geographical divisions of the world.[40]

The drain to India evidently began to fall off in the 1760's, but it did not cease.[41] The Industrial Revolution, by reversing the direction of the flow of textiles in world trade, was to reduce the silver loss to India and ultimately help to eliminate it.[42] But the overall drain to the East did not decline in the 1760's. The slack left by the decline in the drain to India was replaced by a new flow of silver to China, which resulted from expanding British imports of tea.[43] British exports sold poorly in China and an attempt was made to reduce the drain by creating a new multilat-

---

[39] Craig, The Mint, pp. 215, 219, and 408–422, App. 1. It should be noted, however, that the inclusion of the £320,373 output of the Edinburgh mint for 1707–1709 would somewhat alter the comparison, though it would not affect the argument (ibid., p. 417).

[40] Saul, Overseas Trade, pp. 7–8 and p. 7, fig. 1.   [41] Ibid., p. 6.

[42] G. Unwin, "Indian Factories in the 18th Century," Studies in Economic History: The Collected Papers of George Unwin, ed. R. H. Tawney (London, 1927), p. 352; W. Ashworth, A Short History of the International Economy, 1850–1950 (London, 1952), p. 30.

[43] Saul, Overseas Trade, p. 6.

eral trade pattern in the East. The problem was not solved until the first half of the nineteenth century, when exports of opium from India to China helped to redirect the flow of silver.[44]

The loss of bullion had a disastrous effect on the silver coinage of eighteenth-century Britain. The "Great Silver Recoinage" of 1696–1699 had been completely undone by 1717.[45] On the advice of Sir Isaac Newton, the master of the mint, the guinea was revalued at 21s. in the hope of pulling silver from the continent, since there was no hope of drawing it from the East.[46] While the change may have been an important step in the direction of adopting the gold standard and it produced the 21s. guinea, it failed to improve the silver situation.[47]

---

[44] *Ibid.*, pp. 6–7.   [45] Craig, *The Mint*, p. 194.

[46] Sir Isaac Newton, State of the Gold and Silver Coinage (25 Sept. 1717), in W. A. Shaw, ed., *Select Tracts and Documents Illustrative of English Monetary History: 1626–1730* ("Wheeler Economic and Historical Reprints," no. 1; London, 1935), pp. 166–177.

[47] The year 1816 is usually accepted as the date of the *de jure* establishment of a gold standard in England. The *de facto* appearance of a gold standard is another matter. The choice seems to be limited to 1717 or 1774. Everything depends, of course, on the definition of the gold standard, and "in attempting to say what we mean by a gold standard, we are again met by the difficulty that the facts of life have escaped out of the pigeonholes of the makers of text-books" (D. H. Robertson, *Money*, ed. C. W. Guillebaud and Milton Friedman [Chicago, 1962], p. 53). One textbook, for example, insists that one of the "formal requisites" for a "gold coin standard" was "a free flow of gold into and out of the monetary system as well as into and out of the country" (William Howard Steiner and Eli Shapiro, *Money and Banking* [rev. ed.; New York, 1941], p. 47). Before 1819, England only permitted the export of foreign coin and bullion. Does this satisfy the condition? If not, then under this definition the country did not go on a *de jure* gold coin standard in 1816.

In 1717, the guinea was given a statutory price of 21s., which was below its market price. Hawtrey's comment is of interest: "This was not a case where the statutory valuations of gold and silver coins undervalued silver. The price of the guinea was not a statutory valuation at all, but a free market price, though the practice of accepting guineas in payment of taxes at 21s. 6d. gave some official support to the rate. This is one of those cases where we must distinguish between the money of account, in which debts and credits are reckoned, and the legal tender money in which debts are payable. The fault was not that the guinea was overvalued, but that, given the existing level of

By the 1760's, the silver coins were in an almost unbelievable condition: "Long wear had reduced shillings and sixpences to complete blanks. . . . The majority of counterfeiters were content to produce plain white disks, which benches were not certain was an offense against the law, and francs and other foreign coins of suitable size were imported and rubbed smooth to pass as shillings." [48]

The gold recoinage of 1773–1777 and the change in the status of silver coins from unlimited to limited legal tender in 1774, actions that are sometimes regarded as steps toward the adoption of gold standard, probably helped to keep the deteriorating silver coins in circulation, and not to drive them out. [49] Nevertheless, by

---

prices and wages, the monetary unit of account was itself overvalued in terms of silver by the mint price" (Hawtrey, *Gold Standard,* p. 67). After 1717, however, "silver was still undervalued and little of it remained in circulation" *(ibid.)*.

[48] Craig, *The Mint,* pp. 247–248.

[49] Hawtrey chooses 1717 as the point at which the *de facto* gold standard appeared, because gold coin was given a statutory valuation in that year *(Gold Standard,* p. 6). Craig selected the same year on the basis of the brief mild reaction of the gold market, which "England . . . dominated" *(The Mint,* p. 218). It is true that even before the change in the value of the guinea, Newton stated that "gold is now become our standard money and silver is a commodity which rises and falls in its price as it does in Spain" (Craig, *The Mint,* p. 219). Against this statement, however, must be set that of Joseph Harris, the king's assayer, in 1757: "Everybody knows that pounds, shillings and pence denote certain specific quantities of pure silver. We have never heard till lately a word mentioned of gold being the standard of value" (quoted in Craig, *The Mint,* p. 256). A House of Commons resolution of 1718 seems to be ambiguous; perhaps the House was opting for bimetallism: "This House will not alter the standard of the Gold and Silver coins of this Kingdom in Fineness, Weight or Denomination" (quoted in Craig, *The Mint,* p. 219.) Clapham suggested that the recoinage of gold while the poor silver coinage was not touched, "was in effect the introduction of a gold standard" *(The Bank of England: A History, 1694–1914* [Cambridge, 1944], I, 176). Given the past and present uncertainties, perhaps Thomas Smith's statement before the Bullion Committee that a pound could not be defined except by the admission that it was "difficult to explain it, but every gentleman in England knows it," was less lucicrous than Peel thought it to be in 1819 (F. A. Mann, *The Legal Aspect of Money: With Special Reference to*

the end of the eighteenth century, the "silver coinage was dead." [50]
When it was resurrected in 1816, it was as a token coinage.

One peripheral aspect of the silver problem needs to be mentioned in passing, and that is its effect on the East India Company and on trade with India. By the late eighteenth century, the company had a serious remittance problem growing out of its need to remit a considerable amount of tribute. Remittance in bullion would have resulted in loss. As far as possible, remittance took the form of goods, but the company tended to manage its exports from India "in the main as a means of remitting the tribute it drew, with a careless eye to cost and profit." The Company's emphasis on remittance helps to explain the British merchants' confidence that they could make the East India trade pay, and provided one of the motives for their attempts to modify the company's monopoly—attempts that gradually met with success after 1792. Some of the merchants, at least, tended to underestimate or simply ignore the domestic effects of the drain of silver.[51]

If the condition of the silver coinage was poor, that of copper was abominable. The copper coins should have been suitable for wage payments. They were of the right denomination for wage payments and wage earners' disbursements, they were legal tender, and there usually was not a shortage of them in the country. Nevertheless the copper coinage presented a problem to the manufacturer with wages to pay. The root of the silver problem was the inability of the state to keep silver coins in circulation; the root of the copper problem was the inability of the state to distribute the coins.

Comparative, Private, and Public International Law [2nd ed.; Oxford, 1953], p. 41 and nn. 3 and 4).

Viner thought that the hands-off policy was intended to keep the silver coins in circulation ("Clapham," p. 272).

[50] Craig, *The Mint,* p. 255.

[51] S. G. Checkland, "John Gladstone as Trader and Planter," *Economic History Review,* 2nd ser., VII (1954), 216–222 (quote on 217).

A proclamation of 1672 had made copper coins legal tender, but it had added that they were "to contain as much copper as shall be of the true intrinsic value of each less the charges only of coining and uttering." [52] In the production of gold coins and silver coins, the state assumed the burden of the costs of production, which during the first quarter of the eighteenth century averaged 1½ per cent of the face value of silver coins.[53] For the years 1775–1795, the average cost was 1¼ per cent for gold.[54] The cost of coining copper was at least 31½ per cent of the face value of the coins in the first quarter of the century,[55] and probably higher than that in 1770–1775.[56]

The relatively high costs of producing copper coins meant that they were always regarded as token coins.[57] The government's refusal to accept the heavy cost of recoinage meant that counterfeiting would be easy and the legal-tender status of the coin would be undermined. Counterfeiting of coppers flourished in the eighteenth century. In the seventies, estimates by merchants put the counterfeits at two-thirds to one and one-half times the legal issue.[58] In 1787, the mint examined samples of copper coins and found that "only eight percent had some tolerable resemblance to the king's coin; forty-three per cent were blatantly inferior; twelve per cent were blanks; and the balance was 'trash which would disgrace common sense to suppose it accepted for coins.' " [59] The law was far more lenient towards the counterfeiter of copper coin than to the counterfeiter of nobler coins.[60]

The low intrinsic value of the copper coins, counterfeiting, and

---

[52] Proclamation of 16 August 1672, as quoted in Craig, *The Mint*, p. 175. The policy continued in effect until 1821.

[53] Craig, *The Mint*, pp. 199–200.

[54] *Ibid.*, p. 237. There seems to be no comparable figure available for silver coinage, perhaps because so little was coined in these years.

[55] *Ibid.*, p. 200.

[56] Calculated from *ibid.*, p. 428, App. The cost works out to just over 31%, but the mint started from fillets, not bullion. If the cost of turning bullion into fillets is added, the cost of production probably goes over 31.5%.

[57] *Ibid.*, p. 250.   [58] *Ibid.*, p. 253.   [59] *Ibid.*   [60] *Ibid.*, p. 252.

the failure to understand the mechanism of distribution [61] produced a combination of scarcity and surplus as the coins tended to pile up in some areas, particularly London,[62] and to be scarce in other areas where they were needed for wage payments.

Toward the end of the century, merchants and manufacturers issued traders' tokens—metallic promissory notes of uncertain legal standing—in areas that were short of copper (and silver) coins. These "respectable counterfeits," which did not attempt to imitate the king's coins, were not illegal, but they did not solve the problem. Even Matthew Boulton's efforts to remedy the situation by producing coppers for the Treasury—which bypassed the mint—came to naught, and various local authorities issued their own coins. Two of the larger issuers were the Corporation of Sheffield and the Birmingham Poor Law Authority.[63] The malady was an old one, having been known in the Middle Ages,[64] and it was not until 1821 that the mint began to provide an adequate amount of small coins.[65]

---

[61] Cipolla, *Money, Prices, and Civilization*, pp. 27–31. The effect of lack of knowledge or lack of understanding was less important in the Middle Ages than it was in eighteenth-century England. Limited monetary sovereignty in the Middle Ages would have made a "cure" unlikely in any event (*ibid.*, p. 31). English governments of the eighteenth century had a recognized legal right to administer the monetary system.

[62] Craig, *The Mint*, p. 251. In 1754, the butchers, bakers, and grocers appealed to the government to stop coinage of copper and to withdraw the copper coins in circulation. They complained that copper had surplanted gold and silver and that the wages of the workers were almost entirely paid in copper coins, leaving each of them with £50 to £500 of half pence that they could not get rid of because no large transaction could be negotiated with them. The government suspended issue for about seven years. Coppers were piling up again in London in 1809. In 1811, the government tried to ease the provincial shortages of coppers by transferring new coin from the holdings of the London brewers to the provinces, but London traders complained about their surpluses again soon after and the government withdrew some coppers (*ibid.*, pp. 266–267).

[63] *Ibid.*, pp. 254 and 262–267.

[64] Cipolla, *Money, Prices, and Civilization*, p. 32 and n. 15.

[65] Craig, *The Mint*, p. 267.

Cipolla has raised an interesting question that unfortunately can only be alluded to here. In speaking of the "dollars" of the Middle Ages, he said that

their high unitary value . . . was important not only for the prestige it gave, but also for the social implications it brought into play. Since the mass of the people possessed low purchasing power, the high unitary value made the dollars of the Middle Ages "aristocratic coins" in the sense that they circulated only among the upper classes and only in special sectors of economic life. The fact that in the stratified society different classes use different types of money presents a great problem with many consequences.[66]

He evidently thought that things changed in the sixteenth century:

With the beginning of modern times the social implications of the petty coins were completely changed. Through a progressive secular debasement the small coins were now reduced to very low units of value. On the other side, through the sixteenth century, the general level of prices and wages moved markedly upward. Consequently, during the sixteenth century it became more and more common to see gold . . . or big silver coins . . . in the hands of the wage-earning people, just as it became more and more common to see these pieces used as means of payment in local and petty transactions. The gold coins lost the character of "aristocratic money." [67]

If the description of sixteenth-century and later developments is intended to apply to northern Europe in general and England in particular—and it may well not be so intended—it is inaccurate.[68] The monetary situation in eighteenth-century England much more closely resembles Cipolla's description of the one in medieval Europe.

In eighteenth-century England, gold coins were not suitable for

---

[66] *Money, Prices, and Civilization,* pp. 25–26.

[67] *Ibid.,* pp. 36–37.

[68] The discussion is general, but the coins referred to here are all Italian. In addition, the subtitle of the book limits the discussion to southern Europe, but the actual argument seems to be general.

wage payments or for workers' disbursements. They were only useful to those who had large payments to make or receive. Parliament was zealous in preserving the value of gold coins. After the revaluation of the guinea from 21s. 6d. to 21s., Parliament declared in a resolution "that this House will not alter the standard of the Gold and Silver coins of this Kingdom in Fineness, Weight or Denomination." [69]

The state of the silver coinage was looked on with indifference by a merchant like John Gladstone,[70] and in all likelihood by the East India Company. After all, Thomas Mun had been a director of the East India Company.[71] The laws that punished the counterfeiting of gold and silver were harsher than those that punished the counterfeiting of copper coins, and the bracketing of silver with gold may have been due to the earlier position of silver as the standard and to the disagreement, even after 1717, over which metal was the standard.

It can be conjectured that the means-of-payment problem was intensified by the rapid growth of population. Whether or not the standard of living was rising, the levels of income were not very high. Hoarding, therefore, probably involved coins of very small denominations—just those small silver and copper coins that were in shortest supply. Savings banks, as has been indicated, did not offer most members of the rapidly increasing population a real alternative to hoarding.

The problem presented by the faulty silver and copper coinage could have been met by the issue of bank notes of small denominations. The order of magnitude of wages was such that only notes of less than £1 with at least local acceptance could have met

---

[69] Resolution of the House of Commons, Jan. 13, 1718, as quoted in Craig, *The Mint*, p. 219.

[70] Checkland, "John Gladstone," p. 217.

[71] Mun had, of course, argued for the right to export bullion in his famous tract (*England's Treasure by Foreign Trade* . . . [London, 1664], as reprinted in J. R. McCulloch, ed., *Early English Tracts on Commerce* [Cambridge, 1952], pp. 115–209) .

the need. The Bank of England note was too large to serve the purpose. Until 1793, its lowest denomination was £10; in that year a £5 note was introduced. With the coming of suspension in 1797, the Bank began to issue £1 and £2 notes. It retained the power to issue notes of £1 and over until 1829, when £5 became the smallest note it was permitted to issue.[72]

The Bank of England did not take up the slack left by the bad coinage; the country banks attempted to do so with limited success. Notes of less than £1 could not be issued legally by English and Welsh country banks between 1775 and 1797 or after 1808, but they apparently issued them illegally.[73] From 1777 to 1797, bank notes for less than £5 were also illegal. The £1 country-bank note was, therefore, only legal from 1797 to 1829.[74] However, since local bank notes, small or large, did not circulate in Lancashire, where there were few banks of issue, the illegal issues did not solve the problem. In Manchester in particular, where there was no bank of issue at least until the twenties, wages were paid in coins that were often obtained with great difficulty.[75] In Scotland, £1 notes had been in circulation since 1704 and were never made illegal.[76]

Bank notes were treated with suspicion in England and Wales—whether they were issued in Threadneedle Street or in the provinces. Many of them, including those of the Bank of

---

[72] Clapham, *Bank of England,* II, 2–3 and 105–107; E. Cannon, *The Paper Pound of 1797–1821: A Reprint of the Bullion Report* (London, 1919), pp. vii–xlii.

[73] Pressnell, *Country Banking in the Industrial Revolution* (Oxford, 1956), pp. 16–17 and 144–145. Some banks issued tokens for less than £1. In 1816, three-shilling bank tokens were circulating in Liverpool (*Manchester Magazine,* II, no. 21 [Sept. 1816], 427).

[74] Pressnell, *Country Banking,* p. 16; J. H. Clapham, *An Economic History of Modern Britain,* I (Cambridge, 1939), 264.

[75] Clapham, *Bank of England,* II, 90–91; S. Hibbert-Ware, *Remarks on the Facility of Obtaining Commercial Credit* (Manchester, 1806), pp. 34–35.

[76] A. E. Feavearyear, *The Pound Sterling: A History of English Money* (London, 1931), p. 225.

England, were easily forged, but even if they had not been, the frequency of bank failures alone would have engendered caution.[77] The utility of bank notes depended on the existence of a public educated in their use, and such a public could not be created overnight. A sizable part of the wage-earning population had not as yet been conditioned to the use of bank notes. The story told by T. C. Foster seems almost too good an illustration of the point to be true:

> In Galway, I was assured that so little do people know the commercial value of money that they are constantly in the habit of pawning it. I was so incredulous of this that the gentleman who informed me asked me to go with him to any pawnbroker to assure myself of the fact; and I went with him and another gentleman to a pawnbroker's shop kept by Mr. Murray in Galway. On asking the question the shopman said it was quite a common thing to have money pawned; and he produced a drawer containing a £10 Bank of Ireland note pawned six months ago for 10/-; a 30/-Bank of Ireland note pawned for 1/-; a £1 Provincial Bank note pawned for 6/-. . . .[78]

For the more sophisticated, the Bank note had the disadvantage that it was not legal tender until 1811.[79]

Suspension had had a remarkable educative effect on that part of the population that made and received relatively large payments. Success in a world war that England had, to a considerable extent, fought with sacks of gold, and the discovery that a quarter of a century of inconvertibility had not brought the country to

---

[77] Pressnell, *Country Banking*, p. 15.

[78] *Letters on the Condition of the People of Ireland* (1846), p. 314, in J. W. Rogers, *The Potato Truck System of Ireland . . .* (2nd ed.; m. pub., 1847), pp. 6–7, as quoted in K. H. Connell, *The Population of Ireland, 1750–1845* (Oxford, 1950), p. 142, n. 3.

[79] Fom that year until Resumption, the Bank note was legal tender. After an interlude in which legal tender status was revoked, the Bank note finally became legal tender in 1833, subject to the provise that it would retain that status only as long as it was convertible (Mann, *Legal Aspect*, pp. 34–45).

rack and ruin,[80] made the habitual users of the gold coins far less insistent on the actual possession of them than they had previously been. In 1816, the Government, which had intended to keep the guinea as the principal gold coin, was affected by the public's preference for pounds, to which they had become accustomed by the use of bank notes. The preference, which was strong enough to make the government accept the cost of recoining the guinea, resulted in the minting of the twenty-shilling gold sovereign.[81]

The new-found convenience of bank notes and the new-found confidence in them can be seen in the slowness with which they were exchanged for sovereigns in the years 1817–1820, when exchange of £1 and £2 Bank notes for sovereigns was permitted but not required by law. Tourists alone found sovereigns more useful than Bank notes.[82] These developments, however, did not affect the manufacturers' wage-payment problem.

During the restriction period, the Bank of England attempted to solve the problem by issuing tokens—first in denominations of about 5s. and, after 1811, in denominations as low as 1s. 3d. They were intended to provide coins for small payments by evading British laws regulating the intrinsic value of coins, and they were apparently distrusted.[83] The earliest issue, valued at 4s. 6d., was a Spanish dollar countermarked by stamping a small head of George III on the cheek of the king of Spain. The token was described as having "two Kings' heads and not worth a crown." [84]

---

[80] It seemed to some that it would. Sir William Forbes, a Scottish banker, recalled his feelings on being informed of Suspension as follows: "My ideas at various time during the course of the war, had been often not a little gloomy when I thought of the State of things in the Kingdom, and indeed in Europe; but now it was that I certainly did think the nation was ruined beyond redemption, when so novel and alarming a circumstance has taken place at the Bank of England, which had ever been considered as the bulwark of public and private credit" (*The Memoirs of a Banking House* [1803], as quoted in Cannon, *Paper Pound*, p. xv).

[81] Craig, *The Mint*, p. 285.

[82] *Ibid.*, pp. 288–289.   [83] *Ibid.*, pp. 261–263.   [84] *Ibid.*, p. 261.

Even if they had been readily accepted, the Bank of England tokens would probably not have served as a means of paying wages for very long. Although they were token coins in England, their silver content was still too high to prevent them from being drawn to the Far East.[85]

The manufacturers themselves made a number of attempts to adapt their enterprises to the shortage of the means of payment. These attempts were significant because they were valuable contributions to the solution of a nearly intractable economic problem and because, to some extent, they drew the worker, the shopkeeper, and, indeed, the community as a whole into the network of credit without which some enterprises might well have foundered for lack of short-term capital and other enterprises would have been constrained to slower growth.

The short-term capital role of the laborer, the shopkeeper, and the community becomes clear if the wage system is considered. In the cotton factories, as in the domestic industries, wage contracts ran for what were—by later standards—long periods. In the 1770's and 1780's, wage contracts for a year were common. Although the contracts seem to have grown shorter in the course of time, as late as 1827–1828 the Strutts still hired their spinners for three months and required three months notice from an employee if he wished to leave. These long contracts were in fact legally enforced.[86]

Short and long wage payments were made. Weekly or fortnightly subsistence advances were made; in addition, a settlement was made at the end of the contract. In the case of the Strutts, this

---

[85] *Ibid.*, p. 263. I have assumed that the silver-to-gold exchange ratio was 12 to 1 in India during the years of issue. At that ratio it would seem to have been profitable to ship the tokens to India even when their face value was at its highest (5s. 6d.). I have not allowed for shipping and insurance costs, however, since I have no idea of what they were. John Gladstone instructed one of his agents that Madras was the best place to dispose of "dollars"—possibly a reference to Bank tokens (Checkland, "John Gladstone," p. 219).

[86] Fitton and Wadsworth, *The Strutts*, pp. 106 and 233–234.

"Quarterly Gift Money" was paid in cash and amounted to one-sixth of the total wages paid. "Gift Money" served a number of functions: it helped the Strutts maintain factory discipline, and it probably prevented their labor turnover from being even higher than the 16 per cent a year that it was. Fines for misconduct were levied against the "Gift Money," and it was forfeited if the employee left without giving the required three months notice.[87] As the long wage contract tended to disappear from industry during the nineteenth century, so did the settlement payments. Viewed in relation to the manufacturers' short-term capital problems, the settlement payments can be regarded as an involuntary extension of short-term credit to the entrepreneur by his labor force, although the exaction of short-term loans may not have been the employer's chief motive in using this method of payment.

Short and long payments were made in various media of which some were only suitable for one type of payment. A laborer could be paid in coin, Bank of England notes or tokens, country-bank notes, manufacturers' promissory notes or tokens, small bills of exchange, and truck. Although gold coin, Bank of England notes, and country bank notes were not suitable for advances, they could conceivably have been of some use for settlements. A list of eighteen Strutt employees and the "Quarterly Gift Money" due them in the years 1801–1805, however, contains the names of only five who were to receive over one pound.[88]

Samuel Oldknow paid a large part of his wages in shopnotes redeemable in kind on demand at his store, but only some of them were redeemed there by his employees. There were other shops in the town and, since the laborers sometimes wanted cash or goods that were not obtainable at the company store, the practice of discounting these notes soon grew up among the shopkeepers. When the notes were presented to Oldknow by the shopkeepers for redemption, the manufacturer either paid them immediately with a two-month bill drawn on one of his London customers, or

---

[87] *Ibid.*, pp. 232–246.   [88] *Ibid.*, p. 237.

he paid them in cash after two months had elapsed.[89] According to George Unwin, the historian of the Oldknow enterprises, "in this curious way a score of villagers became involuntary amateur bankers in support of Samuel Oldknow's enterprise." [90] These villagers were helping Oldknow to use less cash and to economize on his short-term capital.

It is only a short step from the use of shopnotes to the issue of promissory notes and token coins. Oldknow took this step, and many other cotton manufacturers issued notes or tokens to pay wages. The Peels issued promissory notes, and the Strutts, the Arkwrights, McConnel and Kennedy, and Robert Owen used token coins.[91] Both media could be used for advances or settlement payments, and both cut down on the issuers' cash needs and were economical of short-term capital.

With the advent of the issue of promissory notes, a manufacturer entered the twilight zone between industry and full banking. Some of them eventually abandoned industry for banking. The British Linen Company and Cunliffe, Brooks and Company were banks whose origins can be traced to the circulation of promissory notes issued to pay wages in a branch of the cotton industry.[92]

Bills of exchange were also used in the payment of wages. Small ones could be used for advances, and bills as small as six pence or a shilling were circulated. Somewhat larger bills were used for settlement payments. These bills were often discounted by retailers.[93] By discounting for the worker, the shopkeeper was, in the

---

[89] Unwin, Hulme, and Taylor, *Samuel Oldknow*, pp. 181–182.

[90] *Ibid.*, p. 182.

[91] *Ibid.*, pp. 190–191; Fitton and Wadsworth, *The Strutts*, pp. 243–244; A Manufacturer in the North of England, *A Letter to the Earl of Liverpool . . . regarding Country Banks and the Currency in the Manufacturing Districts* (London, 1826), p. 16.

[92] Unwin, Hulme and Taylor, *Samuel Oldknow*, pp. 178–179.

[93] T. S. Ashton, "The Bill of Exchange and Private Banks in Lancashire, 1790–1830," *Papers in English Monetary History*, ed. T. S. Ashton and R. S. Sayers (Oxford, 1953), pp. 37–49.

first instance, financing the worker's consumption, but he was, at one remove, financing the manufacturer's production, although this was not the legal status of the transaction. As has been indicated in Chapter III, the discount of a bill of exchange was legally a loan by the buyer of the bill to the seller. A loan by a shopkeeper to a factory hand would have been an unlikely transaction, however, had it not been for the contingent liability of the manufacturer and the shopkeeper's wish to keep the custom of the worker. Had the discount rate been flexible in the eighteenth century or had it been lowered in response to an increase in the volume of bills presented for discount, the manufacturer himself might have found it desirable to discount the bills with the shopkeeper or with a banker, but even in that case his means-of-payment problem might have presented an insuperable obstacle. He probably would have had to buy silver coins at a premium in order to pay his employees. As it was, the inflexibility of the rate of discount and the rationing of discounts made it desirable for the employer to pay out his small bills of exchange.

How much of the bill the employee received in cash and how much of it went to cover debts already owed to the shopkeeper or became a book credit at the shop is not clear. Nor is it certain that a shopkeeper, engaged in petty transactions with workers who may have been ignorant of the law, adhered to the discount rate dictated by the usury laws. The answers to the questions posed here are probably as various as human nature, but a great deal must have depended on the amount of competition in the area and perhaps also on whether or not the millowner was able or willing to set up a fair truck system or to threaten to do so.

Truck payments were suitable for advances or settlements. They originated in the colonizing aspects of some of the early factories as well as in the state of the currency. Where a factory was established away from a center of population, as many of them were before steam power was widely used instead of water power, the employer might find it necessary to provide food and housing; this, in turn, meant company-store and rent deductions.

Whatever its drawbacks in the eyes of the laborer, this type of payment did not involve an involuntary extension of credit to the employer. If the entrepreneur collected rent, he also built houses; if he made part of his payments in food, he also had to use his capital to stock the company store.

While it was true that the manufacturer could in times of need borrow against the stock of his truck shop, the store was hardly an advantage to him and it did not improve his capital position. By the late 1820's, the truck system seems to have been an advantage only to the small manufacturer.[94]

It is undoubtedly true that some of these methods of paying wages were subject to abuse. But it is difficult to see how the entrepreneurs, operating within the framework of a poor coinage and often under the necessity of creating new towns, could have completely avoided these abuses.

One thing that is clear, however, is the role of the shopkeeper in aiding the manufacturer. By accepting the manufacturer's promissory notes or tokens and by discounting bills of exchange, he made it possible for the manufacturer to use a smaller amount of the scarce silver coins and poorly distributed copper coins. At the same time, the shopkeeper—by accepting the manufacturer's notes or tokens—was according him some of the benefits of the note-issuing banker. His promises to pay his debts had become currency. Like a note-issuing banker, he had the short-term advantage of the margin between his issue and the reserve that he had to keep against the probable return of his issue for collection. Unlike a banker, he did not make the margin available to someone else by lending it; he used it himself. By using it himself, he added to his supply of short-term capital. To the extent that the

---

[94] G. W. Hilton, "The Truck Act of 1831," *Economic History Review*, 2nd ser., X (1958), 470–479.

community as a whole rather than only a few shopkeepers accepted his notes or tokens as currency, broadened their circulation, and delayed their return to him for collection—to that extent the community was widening the margin and adding to his supply of capital.

The manufacturer used his supply of short-term capital to meet his raw-material costs as well as his wage bill. Hence, for the spinner, the cotton market was comparable in importance to the labor market. In 1779, the cost of the cotton used in making 40-hank yarn was 12.7 per cent of the selling price; in 1834, it was 54 per cent of the selling price.[95] Once the Industrial Revolution was well under way, the size of the stocks of cotton maintained in Great Britain was enormous. From 1811 through 1830, the average number of weeks of cotton consumption in stock in Great Britain on December 31 of each year was thirty-six and one-fourth. Most of this stock of cotton was in the ports; sometimes the proportion of stocks in the ports was as high as 90 per cent of the whole, and it was almost always more than 50 per cent.[96] In any event, the financing of these stocks must have made very heavy demands on the available supplies of short-term capital.

One type of entrepreneur, the cotton broker, helped the spinner meet his short-term capital needs by partly financing his cotton purchases. Unfortunately we do not know very much about the cotton broker's operations during the Industrial Revolution. We do, however, have a summary of the transactions of Nicholas Waterhouse and Company for the years 1799 to 1802.[97] The firm carried on its business in Liverpool and was unusual in that it

---

[95] Simon Kuznets, *Economic Change: Selected Essays in Business Cycles, National Income, and Economic Growth* (New York, 1953), p. 262.

[96] Thomas Ellison, *The Cotton Trade of Great Britain: Including a History of the Liverpool Cotton Market and of the Liverpool Cotton Broker's Association* (London, 1886), n.p., table 1 at end.

[97] The following discussion of Nicholas Waterhouse and Company is based on F. E. Hyde, B. B. Parkinson, and Sheila Marriner, "The Cotton Broker and the Rise of the Liverpool Cotton Market," *Economic History Review*, 2nd ser., VIII (1955), 75–81.

acted both as a seller's broker and a buyer's broker. As a seller's broker, the firm acted for the merchant who imported the cotton; as a buyer's broker, it acted for the yarn manufacturers. In 1799, the firm earned about £4,020 by brokerage, of which approximately £1,270 was earned as a buyer's broker; in the same year the company earned just under £670 as interest and paid out about £360 in interest. In 1800, the company earned about £5,325 by brokerage, of which approximately £1,520 was earned as a buyer's broker; in the same year the firm received just over £1,450 in interest and paid out just over £590 in interest. In 1801, the company earned £4,780 by brokerage, of which £1,150 originated as buyer's brokerage; in the same year, the firm's income from interest was about £1,625, and it paid out approximately £590 in interest.

The most interesting thing about these figures is the size and rate of growth of the interest received. It seems reasonable to assume that these interest payments reflect the Liverpool firm's role as a supplier of short-term capital to both the importer and the spinner. The high level of short-term lending was probably sustained by Nicholas Waterhouse and Company's policy of plowing back about 75 per cent of its profits during the years for which information is available.

There is good reason to believe that the large-scale manufacturer was doing his own importing of cotton by the twenties, at the latest.[98] This development, however, probably tended to cut out the importing merchant rather than the buyer's broker. It was the cotton broker who was to dominate the cotton market of the nineteenth century.[99]

One rather unexpected supplier of short-term capital was the state. Government borrowing place the state in competition with

---

[98] John Gladstone to Kirkman Finlay, Jan. 29, 1823, in Huskisson Papers, Vol. XIII (Additional MSS, no. 38746), ff. 101–102, British Museum; Henry Smithers, *Liverpool, Its Commerce: With a History of The Cotton Trade* (Liverpool, 1825), pp. 139–140.

[99] Hyde, Parkinson, and Marriner, "Cotton Broker," p. 76.

the manufacturers for resources, but there were at least two occasions on which the government aided the entrepreneurs with what were essentially short-term loans. During the crisis of 1793, the government made loans totaling £2,200,000 to tide them over. It is true that these loans were made to the "mercantile interest," but there was, at the time, no distinction made between "merchants," "traders," and "manufacturers." The government repeated the process in 1811 by again lending exchequer bills, this time to the amount of £2,000,000. The Bank of England provided some indirect aid by buying these bills (at a considerable discount) in order to support the market.[100]

Another aspect of the government's fiscal activities was of some consequence: the receivers of public revenues were permitted to invest the public funds in their hands. They used some of this money to discount bills of exchange. Presumably some of these bills originated in the cotton industry. Thus, it is possible that public money was being used by individuals to help finance the cotton industry.[101]

---

[100] Clapham, *Bank of England*, I, 263–266, and II, 33–35.

[101] Ashton, *18th Century*, p. 182. For an account of this use of government revenues by bankers see L. S. Pressnell, "Public Monies and the Development of English Banking," *Economic History Review*, 2nd ser., V (1953), 378–397. Legislation to end the practice starts in 1822 (Pressnell, "Public Monies," pp. 394–395). The same sort of looseness in handling government revenues and expenditures also existed at the center of government (Clapham, *Bank of England,* I, 214–215).

Part III

The Markets for Long-Term Capital

Chapter V

The Personal Element

THE relative backwardness of the long-term capital market with its emphasis on localization and personal contact made personal savings an extremely important element in the long-term capital supply of the entrepreneur.[1] These savings were mobilized by either the individual proprietorship or the partnership, the most personal types of business organization, which had essentially the same standing before the law.

The proprietors and partners whose personal savings were mobilized were drawn from a very wide range of the social spectrum and this range—in conjunction with the great variety of sources from which the cotton industry drew its short-term capital—may help to account for the sustained growth that characterized the industry. The supply of capital was not dependent on the fortunes of any single group or institution outside the industry.

Whatever the sources of its capital, a cotton-factory firm needed a capital structure different from that required by a putting-out firm, and as a result entrepreneurs of the different types of firms enjoyed different degrees of freedom. The domestic firm kept most of its capital in a circulating form. The domestic-industry entrepreneur invested in stocks of cotton, yarn, and unfinished cloth, rather than in extensive buildings or machinery. The houses of the spinners and weavers, which can be considered in part as industrial plant, were variously owned; in some regions they were

---

[1] See Chapter II above; M. M. Postan, "Recent Trends in the Accumulation of Capital," *Economic History Review*, VI (1935), 6–7; A. H. John, "Insurance Investment and the London Money Market of the 18th Century," *Economica*, N.S., XX (1953), 143.

the property of the spinner or weaver, in others they belonged to the landowner or entrepreneur. These regional variations in ownership also existed with respect to machinery and tools. The organizer of domestic production could, therefore, move from industry to industry or from one sector of the cotton industry to another much more easily than his factory counterpart.[2] The newer entrepreneur was almost certain to own his machinery, and he often, though by no means always, owned his factory.[3] In any event, the fixed capital was never the property of the laborers.

The entrepreneurs discussed above were, of course, ideal types and the real factory owner did not always conform precisely to type. He could very well put out, to domestic weavers, yarn that had been spun on his power-driven machinery.[4] Indeed, it was not until the late 1820's and early 1830's that many millowners were tempted into extensive long-term investment in power-loom factories by low and falling profit margins in spinning. This investment had the effect of turning many of the firms that had combined factory spinning with domestic weaving into integrated factory enterprises.[5]

These additional demands on long-term capital came, however,

---

[2] T. S. Ashton, *An Economic History of England: The 18th Century* (London, 1955), p. 100; T. S. Ashton, *The Industrial Revolution, 1769–1830* (Oxford, 1948), p. 50.

[3] John Kennedy, "Brief Notice of My Early Recollections," *Miscellaneous Papers on Subjects Connected with the Manufactures of Lancashire* (Manchester, 1849), p. 4. In this paper, which seems to have been written in 1827, John Kennedy, who was a partner in B. and W. Sanfords, McConnel and Kennedy and later was a partner in McConnel and Kennedy, states that early in his spinning career he set up his machines in "any garret we could find." Later, his partnership built and owned its own extensive mills.

[4] For examples see *James Finlay and Company Limited: Manufacturers and East India Merchants, 1750–1950* (Glasgow, 1951), pp. 54–55, and F. Collier, "Samuel Greg and the Styal Mill," *Memoirs and Proceedings of the Manchester Literary and Philosophical Society*, LXXXV (1941–1943), 141.

[5] R. C. O. Matthews, *A Study in Trade-Cycle History: Economic Fluctuations in Great Britain, 1833–1842* (Cambridge, 1954), pp. 129–134.

at the very end of the period. During most of the period, the effects of improvements in transportation, which tended to be economical of short-term capital in the cotton industry, probably also led to far more efficient use of long-term capital by preventing factories from standing idle for want of raw materials and fuel. These improvements in transportation, of course, made heavy demands for long-term capital on the economy as a whole, but these demands did not necessarily fall on the shoulders of the factory spinner or weaver. In addition, the economy of short-term capital that was made possible by improved transportation and by some of the technical innovations in the cotton industry may have freed some of the capital previously embodied in stocks for investment in plant.[6]

In his search for long-term capital the entrepreneur faced competition from government, canal companies, enclosing landowners, and, toward the very end of the period, the railway companies. In 1830, the long-term funded debt alone was almost six times as large as the entire national debt had been in 1763.[7] By 1825, over £16,000,000 had been invested in canal companies that were still in existence.[8] Enclosure, too, absorbed large quantities of long-term capital despite long periods—like that from 1781 to 1795—in which long-term capital for enclosure was difficult to find.[9] Railways also were large users of long-term capital; between 1825 and 1835, fifty-four railway acts were passed by Parliament

[6] Ashton, *18th Century*, p. 90.

[7] J. R. McCulloch, *A Descriptive and Statistical Account of the British Empire* (4th ed.; London, 1854), II, 435.

[8] J. H. Clapham, *An Economic History of Modern Britain*, I (2nd ed.; Cambridge, 1939), 82.

[9] J. D. Chambers, *The Vale of Trent 1670–1800: A Regional Study of Economic Change (Economic History Review*, supp. no. 3; London, n.d.), p. 47; R. E. Prothero, *English Farming Past and Present* (London, 1912), p. 163; Ashton, *18th Century*, pp. 40–41; Ashton, *Industrial Revolution*, pp. 24–25 and 59–61. Enclosure often required expenditure on legal expenses and surveys, farm buildings, fencing, drainage, etc.

authorizing lines varying from the 3¼-mile Paisley and Renfrew with a capital of £33,000 to the 112½-mile London and Birmingham with a capital of £5,500,000.[10]

It would not be justified to conclude that all this long-term investment in government securities, canals, enclosure, and railways was undertaken at the expense of investment in the cotton industry. The long-term capital that flowed into these channels would not have automatically found its way into the cotton industry, or any industry for that matter, even if one of these channels had been closed. Savings were too specific and investment too localized for this to have occurred.

In 1789, when the Liverpool and Leeds Canal was organized, 71 per cent of the shareholders, holding almost 56 per cent of the shares, were from Yorkshire and Lancashire—the area served by the canal. This localization of ownership was still evident in 1800, when almost 64 per cent of the shareholders, owning nearly 46 per cent of the shares, were residents of these two counties.[11] Although the figures indicate some decline in the geographical concentration of ownership once the project was well under way, the degree of local ownership in 1800 was still remarkably high. The local character of canal investment was not restricted to this particular case; a similar geographical concentration of investment seems to have been involved in the construction of the Grand Trunk Canal, which was the other very large undertaking in this field.[12] Indeed, there seems to have been only a single instance before 1793 in which investors who were not locally interested in a canal were responsible for its beginning.[13]

In the earliest years of railway construction, long-term railroad investment was also highly local in nature.[14] The significance of

---

[10] Clapham, *Economic History*, I, 387.

[11] George Heberton Evans, *British Corporation Finance, 1775–1850: A Study of Preference Shares* ("The Johns Hopkins University Studies in Historical and Political Science," extra vols., N.S., no. 23; Baltimore, 1936), pp. 31–32 and 6. [12] *Ibid.*, p. 7. [13] *Ibid.*, p. 9.

[14] *Ibid.*, pp. 6, and 9–10; Clapham, *Economic History*, I, 386.

localization is much less clear for railways than for canals. For example, although the initial promise of London capital was of considerable importance in the promotion of the Liverpool and Manchester Railway, actual investment in the railroad may have been dominated by Lancashire.[15] S. A. Broadbridge has argued that "it is not local finance that should be emphasized . . . , but rather the part played by Lancashire in the financing of the railways." He takes the fact that early railroad investment by Lancashire extended beyond the boundaries of the county as evidence that localization was only the product of a coincidence between the relatively large number of early railways built in Lancashire and the search for outlets for the excess capital of Liverpool and Manchester. "Nor is it surprising that an area which was undergoing the most rapid industrialization, and which supplied the bulk of Britain's exports, should have had large reserves of capital." The cotton trade is specifically mentioned as one of the streams that flowed into "the main reservoir of capital" from 1827 to 1844. Therefore, the argument concludes, "the [long-term capital] market was to a certain extent perfect [by 1845] in the sense that once shares were put on the market they flowed over the country." [16]

It is possible to accept the special position of Lancashire in railway investment without drawing the same conclusions. The wealth was certainly there. It has been estimated that Lancashire was the thirty-fifth wealthiest English county in 1693, third in 1803, fourth in 1814, and second in 1843.[17] However, investment in railways did not necessarily come to any great extent from the cotton industry. The demand for long-term capital in the cotton industry fluctuated, but there is little reason to think that it

---

[15] Harold Pollins, "The Finances of the Liverpool and Manchester Railway," *Economic History Review,* 2nd ser., V (1952), 90–97.

[16] "The Early Capital Market: The Lancashire and Yorkshire Railway," *Economic History Review,* 2nd ser., VIII (1955), 200–212.

[17] E. J. Buckatzsch, "The Geographical Distribution of Wealth in England, 1086–1843," *Economic History Review,* 2nd ser., III (1950), 187, table 1.

diminished between the twenties and the forties.[18] There were few power looms in the United Kingdom in 1825, 100,000 in 1834, and 250,000 in 1845.[19]

The significance of localized investment lies in localization as a symptom of imperfection in the long-term capital market. There is a good deal of evidence of the personal and hence imperfect nature of the market for long-term railroad investment. Many shares were never available to the public; some were earmarked for investors in towns along the right of way, some for the landowners along the right of way (to prevent them from "being seduced into an opposition"), and some for purchase by larger railroads.[20]

In 1834, *The Circular to Bankers* complained of the lack of a market for the old and new securities of companies engaged in public works and contrasted this situation unfavorably with the state of affairs in the market for government securities.[21]

Investment in enclosure was, of course, localized. Although the traditional belief that the costs of enclosure were excessively high has been proved mistaken, the total amount of capital involved was nevertheless quite large.[22]

While long-term investment in canals, enclosures, and railroads was concentrated in the provinces, long-term investment in government securities seems to have been concentrated in London before 1793. During the course of the Napoleonic Wars, however, provincial investment in the public funds grew by leaps and

---

[18] Matthews, *Trade-Cycle History*, pp. 127–144.

[19] M. Blaug, "The Productivity of Capital in the Lancashire Cotton Industry during the Nineteenth Century," *Economic History Review*, 2nd ser., XIII (1961), 379, App. C.

[20] Harold Pollins, "The Marketing of Shares in the First Half of the Nineteenth Century," *Economic History Review*, 2nd. ser., VII (1954), 230–239; quotation is from Liverpool and Manchester Railway Company, *A Synopsis of the Proceedings Necessary in Soliciting the Bill, with Observations* (Liverpool, 1824).

[21] Cited in Evans, *British Corporation Finance*, pp. 15 and 17.

[22] W. E. Tate, "The Cost of Parliamentary Enclosure in England (with Special Reference to the County of Oxford)," *Economic History Review*, 2nd ser., V (1952), 258–265.

bounds.[23] The heavy concentration of investment in long-term government securities in London was probably due to the special role of the funds in the money market, which was concentrated in London, and to London's importance as a mercantile center.[24] The decline in the relative importance of London in this respect may have been partly due to the relative decline of London as a mercantile center,[25] partly to the fact that London did not have a monopoly on patriotic sentiment, and partly to the relative increase in the wealth of the Midlands and the North as a result of the Industrial Revolution.[26]

The fairly high degree of localization of long-term investment in government securities, canals, enclosures, and railroads suggests that the large size of the national aggregates of long-term capital invested in these enterprises may not be a true measure of the degree of competition that the cotton manufacturer faced in his search for long-term capital. That these enterprises provided some competition seems plausible; that this competition was not in any sense proportional to the amounts of capital invested in these enterprises seems probable.

More important than external competition for capital was the entrepreneur's lack of complete singleness of purpose, and this, of course, is not surprising. Many factory owners invested in land and great houses. Arkwright bought the manors of Cromford and Willerslay for £41,000.[27] Bott built himself a house for £10,000.[28] Samuel Oldknow's near bankruptcy can be traced, in part, to his

---

[23] Arthur D. Gayer, W. W. Rostow, and Anna Jacobson Schwartz, *The Growth and Fluctuation of the British Economy, 1790–1850* (Oxford, 1953), I, 409–410.

[24] John, "Insurance Investment," pp. 138–139.

[25] There is some evidence of the actual deterioration of the port of London by the 1790's (Walter M. Stern, "The Isle of Dogs Canal: A Study in Early Public Investment," *Economic History Review*, 2nd ser., IV (1952), 359.

[26] See Buckatzsch, "Geographical Distribution."

[27] Abstract of Sir Richard Arkwright's Title to the Manor of Cromford, 1789, Additional MSS, no. 6689, f. 378, British Museum; Additional MSS, no. 6687, f. 112, dated 1782, British Museum.

[28] William Henry Chaloner, *The History of the Cotton Manufacture in Nantwich, 1785–1874* (Nantwich, ca. 1930), p. 142.

activities as an agricultural-estate builder and improving land-lord.[29] Kirkman Finlay's sad Scottish lament, which he wrote in his diary in 1831, as an indication of what could happen to a manufacturer who indulged his instinct to acquire broad acres.

In 1819, I had a fortune which would have allowed me to spend £5–6,000 yearly, and since that period my profits have accumulated to a sum which, had all been accumulated, would have put me in posses-sion now of £180,000–£200,000. But what has been my conduct? By a purchase of the lands of Achenwillen in 1819 for £14,050 a commence-ment was made for the most wild and inconsiderate outlay. I was induced to make an addition to the House and my own pride and vanity and the selfish conduct of the Architect who considered only how his own reputation could be advanced, led me to a very large and expensive building filled my mind with new and extravagant ideas and induced me to purchase more land, and to spend upon the property an immense and most imprudently large sum of money.[30]

While it is true that these estates could be mortgaged and the proceeds used for industrial purposes, mortgages were very diffi-cult to obtain in periods when the interest rate was high enough to press against the upper limit set by the usury laws. Since the agricultural boom years of the Napoleonic Wars were also years of particularly high long-term interest rates, it was especially difficult for an agricultural investor to obtain mortgages at the time when the economic appeal of landholding was at its strongest (see Chapter II and Appendix 11).

Local transportation improvements also siphoned off some of the cotton-factory owner's long-term capital. Samuel Oldknow, for example, built a bridge and road in 1790 at a cost of £3,000; his return on this investment was 1⅔ per cent per year.[31] That this investment was not essential to him is indicated by its coming some time after his cotton factory was in operation. Oldknow was

---

[29] George Unwin, Arthur Hulme, and George Taylor, *Samuel Oldknow and the Arkwrights* (Manchester, 1924), pp. 200–202.

[30] *James Finlay and Company Limited*, p. 127.

[31] Unwin, Hulme, and Taylor, *Samuel Oldknow*, pp. 222–223.

also one of the leading promoters of the Peak Forest Canal; he acquired 52 shares of £100 each at first and later added another 164 shares.[32]

The use of water power was responsible for a considerable diversion of long-term capital from factory and machine investment. The factory owners were men who, in John Kennedy's phrase, "colonized near the waterfalls." [33] These men often were, therefore, community builders, and as such, they frequently had to provide facilities of a sort that their domestic-industry counterparts did not have to supply at all and that a steam-factory owner could avoid providing by locating in an urban rather than a rural area. It is not surprising that utopian schemes like those of Robert Owen had their roots in an era in which new, compact, relatively isolated communities were in fact coming into being and were proving to be economically viable. Perhaps the triumph of the steam engine had a great deal more to do with the undermining of utopian socialism than Friedrich Engels' *Socialism, Utopian and Scientific.*

Housing was the most obvious community investment. The Finlays for example, built half of Deanston Village in 1811 and the other half in 1820 at a total cost of £20,000.[34] Dale and Owen, Greg, the Oldknows, and the Strutts are other obvious examples of factory owners functioning as community builders.

The logic of technological development in the cotton industry, which for a time made it profitable to use women and children in cotton factories to the extent of almost excluding adult male labor, also created subsidiary demands on the entrepreneur's supply of long-term and short-term capital. Thus, Samuel Oldknow

---

[32] *Ibid.,* p. 194.

[33] John Kennedy, "Observations on the Rise and Progress of the Cotton Trade in Great Britain: Particularly in Lancashire and the Adjoining Counties," *Memoirs of the Literary and Philosophical Society of Manchester,* 2nd ser., III (1819), 122. On the nineteenth century see W. Ashworth, "British Industrial Villages in the Nineteenth Century," *Economic History Review,* 2nd ser., III (1951), 378–387.

[34] *James Finlay and Company Limited,* pp. 67–73.

was drawn into a number of secondary enterprises by the need to provide employment for the adult male members of the families of the women and children he employed. His employment of colliers, lime-burners, builders, and farm laborers must be viewed in this light, as must his various forays into road making, bridge building, and other improvements on his estates.[35] Conversely, some of the backbarrow ironmasters set up textile works near their furnaces in order to provide employment for the wives and children of their adult male employees.[36] In bidding for labor, the ability of an entrepreneur to provide employment for an entire family was undoubtedly of great importance, although it made demands on his supply of capital.

The instruments for the mobilization of capital to meet the primary and secondary demands on the entrepreneur's capital were the partnership and the individual proprietorship.[37] Although the most famous firms in the industry were partnerships, the incidence of individual proprietorship was fairly high, as Table 15 indicates. These figures refer to bankruptcies and therefore might be expected to cover only the least viable firms in the

Table 15. Bankruptcies in the cotton industry, 1786–1846

Years	No. of firms	No. of partners	Partners/firm
1786–1790	4	5	1.3
1791–1800	49	71	1.4
1801–1810	141	182	1.3
1811–1820	102	141	1.4
1821–1830	113	144	1.3
1831–1840	227	308	1.4
1841–1846	142	209	1.5

Source: Richard Burn, *Statistics of the Cotton Trade* (London, 1847), n.p., table 25.

---

[35] Unwin, Hulme, and Taylor, *Samuel Oldknow,* pp. 167–168.

[36] Ashton, *Industrial Revolution,* p. 112.

[37] Ashton, *18th Century,* p. 118; G. M. Mitchell, "The English and Scottish Cotton Industries: A Study in Interrelation," *Scottish Historical Review,* XXII, no. 86 (Jan. 1925), 105.

industry, but they are nevertheless of some value. Since the statistics include the number of partners, they are almost certainly figures for firms that actually went through bankruptcy proceedings and therefore almost certainly exclude the very weakest firms—those whose assets at the time of failure could not support these rather expensive proceedings. The figures are interesting both because they indicate no trend over time of partners per bankrupt firm and because the averages of 1.3 to 1.5 partners per firm indicates the existence of a large number of unsung individual proprietorships. In Scotland, too, individual proprietorships and partnerships were the dominant form of business organization in the cotton industry, although there was a somewhat greater tendency there to resort to unincorporated joint-stock companies.[38]

The partnership had a higher degree of flexibility than it is sometimes credited with. James and Kirkman Finlay built up a very elaborate system of commercial and industrial partnerships centering on themselves and their relatives. Some of these were *ad hoc* enterprises, lasting a relatively short time; others were more or less permanent.[39] Richard Arkwright, specifically prohibited by the terms of one of his patents from entering into a partnership with more than five members,[40] entered a number of smaller ones. At one time he participated in and ran mills at Notthingham, Cromford, Belper, Bakewell, Wirksworth, Derby, Chorley, Manchester, and Lanark.[41] His partners at any one time must have

[38] W. H. Marwick, "The Cotton Industry and the Industrial Revolution in Scotland," *Scottish Historical Review,* XXI, no. 83 (April 1924), 209.

[39] Evidence of Kirkman Finlay, *Report from the Select Committee on Manufactures, Commerce and Shipping (Reports,* 1833 [690]), Vol. VI, pt. 1, qq. 618–619; *James Finlay and Company Limited,* pp. 4, 7, 10–12, 14–15, 22, and 30.

[40] *The Trial of a Cause . . . to Repeal a Patent Granted . . . in 1775 to Mr. Richard Arkwright . . . at Westminster-hall, on Saturday the 25th of June, 1785* (London, 1785), p. 6.

[41] Paul Mantoux, *The Industrial Revolution in the Eighteenth Century: An outline of the Beginnings of the Modern Factory System in England,* trans. Marjorie Vernon (2nd ed.; London, 1928), p. 254, n. 3.

numbered considerably more than five, though there may not have been more than five in any one partnership. His partners, at one time or other, included John Smalley, Samuel Oldknow, David Dale, Samuel Need, the Strutts, Richard Arkwright, Jr., Thomas Walshman, John Cross, a Mr. Simpson of Manchester, a Mr. Whittenbury of Manchester, and, in all probability, others.[42]

This predominance of individual proprietorship and partnership is not surprising in view of the strength of local ties and the importance of feelings of kinship in eighteenth-century English society.[43] One need only think of the Strutts, the Arkwrights, the Peels, the Oldknows, and the Finlays, to choose the most prominent examples, to appreciate the extent to which family ties figure in cotton-industry partnerships. The importance of family ties is indicated, for example, by the appointment of James Smith to manage the large Deanston Mills at the age of eighteen. Smith was a nephew of Archibald Buchanan, who in turn was a cousin and business associate of the Finlays, who were partners in the company that owned the Deanston Mills. James Smith proved to be a man of great ability and became, in his later years, an industrial and agricultural innovator. The career of Samuel Greg provides another example. He was one of the younger members of the large family of a Belfast shipowner. His prospects might have been bleak had he not been invited to England by his mother's family, who underwrote his first spinning enterprise.[44]

---

[42] *Ibid.*, p. 232, n. 2; R. S. Fitton and A. P. Wadsworth, *The Strutts and the Arkwrights, 1758–1830: A Study of the Early Factory System* (Manchester, 1958), p. 78. The Mr. Simpson was probably Samuel or John Simpson, who were in partnership with John Barton in 1794, when Samuel died. Richard Arkwright, Jr., was an executor of the estate when the partnership was reconstructed in 1794 (Arkwright Deed [an apparent misnomer], Manchester Central Library).

[43] Ashton, *18th Century*, p. 18.

[44] *James Finlay and Company Limited*, pp. 12 and 67–73; William Hutton Marwick, *Economic Developments in Victorian Scotland* (London, 1936), pp. 95–96; Collier, "Samuel Greg," p. 139.

The importance of family ties is hardly surprising. The era of the Industrial Revolution was also the age of placemen and family influence in administration and politics. It was also an aristocratic age in which society was highly localized, hence the importance of bonds that transcended locality—bonds like those supplied by the institutions of the family, of class, and (in the case of the Dissenters) of religion.[45] With more men than business opportunities available, some mechanism was necessary for distribution of these opportunities. Family ties played a part in this distribution. It may be conjectured that the pressure generated by the competition for the available places and business opportunities was reduced by a fall in family size and by an increase in business opportunities generated by industrialization.[46]

The entrepreneurs' natural predilections for personal business organizations were reinforced by historical experience. The vague Bubble Act of 1720, which was a consequence of the speculative mania associated with the South Sea Company, prohibited, under very heavy penalties, the creation of joint-stock companies without the consent of Parliament.[47] As F. W. Maitland put it: "A panic-stricken Parliament issued a law, which, even when we now

---

[45] See Sir Lewis Namier, *The Structure of Politics at the Accession of George III* (2nd ed.; London, 1957), pp. 1–61; also see Isabel Grubb, *Quakerism and Industry before 1800* (London, 1930).

[46] See H. J. Perkin, "Middle-Class Education and Employment in the Nineteenth Century: A Critical Note," *Economic History Review*, 2nd ser., XIV (1961), 122–130; C. F. Musgrove, "Middle-Class Education and Employment in the Nineteenth Century," *Economic History Review*, 2nd ser., XII (1959), 99–111. An indication of decreasing family size from the 1820's through the 1840's is given in J. T. Krause, "Changes in English Fertility and Mortality, 1781–1850," *Economic History Review*, 2nd ser., XI (1958), 67. For an extremely interesting general discussion of the significance of family size and inheritance laws, see H. J. Habakkuk, "Family Structure and Economic Change in Nineteenth-Century Europe," *Journal of Economic History*, XV (1955), 1–11.

[47] Ashton, *18th Century*, p. 18. Two cotton-manufacturing companies were projected during the mania (W. R. Scott, *The Constitution and Finance of English, Scottish, and Irish Joint-Stock Companies to 1720* [Cambridge, 1911], III, 451–452).

read it, seems to scream at us from the statute book." [48] Although the act seems to have had some inhibiting effect on the creation of joint-stock companies, there were in fact very few prosecutions under it.[49] Changing conditions and changing legal interpretations had moderated the impact of the statute: "When the great catastrophe was forgotten, lawyers began coldly to dissect the words of this terrible act and to discover that after all it was not so terrible. . . . Before the 'Bubble Act' was repealed . . . most of its teeth had been drawn." [50] By 1825, it was no longer possible to keep the act on the statute books. A small but increasing number of prosecutions had begun, a large number of unincorporated joint-stock companies had recently come into being, and the attorney-general declared that "it appears to be agreed on all sides that its meaning and effect are altogether unintelligible." [51] Repeal of the Bubble Act in 1825, however, achieved very little; the unincorporated joint-stock company was still illegal under the common law and the great goal of limited liability had not been made more attainable.[52] "It was a day of half-measures." [53] Indeed, it was not until the passage of the acts of 1855, 1856, and 1857 that the decisive steps toward limited liability were taken.[54]

During the era of the Industrial Revolution, very few joint-stock companies—chartered or unchartered—were projected, and fewer still came into existence in the cotton industry. There was talk of creating a "Cotton Manufacture Company of Manchester"

[48] F. W. Maitland, "Trust and Corporation" (1904), *Maitland: Selected Essays*, ed. H. D. Hazeltine, G. Lapsley, and P. H. Winfield (Cambridge, 1936), p. 208.

[49] H. A. Shannon, "The Coming of General Limited Liability," *Essays in Economic History: Reprints Edited for the Economic History Society*, ed. E. M. Carus-Wilson, I (London, 1954), 359–360.

[50] Maitland, "Trust and Corporation," p. 209.

[51] *Hansard* (1825), XIII, 1019, as quoted in Shannon, "General Limited Liability," p. 360.

[52] *Ibid.*, pp. 365–379; W. S. Holdsworth, *A History of English Law*, ed. A. L. Goodhart and H. G. Hanbury, XIII (London, 1952), 269–270.

[53] Maitland, "Trust and Corporation," p. 210.

[54] Shannon, "General Limited Liability," pp. 366–379.

during the years 1776 to 1778.[55] This may have been the same company whose application for incorporation as a company to manufacture cotton and linen cloths was rejected in 1779 and never renewed again.[56] In 1788, the Committee of the Privy Council for Trade and Foreign Plantations rejected a proposal for the incorporation of a company to promote cotton manufactures by creating warehouses and sales facilities for cotton goods in London.[57] It is conceivable that Spencer and Company, a cotton-printing firm that was in existence from 1815 to 1834 and that was commonly referred to as "The Long Firm" because it contained eleven partners, was an unincorporated joint-stock company.[58] In 1836, Kirkman Finlay, the great Scottish merchant and manufacturer, mentioned a prospectus for a spinning and power-loom–weaving company with a proposed capital of £500,000.[59]

Only one of the 947 joint-stock companies in existence in September of 1844 was engaged in cotton manufacturing.[60] Robert Owen's New Lanark Company of 1813 seems to have been the only prominent firm in the cotton industry that operated as a joint-stock company. In 1813, Owen and six distinguished partners purchased the New Lanark mills, in which Owen already was a partner and the manager, for £114,000.[61] This enterprise was organized as an unincorporated joint-stock company. Under the Bubble Act, the legal test of whether or not a partnership was a joint-stock company was the transferability of the firm's shares,[62]

---

[55] Armand Budington Dubois, *The English Business Company after the Bubble Act, 1720–1800* (New York, 1938), p. 81, n. 231.

[56] *Ibid.*, pp. 37, 151, n. 71, and 156–157, n. 92; Postan, "Recent Trends," p. 4.

[57] Dubois, *English Business Company*, pp. 34–35.

[58] J. Graham, "The Chemistry of Calico Printing from 1790–1835 and the History of Print Works in the Manchester District from 1760–1846," MS book, n.d. [1847–1848], p. 415, Manchester Central Library.

[59] Kirkman Finlay to A. S. Finlay, April 25, 1836, in *James Finlay and Company Limited*, p. 146, App. II.

[60] Gayer, Rostow, and Schwartz, *Growth and Fluctuation*, I, 415–416.

[61] Margaret Isabel Cole, *Robert Owen of New Lanark* (New York, 1953), pp. 68–69.

[62] Dubois, *English Business Company*, p. 4.

and there is no doubt that the shares of the New Lanark Company were transferable.[63]

There are various reasons why this Scottish firm was so exceptional. An unincorporated joint-stock company operated essentially under the law of partnership, and Scottish partnership law placed fewer obstacles in the way of such an enterprise—in spite of the fact that the Bubble Act applied to Scotland.[64] For various reasons, it was safe to assume that the enterprise would be entirely free from prosecution. Prosecution was rare in any event and the New Lanark cotton mills had had a philanthropic aura about them from their very inception, an aura that must have become stronger when the mills were taken over by the new partners. These were Jeremy Bentham; Joseph Foster and William Allen, two leading Quaker philanthropists; John Walker, a gentleman of great wealth and a distinguished amateur in the arts and sciences; Joseph Fox, a Dissenting dentist; and Michael Gibbs, a leading Churchman who later became Lord Mayor of London.[65]

While the partnership and unincorporated joint-stock company carried on business under important legal disabilities,[66] the incorporated joint-stock company, before 1855 or 1857, faced one practical difficulty that in itself would have been decisive in preventing incorporation of cotton firms: the cost of incorporation was ridiculously high. Until 1841, the legal and Parliamentary expenses of the Great Western Railway were at least £100,000; when the

---

[63] R. Owen to J. Bentham, Dec. 31, 1823, Bentham Papers, Vol. IX (Additional MSS, no. 33545), f. 651, British Museum; William Allen to J. Bentham, Sept. 24, 1828, Bentham Papers, Vol. X (Additional MSS, no. 33546), ff. 237–238; William Allen to J. Bentham, March 19, 1829, Bentham Papers, Vol. X, f. 267.

[64] Shannon, "General Limited Liability," p. 358 and n. 2.

[65] Cole, *Robert Owen*, pp. 66–67. James Mill may have been a shareholder in 1823 (William Allen to James Mill, July 25, 1823, Bentham Papers, Vol. IX, f. 629).

[66] Shannon, "General Limited Liability," pp. 358–359 and 361–364; Holdsworth, *History of English Law*, XII, 531–532, and XIII, 366–369.

shareholders of the Liverpool, Manchester, and Newcastle Junction Railway met to dissolve the association, they discovered that the company had already spent £100,000 on legal expenses relating to incorporation. Expenditures of £50,000 to £100,000 before incorporation do not seem to have been unusual.[67] Considering the fact that the New Lanark mills, which were regarded as quite large, had sold for about £114,000 in 1813, one can conclude that the cost of incorporation was prohibitive.

The partnership and the individual proprietorship were the prevailing forms in the cotton industry during the Industrial Revolution. It was through these that personal savings, which formed an important element in the long-term capital supply of new cotton firms, were mobilized. Taking England and Scotland together, the people who went into these partnerships came from every stratum of society except the very top and the very bottom.[68] An analysis of the social origins of the entrepreneur in the cotton industry would make it possible to determine the sources from which some of the initial long-term capital in the cotton industry were derived. Although the evidence on which to base a statistical analysis of the origins of this group of entrepreneurs does not exist, it is possible to identify some of the groups which made important contributions of personnel, and hence of personal savings, to the cotton industry.[69]

The nobility and the large English landowners made no direct

---

[67] Evans, *British Corporation Finance*, pp. 12–13 and 25.

[68] Wales need not be considered separately; most of its industrial capital was English (Arthur Herbert Dodd, *The Industrial Revolution in North Wales* [Cardiff, 1933], p. 306; David Jeffrey Davies, *The Economic History of South Wales Prior to 1800* [Cardiff, 1933], p. 114).

[69] By using the *Dictionary of National Biography* and other standard biographical sources, Neil J. Smelser attempted to identify the businessmen who petitioned Parliament on behalf of Samuel Crompton in 1812. He was able to identify only "a tiny proportion" of them (*Social Change in the Industrial Revolution: An Application of Theory to the British Cotton Industry* [Chicago, 1959], p. 68, n. 3). I made a similar attempt with no success.

contribution to the new class of factory owners.[70] The aristocracy's closest economic contacts with the industrialists in the cotton industry came when the master spinner or weaver rented land, and perhaps buildings, from the local aristocracy. Various cotton manufacturers rented land from, among others, the Earls of Wilton, Stamford, and Derby, the Marquis of Cholmondeley, Lord Grantham, and Sir Harbord Harbord.[71]

Some leases contain a curious mixture of the old and the new. In 1784, when Daniel Burton rented twelve acres from Sir Harbord Harbord, he obtained the use of the land, a barn that could be used as a factory, and the right to construct a weir on the river Irk for water power; in addition to paying rent, Burton agreed to plant two trees of oak, elm, or ash every year, to grind his corn at Sir Harbord Harbord's mill, and to keep one hound for the use of the lord of the manor.[72]

In a few cases, English landowners invested in the conversion of corn mills or woolen mills into cotton mills and rented these mills to cotton spinners.[73] Although this sort of investment sometimes included the power source and the transmission system, it understandably did not include the actual machinery; [74] the power source and transmission system could conceivably be used to drive other machinery, but the cotton machinery itself was so special-

---

[70] On the general problem of aristocracy and "trade" see H. J. Habakkuk, "England," in A. Goodwin, ed., *The European Nobility in the Eighteenth Century* (London, 1953) , p. 19.

[71] Graham MS, pp. 341, 360–361, 369, 411, and 422; Chaloner, *Cotton Manufacture in Nantwich*, p. 142; Indenture between Sir Harbord Harbord . . . and Daniel Burton . . . , Jan. 1, 1784, Burton Deeds, no. 3, Manchester Central Library.

[72] Indenture, Jan. 1, 1784, Burton Deeds, no. 3.

[73] Unwin, Hulme, and Taylor, *Samuel Oldknow*, p. 121.

[74] *Ibid.*, p. 118; Graham MS, p. 429; McConnel and Kennedy to A. Lane (their landlord) , Jan. 22, 1796, McConnel and Kennedy MSS, Letter Books, Lewis Library of Commerce, University of Manchester. On this point of the division of risk, an extremely interesting parallel could be drawn between the cotton industry during the Industrial Revolution and the early American automobile industry (see Lawrence Seltzer, "The Mobility of Capital," *Quarterly Journal of Economics*, XLVI [1931–1932], 496–508) .

ized that investment in it, even for the purpose of rental, was relatively risky. In spite of the exclusion of machinery, investment by landowners was significant because it was economical of the cotton manufacturer's long-term capital.

There are at least two instances in which members of the landed gentry may have participated in firms in the cotton industry. In 1816, a Major Halcombe Brooke started a small cotton-printing factory near Rainsbottom and engaged in printing for a few years.[75] Given the make-up of the British army officer corps at the time, it is probable, though not certain, that the Major was a member of the landed gentry.[76] One can be more nearly certain about a Colonel Mordaunt, who, in 1781, was one of the nine defendants named in Richard Arkwright's action for patent infringement. He was described by Mr. Bearcroft, the counsel for the crown, as "a gentleman of family, but not of much fortune, who did not mend it by dabbling in this kind of manufacture." [77]

The substantial Scottish landowner seems to have been far more active than his English counterpart in promoting and participating in the creation of cotton factories.[78] At Kelton, Sir William Douglas, "the principal heritor," became a partner in a cotton firm that ultimately failed.[79] At Kirkentilloch, a cotton mill was erected by Sir John Stirling, "a public spirited gentleman of the neighbourhood." [80] In 1787, Mr. Alexander of Ballochnyle, a local landowner, built a spinning mill at Catrine in partnership with David Dale.[81] In the late eighties, Robert Dunmore, Laird of Ballindalloch and Ballikinrain, in association with two sons of James Buchanan (another landowner), built a cotton mill at

---

[75] Graham MS, p. 344.

[76] Elie Halévy, *A History of the English People in the Nineteenth Century,* I (2nd ed. rev.; London, 1949), 79–83.

[77] *Trial of a Cause,* p. 22.

[78] Henry Hamilton, *The Industrial Revolution in Scotland* (Oxford, 1932), p. 129; Marwick, "Cotton Industry," pp. 207–208; Mitchell, "English and Scottish Cotton Industries," p. 105.

[79] Marwick, "Cotton Industry," p. 208.   [80] *Ibid.,* p. 209.

[81] Hamilton, *Industrial Revolution in Scotland* (Oxford, 1932), p. 126.

Ballendoch. Dunmore, who was described in the *Statistical Account of Scotland* as "uniting the activity of the country gentleman with the liberality of the merchant," had already tried his hand at calico manufacture but had met with little success.[82] The Buchanans, who joined Dunmore in this project, were cousins and landlords to the Finlays, whom they later joined in various commercial and industrial undertakings.

The characteristic enterprise of the Scottish landowners was clearly recognized. In 1806, in referring to western Scotland, where the cotton industry was concentrated,[83] Robert Forsyth stated that, "as the mercantile character predominates, the country gentlemen in this district were uncommonly ready to encourage every improvement and many of them have at times caught the infectious rage for mercantile speculation.[84] It was, perhaps, this enterprise—this willingness to invest outside of agriculture —that accounted for the difference between England and Scotland. Both the myth of Scottish democracy and the underlying reality made it easier for a Scottish landowner to fully enter into the new kind of industrial enterprise represented by the cotton factory.[85]

The burdens on the land were considerably lighter in Scotland than in England. In 1840, the per capita expenditure for poor-law assistance in Scotland was only one-fifth that of England.[86] By the beginning of the eighteenth century, poor relief in Scotland had

---

[82] *Ibid.*, p. 127; *James Finlay and Company Limited*, pp. 60–66. Another example is to be found in Marwick, "Cotton Industry," p. 209. For an idealized fictional version of the role of the Scottish landowner in the inception of a cotton mill, see John Galt, *The Annals of the Parish* (1st pub. 1821), in D. S. Meldrum and William Roughead, eds., *The Works of John Galt* (Edinburgh, 1936), I, 181–182. Galt was an employee of Kirkman Finlay and the inventor of the term "Utilitarianism" (not quite as small a distinction as the authorship of the *Annals*).

[83] Clapham, *Economic History*, I, 51–52.

[84] R. Forsyth, *The Beauties of Scotland* (Edinburgh, 1805–1808), III, 326.

[85] Laurence James Saunders, *Scottish Democracy, 1815–1840: The Social and Intellectual Background* (Edinburgh, 1950), p. 1.

[86] *Ibid.*, pp. 198–199.

long been a function of the Church, and one which depended for the most part on voluntary subscriptions administered by it. During the course of the century, some parishes found the voluntary contributions so inadequate that they were forced to adopt a policy of assessment in order to raise funds. By 1800, however, only 92 parishes (mainly urban) out of a total of 878 had accepted assessment.[87] Even in the 1830's, voluntary contributions were the rule and assessments the exception.[88] In addition, in those Scottish parishes where assessment had been adopted, the burden did not fall very heavily on the landowner, who was legally empowered to pass one-half of his assessment on to his tenants.[89]

In England, in accordance with Elizabethan legislation that was still in effect, the poor rate was paid by "every occupier of lands, houses, tithes impropriate, or appropriations of tithes, coalmines and saleable underwoods." [90] By the mid-eighteenth century, the owners of sizable landed estates in England no longer occupied much land [91] and were therefore directly liable for only a small part of the large and growing burden of the poor rates.[92] On the other hand, there was a common impression abroad that the rates were "eating up all the rent." [93] It seems almost certain that the poor rates adversely affected rents, in the sense that they were kept lower than they might otherwise have been, in spite of the fact that the rates were paid by the occupiers rather than the owners.[94] The incidence of the tithe was also lower in Scotland

---

[87] Thomas Ferguson, *The Dawn of Scottish Social Welfare: A Survey from Medieval Times to 1863* (London, 1948), pp. 5–6 and 187.

[88] Saunders, *Scottish Democracy*, p. 197. [89] *Ibid.*, pp. 21–22 and 197.

[90] Quoted in S. and B. Webb, *English Poor Law History*, pt. 2, I (London, 1929), 2–3. On legal liability for poor rates see Holdsworth, *History of English Law*, X (1938), 276–295.

[91] G. E. Mingay, *English Landed Society in the Eighteenth Century* (London, 1963), pp. 167–170.

[92] S. and B. Webb, *English Poor Law History*, pt. 2, I, 1–4.

[93] *Ibid.*, p. 3, n. 1.

[94] The Webbs present evidence that rents were rising during the Revolutionary and Napoleonic Wars and conclude that "the common impression

than in England.[95] Here, too, the landlord was affected through his rents.

The Scottish landowner had at least one direct financial advantage over the English landlord: the incidence of the land tax was lower in Scotland than in England.[96] The lower incidence in Scotland of those burdens on the land that were borne by the landlord meant that at a given income level, the Scottish landowner was in a better position to invest in the cotton industry than the English landowner.[97] The lower incidence in Scotland of those increasing burdens on the land that were borne by the occupier meant that as time went on and rents were affected the Scottish landowner's relative position as a potential investor in the cotton industry probably improved.

A more direct participant in the creation of English cotton firms was the yeoman—the modest owner-occupier or fairly substantial tenant farmer.[98] Down to the end of the Napoleonic Wars, at least, the yeoman was under no pressure to leave the land. Indeed, the high agricultural prices during the war may have helped to supply him with some of his capital. The economic pressure on him, which had been severe in the late seventeenth century and early eighteenth century, was renewed when prices

---

that the rates were 'eating up all the rent' was entirely unfounded" (*ibid*). The quoted phrase, however, does not necessarily imply that money rents fell. Given the price inflation in this era, the phrase can be taken to imply that real rents fell or that the landowners did not share in the agricultural prosperity of these years to the extent that they would otherwise have expected.

[95] Saunders, *Scottish Democracy*, pp. 21–22 and 197.   [96] *Ibid.*, p. 21.

[97] The income referred to is income before deduction of those burdens on the land that are discussed above.

[98] In the eighteenth century, the term, which had originally applied to the small owner-occupier, was coming to include tenant farmers (W. H. B. Court, *A Concise Economic History of Britain: From 1750 to Recent Times* [Cambridge, 1954], pp. 27–28; P. Gaskell, *Artisans and Machinery: The Moral and Physical Condition of the Manufacturing Population Considered with Reference to Mechanical Substitutes for Human Labor* [London, 1836], pp. 30–33).

tumbled after the end of the Napoleonic Wars.[99] In Scotland, the analogous class probably was under greater pressure to leave the land between 1750 and 1850. The pressure was unevenly distributed over the country, but it seems on balance to have operated to create a large number of tiny holdings.[100]

The Peels, Jedediah Strutt, James McConnel, John Kennedy, Samuel Oldknow, and the Ashtons were members of yeoman families. Each of these families went through a stage between yeoman farming and entry into the cotton industry; they did not, as has sometimes been suggested, simply exchange agriculture for the cotton industry.[101]

The description of the Peels as members of "the lesser gentry" is a flattering exaggeration; they were yeomen holding land at Bury.[102] The Prime Minister's grandfather became a domestic woollen weaver and hand printer of cottons, while maintaining his contact with the land.[103] The four Peel brothers, William, Lawrence, Edmund, and Robert (the first baronet) entered the cotton-printing branch of the industry. They split up and expanded their interests, forming a series of related partnerships covering many processes of the cotton industry.[104] The first Sir Robert Peel was the most successful of the brothers; when he died in 1830, his personal estate came to £1,400,000.[105]

Samuel Oldknow's grandfather Thomas was a yeoman holding

---

[99] Court, *Concise Economic History*, pp. 26–30; E. Davies, "The Small Landowner, 1780–1832, in the Light of the Land Tax Assessments," *Essays*, ed. Carus-Wilson, I, 270–294.

[100] Malcolm Gray, "The Abolition of Runrig in the Highlands of Scotland," *Economic History Review*, 2nd ser., V (1952), 46–57.

[101] Gaskell, *Artisans and Machinery*, pp. 30–33 and 33, n.; Ashton, *Industrial Revolution*, p. 25.

[102] Quotation from A Biographical Sketch of Sir Robert Peel, 1st Baronet (dated 1826, no signature), Additional MSS, no. 40388, f. 34.

[103] Mantoux, pp. 221, 379 and 407.   [104] Graham MS, p. 357.

[105] Mantoux, *Industrial Revolution*, p. 379, n. 1; this is not inconsistent with a statement that his total worth at his death was £2,250,000 (E. Helm, *Chapters in the History of the Manchester Chamber of Commerce* [London, n.d.], p. 13).

land near Nottingham. Thomas Oldknow and one of his sons set up a draper's shop in Nottingham, while Samuel's father was sent to Anderton in Lancashire to study the domestic cotton industry. Samuel Oldknow's father remained at Anderton and set up in business there. The link with the land was kept and, indeed, strengthened when Samuel's mother inherited a small leasehold estate from her father. Samuel was apprenticed to his uncle and later made a partner in the draper's shop. It was as a partner in a draper's firm that Samuel went to Anderton to establish the muslin works that began his meteoric career as a cotton manufacturer and spinner.[106]

John Kennedy, of the great spinning firm of McConnel and Kennedy, also came from a yeoman family. His grandfather David had been a shopkeeper who purchased an estate in New Galloway; David Kennedy also seems to have been a publican. The estate was inherited and farmed by Robert Kennedy, John Kennedy's father. In 1784, John Kennedy, pursuing a course that was also followed by other important spinners born in Scotland (for example, his partner, James McConnel, and George and Adam Murray),[107] went to Chowbent, where he was apprenticed to Messrs. Cannon and Smith, machine makers. At the end of his apprenticeship, he went to Manchester and entered a partnership with B. and W. Sanford, a firm of fustian warehousemen, and James McConnel; the firm carried on machine manufacturing and cotton spinning. In 1795, McConnel and Kennedy separated from B. and W. Sanford. For a few years, the Scots continued to combine machine making with spinning. About 1800, however, they had ceased making machines for sale, although they continued to build them for their own use.[108]

[106] Unwin, Hulme, and Taylor, *Samuel Oldknow,* pp. 1–2.
[107] Ashton, *Industrial Revolution,* p. 19.
[108] Kennedy, "Brief Notice," pp. 2–4, 9–10, 13, and 17–18; McConnel and Kennedy to the Underwood Spinning Company, Aug. 27, 1801, and McConnel and Kennedy to Richard Manley, Dec. 12, 1804, McConnel and Kennedy MSS, Letter Books.

James McConnel's career was similar to John Kennedy's. McConnel's family occupied a farm at Kirkbridgeshire. He was apprenticed to his uncle William Cannon of Cannon and Smith. It was undoubtedly at Chowbent that he met John Kennedy. At the end of his apprenticeship, McConnel went to Manchester, where he worked for a cotton spinner before setting up on his own as a machine maker. He contributed part of the initial capital of Sanfords, McConnel and Kennedy; his contribution was made up of one carding engine valued at £6, two mules (for which a customer had been unable to pay) valued at £70, and £92 in money and other assets. Ten years later, his half of McConnel and Kennedy was valued at over £10,000.[109]

Jedediah Strutt was the son of William Strutt, a small farmer and maltster of South Normanton, Derbyshire; his mother was the daughter of a yeoman. He was apprenticed to a wheelwright near Derby. At the end of his apprenticeship, he moved to Belgrave near Leicester and started to work as a journeyman wheelwright. In 1754, Strutt's uncle, a farmer, died, and he inherited his uncle's farm stock; he then set himself up as a farmer. Several years later Strutt and his brother-in-law, William Woollat, who was a minor Derby hosier, invented, or rather perfected, the Derby rib machine. Their combined capitals were evidently too small to patent and exploit the invention, and they began a frantic effort to find additional capital. They finally entered a partnership with John Bloodwaith and Thomas Stamford, two leading Derby hosiers. In 1762, after about three years, this partnership was dissolved. Strutt and Woollat retained the patent and contracted a partnership with Samuel Need, a wealthy Nottingham hosier. Some seven years later, Need and Strutt entered into partnership with Richard Arkwright in order to develop his first invention.[110]

---

[109] J. W. McConnel, *A Century of Fine Cotton Spinning* (Manchester, 1906), pp. 8–9; McConnel and Kennedy MSS, Inventories.

[110] Fitton and Wadsworth, *The Strutts*, pp. 3, 9, 11, 25, 36–37, and 65; E. I. Carlyle, "Jedediah Strutt," *Dictionary of National Biography* (London,

Samuel Crompton, the inventor of the spinning mule, came from a family that may at one time have been small yeomen. By the time Samuel was born, however, the land had been sold. The family stayed on, farming the land it had once owned. Whatever the family's pretensions may have been, by Samuel's day they were forced to supplement their income by spinning.[111] They could scarcely be regarded as a yeoman family. In spite of several efforts to capitalize on his invention, Crompton was never at all successful as a manufacturer, and he died fairly poor. He was never quite able to mobilize enough capital either to defend or exploit the mule.[112] Crompton, perhaps, marks the lowest stratum of agricultural society from which the entrepreneurs were drawn.

There has been some disagreement over the role played by mercantile capital in the cotton industry during the Industrial Revolution. Dodd suggested that "in England this capital, the fruit of years of expanding foreign trade, lay ready, accumulated in the hands of prosperous merchants, needing only the assurance of profit and the removal of restrictions to bring it to the service of industry." [113] Pares and Ashton—for different reasons—believed that merchants did not play an important part in the Industrial Revolution. Referring specifically to merchants engaged in colonial trade, Richard Pares pointed out that:

Since the most lucrative and important branches of colonial trade were those in which the English merchants acted as factors for the planters, and since whatever the size of their commissions they had to employ all their capital and all they could get from their banks in financing the trade itself, they can hardly have had much to spare for the Industrial

---

1961), article based on, among other things, "private information"; Edward Wedlake Brayley and John Britton, *The Beauties of England and Wales* (1801–1816), III, 540–542.

[111] Samuel Crompton to the President of the Royal Society, Nov. 30, 1807, in the Correspondence of Samuel Crompton, 1801–1812, Eggerton MSS, no. 2409, f. 5, British Museum; Hector Charles Cameron, *Samuel Crompton* (London, 1951), p. 22.

[112] Clapham, *Economic History*, I, 51–52; Mantoux, *Industrial Revolution*, pp. 240–241.

[113] *Industrial Revolution in North Wales*, p. 306.

Revolution. Indeed the manufacturers were lucky if they did not have to give them credit. The planters themselves seem to have been recipients of capital rather than sources of it. True, if a Beckford could build a Fonthill or buy a borough seat, he could have set up a factory; but from what can be learnt of the way the West India millionaires spent their money there seem to have been more Fonthills than factories among them and more over-drafts and protested bills than either.[114]

Ashton believed that, although a few men turned to manufacture after making a fortune in trade, "generally the progression was from trading in commodities to dealing in money and shares." [115]

Pointing to an individual merchant, like Drinkwater,[116] will not, of course, refute Pares's or Ashton's arguments. On this point, however, Scottish experience is extremely enlightening. There is a great deal of evidence to indicate that the American Revolution, by disrupting Glasgow's important tobacco trade, aided the transfer of capital to the cotton industry. The American trade was important to Scotland, and the tobacco trade was the most important part of the American trade. By 1775, imports from America were 43 per cent of total imports. Tobacco alone accounted for 38 per cent of total imports and 56 per cent of total exports. By 1777, the Revolution had reduced tobacco imports and re-exports to a trickle.[117] The question of possible transfer of capital would scarcely have arisen, however, had it not been for the remarkable efficiency with which the agents of the "Tobacco Lords" handled the impending crisis in 1775, collecting debts, buying large quantities of tobacco, and rushing the tobacco home or to Holland. Most debts were collected and enormous profits made on the

---

[114] "Economic Factors in the History of Empire," *Essays*, ed. Carus-Wilson, I, 425–426.

[115] *18th Century*, p. 138.

[116] Robert Owen, *The Life of Robert Owen by Himself* (New York, 1920), p. 36.

[117] M. L. Robertson, "Scottish Commerce and the American War of Independence," *Economic History Review*, 2nd ser., IX (1956), 123.

heavy imports of 1774 and 1775, so that there probably was no loss of capital in the trade, and there may even have been further accumulation. In 1775, some Scottish banks reduced the interest rate on money deposited for one year to 3 per cent and others were lending at 3 per cent.[118]

All the capital released by the disruption of the tobacco trade did not find its way into the cotton industry—perhaps even most of it did not. Even that part of it that eventually found its way into the industry seems to have spent about a decade wandering from one nonindustrial occupation to another.[119] However, in the 1780's and 1790's, two decades of remarkable growth in the industry, some of this capital was absorbed by the cotton industry.

Robert Dunmore, a former "Virginia Merchant," built a mill at Balfon and later became a partner of the Buchanans' in the Ballindalloch Cotton Works. In 1791, he and Robert Bogle, another former tobacco merchant, unsuccessfully attempted to introduce cotton spinning to the Highlands.[120] In 1792, Stirling, Gordon and Company, a West Indian house, entered into partnership with James Finlay and Company, and this partnership was to eventually become one of the largest cotton-manufacturing firms in Scotland.[121]

The Revolution also interrupted Glasgow's somewhat less important trade with the colonies in coarse linens. The resulting transfer of capital was probably furthered by the natural decline of the domestic linen industry in the face of competition from the cotton factories. Since the domestic linen industry was—like any domestic industry—inextricably linked to mercantile capital, such a transfer was necessarily a transfer of mercantile capital.[122]

---

[118] *Ibid.*, pp. 124–126 and 126, n. 1.   [119] *Ibid.*, pp. 125–128.

[120] *Ibid.*, p. 130.   [121] *James Finlay and Company Limited*, p. 7.

[122] John Knox, *A View of the British Empire, More Especially Scotland* (3rd ed.; London, 1785), I, xxxvii; David McPherson, *Annals of Commerce, Manufactures, Fisheries and Navigation* (London, 1805), pp. 34–35; Forsyth, *Beauties of Scotland*, III, 281; Marwick, "Cotton Industry," p. 211; Mitchell, "English and Scottish Cotton Industries," pp. 137–138; *James Finlay and Company Limited*, p. 3.

The linen industry provided some of the titans of the Scottish cotton industry—the Buchanans and the Monteiths, for example.[123] At one stage in his career, David Dale was a dealer in linen yarn. In the seventies, when yarn had to be imported into Scotland, Dale became one of the leading Glasgow importers of Flemish and French linen yarn, which he put out to lawn or cambric weavers; he later founded the New Lanark cotton mills.[124] This type of development is scarcely surprising, given the uneven technological development of cotton-spinning and weaving. The development of power spinning before power weaving meant that there would be a resemblance between the organization and marketing practices of linen and cotton industry firms.[125] Hence, transfer of capital from linen to cotton was probably easier than the transfer from tobacco to cotton.

The interruption of these two important branches of Scottish commerce evidently induced a transfer of capital to the new cotton industry—a transfer that partly explains the frequent assertions that the industry was owned in Glasgow, where the tobacco and linen trades had been concentrated. The Glasgow chamber of commerce certainly showed an early and active interest in the cotton industry. In 1785, it petitioned for the removal of various taxes that had been levied on cotton goods. In 1786, it urged the board of trustees to give financial aid to spinners who wished to purchase jennies; this was the same year in which important mills were founded in New Lanark, Deanston, Catrine, and many other places.[126]

The Scottish pattern suggests the possibility that transfers of capital from trade to the cotton industry occurred in areas where a particular branch of trade was disrupted and the area had the other prerequisites for the introduction of cotton factories. In the case of Scotland, the Glasgow area had a partly trained labor force in the domestic linen producers. The applicability of this analysis

---

[123] Robertson, "Scottish Commerce," p. 130.
[124] Hamilton, *Industrial Revolution in Scotland,* p. 125.
[125] Robertson, "Scottish Commerce," p. 130.   [126] *Ibid.,* p. 129.

to Manchester is suggested by the partnership between B. and W. Sanford, fustian warehousemen, and McConnel and Kennedy.[127] After 1760, the domestic-linen industry was driven rapidly out of Lancashire.[128] This suggests that the place to look for merchants who transferred capital to the cotton industry is among the merchant-manufacturers engaged in declining domestic industries and the overseas merchants engaged in trades seriously disrupted by the American and French Revolutionary Wars.

At a time when the amount of capital required to start an enterprise in the cotton industry could be quite small, almost any middle-class connection, business, or position might make it possible for a man to embark as an industrialist in the cotton industry. Samuel Greg was one of the younger members of a large Belfast shipowning family and was invited by his mother's family to come to England and start a spinning mill with their assistance.[129] John Smalley, Arkwright's first partner, was a "liquor merchant and painter," and Arkwright himself had been a barber, peruke-maker, hair merchant, and publican.[130] Examples can be found of cotton manufacturers who had been grocers, salesmen, horse dealers, and excise officers, and others who can only be identified as innkeepers' sons and bankers' sons.[131]

At certain times, a strategically placed laborer or petty capitalist in the domestic or factory cotton industry might, because of high wages or high prices, save enough to enter a factory partnership. The innovations associated with the Industrial Revolution were partly a product of bottlenecks, and they, in turn, helped to

---

[127] Fustian was a cloth made of linen and cotton. A warehouseman was a wholesale trader.

[128] Alfred P. Wadsworth and Julia De Lacy Mann, *The Cotton Trade and Industrial Lancashire, 1600–1780* (Manchester, 1931) , p. 278.

[129] Collier, "Samuel Greg."

[130] Fitton and Wadsworth, *The Strutts*, pp. 60–64. Seven years after his death, Arkwright was described as having been "very capital in Bleeding and Toothdrawing" (*ibid.*, p. 62) .

[131] Graham MS, pp. 342, 347, 357, 435, and 441; and Leo H. Grindon, *Manchester Banks and Bankers* (Manchester, 1877) , pp. 98–99.

produce new bottlenecks. Domestic spinners' wages or profits must have been fairly high when handloom weavers were tramping the countryside in search of yarn for their hungry looms. After this bottleneck was broken by innovations in spinning, the position of the handloom weaver improved until it was later undermined by the adoption of the power loom. High wages, and hence the possibility of savings, were also associated with the earliest application of a new invention. It is to these circumstances that we owe statements like the one made by William Radcliffe that "any man who was industrious and careful might then, from his earnings as a weaver, lay by sufficient to set him up as a manufacturer." [132] John Kennedy wrote that "from the circumstances of the high wages which could be obtained for working the mule, shoemakers, joiners, hatmakers left their previous employment. By their industry, skill and economy, these men first became proprietors of perhaps a single mule, and persevering in habits so intimately connected with success were afterwards the most extensive spinners in the trade." [133]

Capital was not absolutely essential to participation as an entrepreneur in the cotton industry. There are numerous examples of men who were full partners in a firm and who contributed no capital to it.[134] Innovation placed a premium on knowledge. Robert Owen, in 1794 or 1795, turned down an offer of a partnership in a projected large firm because he was offered only one-third of the profits; he had not been asked to contribute any capital, but he nevertheless felt that he should have been offered one-half of the profits.[135]

If capital was needed, a long-term loan could sometimes be

---

[132] Quoted in Mitchell, "English and Scottish Cotton Industries," p. 108.

[133] Quoted in *ibid.*, p. 107.

[134] Evidence of Lewis Loyd, *Report from the Select Committee on Manufactures, Commerce and Shipping* [1833], q 414; Unwin, Hulme, and Taylor, *Samuel Oldknow*, p. 51; John Bell and Co. to McConnel and Kennedy, Nov. 20, 1803, McConnel and Kennedy MSS, Letters Received; Owen, *Life*, pp. 43–44.

[135] Owen, *Life*, pp. 57–58.

obtained. There frequently was a personal aspect to such a loan. Robert Owen got most of his initial capital by borrowing £100 from his brother, a London saddler.[136] If the price of the funds had not fallen, Jedediah Strutt, a Nonconformist, would have been able to borrow the capital needed to exploit his Derby rib machine from Doctor George Benson, a Nonconformist clergyman who had employed Strutt's wife as a servant.[137]

Profits undoubtedly were a much more important source of long-term capital, although there does not seem to have been any agreement among entrepreneurs on a definition of profits.[138] In spite of the absence of an agreed definition, it is possible that most businessmen would have endorsed Malthus' statement that profits were the main source of capital accumulation.[139]

The entrepreneurs' attempts at definition produced widely different results. George Walker's attitude toward profits seems to have been analogous to David Ricardo's view of rent. In 1803, Walker stated that, "we will find weavers making a *difference equal* to a *profit* betwixt *good* and bad *twist*." [140] William Radcliffe regarded profit as being made up of two components, interest on money and a sort of entrepreneurial wage.[141] Judging by Robert Owen's letters, he and his partners regarded profits as the return on their capital after they had paid themselves 5 per cent interest on their initial capital.[142] McConnel and Kennedy had

---

[136] *Ibid.*, pp. 15 and 30–32.

[137] Fitton and Wadsworth, *The Strutts,* pp. 30–31.

[138] Profit can be defined as the residual share of the product of enterprise accruing to the entrepreneur after all payments have been made for the use of the factors of production. As an accounting rather than a theoretical term, it broadly designates an increase in wealth resulting from the operation of an enterprise.

[139] Piero Sraffa, ed., *The Works and Correspondence of David Ricardo,* II (Cambridge, 1951), 182.

[140] *Observations . . . upon . . . Exporting of Cotton Twist* (London, May 5, 1803), p. 16. The odd italics are Walker's.

[141] "Letter of Radcliffe to Addington" (dated May 1, 1804, never sent), *Letters on the Evils of the Exportation of Cotton Yarns* (Stockport, 1811).

[142] R. Owen to J. Bentham, Feb. 8, 1818, Additional MSS, no. 33545, f. 260.

little to say about their profits, but their ledgers speak for them.[143] On December 31 of each year they took an inventory of the partnership's assets and liabilities. In this inventory they allowed themselves an entrepreneurial wage or bonus if they had built a new factory or new machinery for their factories. This they certainly earned, since they not only built their own machinery, but even manufactured their own bricks when they constructed a factory.[144] The partnership's profit was the difference between two successive inventories. Drawings by the partners played no part in the calculation of profit. In the course of a year, each of the partners drew whatever money he needed. Since these drawings were never even approximately equal, one of the partners was treated as a creditor of the partnership and was paid 5 per cent interest on the amount the partnership owed him. The profit retention policy of McConnel and Kennedy can also be gleaned from the firm's ledgers. Everything beyond the *ad hoc* drawings of the partners was retained. No attempt was ever made to systematically realize the earnings of the partnership.

Strenuous as the practice of McConnel and Kennedy may seem, it is considerably milder than that adopted by B. and W. Sanfords, McConnel and Kennedy, the firm from which McConnel and Kennedy sprang. The partnership deed of the parent company provided that the Sanfords were to provide £350 between them and McConnel and Kennedy were to supply a total of £250. The partnership was to run for four years from March 1, 1791. Profits were to be shared equally at the end of the four years, "it being intended that the profits of the said trade . . . shall accumulate and not be taken out of the said joint trade . . . except in cases of necessity." McConnel and Kennedy, however, were each to receive £40 a year for "their Trouble and Time in the management of

---

[143] Unless otherwise stated, the rest of the discussion of the firm of McConnel and Kennedy is drawn from the McConnel and Kennedy MSS, Ledgers. For a summary of some of this material see Appendix 12 below.

[144] McConnel and Kennedy to Mr. Duckworth, Nov. 27, 1804, McConnel and Kennedy MSS.

the said Trade or Business." Any additional capital brought in would receive 5 per cent interest.[145] When the partnership was dissolved in 1795, McConnel and Kennedy's share was worth £1,633. Their capital was six and one-half times as large as it had been in 1791. They had also been able to save an additional £133 between them from the £320 they had been paid to manage the firm.[146]

The profit-retention policy of Robert Owen's New Lanark Company was different from that followed by McConnel and Kennedy, possibly due to differences in business organization. The New Lanark mills distributed interest on the initial capital at the rate of 5 per cent at the end of the year in which the interest had been earned. The "profit" above and beyond this 5 per cent was retained, in its entirety, however, for one year after the year in which it had been earned, and it was then distributed in three equal installments.[147] Owen's firm, therefore, retained all its profits above 5 per cent for one to two years after the year in which it was earned.

The New Lanark partnership was, in organization, a more advanced firm than McConnel and Kennedy. Except for Robert Owen, all the New Lanark partners were permanently resident in London; the mill was in Scotland. Although several of the partners were businessmen, only Robert Owen had experience in the cotton industry. Therefore, in spite of their philanthropic activities in connection with the mill, the partners as a group did not have the same sort of personal business interest in the firm that McConnel and Kennedy had in their venture. Hence, the New Lanark firm's policy called for a slow, cautious, but inevitable withdrawal of profits.

The different profit-retention policies can also be accounted for in social terms. McConnel and Kennedy were in a completely

---

[145] B. and W. Sanfords, McConnel and Kennedy Partnership Deed, March 1, 1791, McConnel and Kennedy MSS, Misc. Papers.

[146] McConnel, *Fine Cotton Spinning.*

[147] R. Owen to J. Bentham, Feb. 8, 1818, Bentham Papers, Vol. IX, f. 260.

different social position from that enjoyed by the distinguished New Lanark partners. Without their mills, McConnel and Kennedy ran the danger of becoming, as a pamphleteer put it, "what they originally were, almost ciphers in society." [148] This was a risk to which an Allen, an Owen, a Mill, or a Bentham was not exposed; their self-esteem and their social standing were not, in any sense, proportional to their capital.

The intimate association of personality with capital, which is a characteristic of a backward capital market, helped to provide the impetus for a high rate of profit retention. Even after McConnel and Kennedy had passed the stage of almost total profit retention represented by their first venture (B. and W. Sanfords, McConnel and Kennedy), they continued to plow back a considerable portion of their profits. In the years 1803 through 1808, after they had been in business for over a decade, they still retained 65 per cent of their profits. But the importance of the personal impulse, which dictated the policy of plowing back a large part of profits, should not be exaggerated; it was the relatively impersonal forces of the market that determined the size of profits.

---

[148] John Wright, *An Address to . . . Parliament on the late Tax . . . on Fustian and other Cotton Goods* (Warrington, 1785), pp. 27–28.

Chapter VI

The Impersonal Forces

THE growth of the cotton industry in the late eighteenth and early nineteenth centuries was truly extraordinary. In that growth the years 1780–1789 were of even greater significance than they were in the history of the growth of total industrial production or industrial consumers' goods production (see Chapter I). Table 16 suggests the crucial importance of the decade in the growth of industry.[1] The average annual output of yarn soared in the eighties; it was over 200 per cent larger than it had been in the previous decade. The 227 per cent increase in cotton yarn production was almost six times as large as that for 1700–1779, which had been the largest increase before 1780–1789, and was more than nine times as large as the average of the percentage increases from 1710–1719 through 1770–1779. The 208 per cent increase in raw cotton consumption for 1780–1789 was more than seven and one-half times as large as the increase for the previous decade, six

---

[1] Because of the practice of mixing cotton with other yarns during most of the eighteenth century, it is not possible to obtain reliable statistics from which to construct an index of the volume of cotton cloth production. Walther G. Hoffmann constructed such an index, but it is practically worthless for the years before 1780 (*British Industry, 1700–1950,* trans. with notes by W. O. Henderson and W. H. Chaloner [Oxford, 1955], p. 257). It is possible, however, to measure the output of the spinning branch of the cotton industry, one of the branches that was really revolutionized during the Industrial Revolution. Even the weaving sector of the cotton industry was considerably less mechanized than the spinning branch. In 1834, 200,000 hand looms were still in use and only 100,000 power looms; by 1845, there were 60,000 hand looms and 250,000 power looms in use (M. Blaug, "The Productivity of Capital in the Lancashire Cotton Industry during the Nineteenth Century," *Economic History Review,* 2nd ser., XIII [1961], 379, App. C).

and one-half times the peak prior to 1780–1789, and more than nine times the average of the percentage increases for 1710–1719 through 1770–1779, as computed from Table 16.

Table 16. Growth of the British cotton industry, 1710–1899

| | % increase in average annual index of volume | | | |
| | A | B | C | D |
Years	Cotton yarn output, U.K.	Cotton consumption, England and Wales	Per capita cotton consumption, England and Wales	Imports of raw cotton, U.K.
1710–1719	20	25	24	
1720–1729	17	5	4	
1730–1739	14	9	7	
1740–1749	25	23	21	
1750–1759	30	32	26	
1760–1769	23	22	16	
1770–1779	38	37	28	
1780–1789	227	208	188	
1790–1799	64	89	73	75
1800–1809	125			108
1810–1819	53			70
1820–1829	89			81
1830–1839	92			87
1840–1849	64			71
1850–1859	51			53
1860–1869	2			18
1870–1879	49			35
1880–1889	21			16
1890–1899	12			3

Source: Based on Appendixes 13, 14, 15, and 16.

For 1790–1799, the percentage increase in the average annual production of cotton yarn [2] fell to less than three-tenths of what it had been in 1780–1789, while the percentage increase in the average annual consumption of cotton [3] fell to little more than

[2] Index covers the United Kingdom.
[3] Index covers England and Wales.

four-tenths of the exceptionally high figure reached in the previous decade. Nevertheless, the increase for 1780–1789 clearly marks a major turning point in the growth of the industry. The pre–1780–1789 peak increase in yarn output was 38 per cent in 1770–1779. From 1780–1789 through 1850–1859, the rate of growth was always, and often very substantially, above 38 per cent. In 1860–1869, the rate of increase fell below the pre–1780–1789 peak for the first time, but this fall can clearly be attributed to the "Cotton Famine" accompanying the American Civil War.[4] In 1870–1879, the rate of increase in cotton-yarn production rose to 49 per cent, which, while it was above the pre–1780–1789 peak, was the lowest rate recorded in the century after 1770–1779, if 1860–1869 is excluded. In 1880–1889, the rate of growth definitely fell below the peak prior to 1780–1789, and in 1890–1899, the rate fell even further. Indeed, except for 1860–1869, the 12 per cent rate for 1890–1899 was the lowest recorded in the eighteenth and nineteenth centuries. The downward trend in the rate of increase of cotton-yarn production in the last three decades of the nineteenth century forms a significant aspect of the Great Depression.[5]

Per capita cotton consumption rose throughout the eighteenth century. Neither the growth, stagnation, or slight decline of population in various decades of the century affected the basic upward trend in production to the extent of producing a decline in the volume of this consumption (see Table 16). The percentage increases in the average annual per capita consumption of cotton, however, were below those for cotton consumption throughout the eighteenth century. Therefore, taking the growth of popula-

---

[4] J. H. Clapham, *An Economic History of Modern Britain,* II (London, 1932), 80, 220–225, 384 and 434. See also William Otto Henderson, *The Lancashire Cotton Famine, 1861–1865* (Manchester, 1934).

[5] H. L. Beales, "The 'Great Depression' in Industry and Trade," *Essays in Economic History: Reprints Edited for the Economic History Society,* ed. E. M. Carus-Wilson, I (London, 1958), 406–415; W. W. Rostow, *The British Economy of the Nineteenth Century* (Oxford, 1948), pp. 58–89 and 145–160.

tion into account does not affect the upward trend in production, and although it deflates the rate of growth somewhat, it does not change the rise and fall in the rates of change in output or their orders of magnitude (see Table 16).

Like the other indicators of the growth of the cotton industry, the per capita consumption of cotton in England and Wales rose very sharply in 1780–1789, when the rate of increase jumped to 188 per cent. Although this was not quite as large as the 227 per cent increase in the production of cotton yarn in the United Kingdom or the 208 per cent increase in the consumption of cotton in England and Wales, it was 6.7 times the increase for 1770–1779; the comparable figures for raw-cotton consumption and cotton-yarn production were 7.7 and 5.9. The ratios of the 1780–1789 percentage increases to the peak increases before 1780–1789 were 6.7 to 1 for per-capita raw-cotton consumption, 6.5 to 1 for raw-cotton consumption, and 5.9 to 1 for cotton-yarn production, as computed from Table 16. Hence, the 1780–1789 jump in the rate of increase in per capita raw-cotton consumption is as impressive as the leap in the other indicators of the rate of growth of production.

A comparison between the rates of increase in the volume of industrial consumers' goods production and in the volume of cotton-yarn production in the United Kingdom, which appear in Table 17, suggests the early date by which the output of the cotton industry began to grow more rapidly than consumers' goods production and the long period over which this higher rate of growth was sustained.

In the eighteenth and nineteenth centuries, the rates of growth of the volume of production in the cotton industry almost always exceeded the rates of growth of the output of all industrial consumers' goods. In every decade from 1710–1719 through 1890–1899, except for 1860–1869 and 1890–1899, the rate of increase in cotton-yarn production exceeded the rate of increase in the volume of industrial consumers' goods production in the United Kingdom (see Table 17). The exceptional rates of

1860–1869 can be traced to the "Cotton Famine" and those of 1890–1899 to the "Great Depression." [6]

The percentage increases in the output of the cotton industry were often much larger than the rates of increase in total indus-

Table 17. Growth of the volume of total industrial consumers' goods production and of the volume of cotton-yarn production, United Kingdom, 1710–1899, and the increase in the volume of raw-cotton consumption of England and Wales, 1710–1799

	% increases in average annual index of volume		
Years	A Industrial consumers' goods production, U.K.	B Cotton yarn production, U.K.	C Raw cotton consumption, England and Wales
1710–1719	11	20	25
1720–1729	11	17	5
1730–1739	4	14	9
1740–1749	5	25	23
1750–1759	17	30	32
1760–1769	4	23	22
1770–1779	14	38	27
1780–1789	34	227	208
1790–1799	38	64	89
1800–1809	39	125	
1810–1819	23	53	
1820–1829	37	89	
1830–1839	45	92	
1840–1849	28	64	
1850–1859	30	51	
1860–1869	16	2	
1870–1879	30	49	
1880–1889	14	21	
1890–1899	17	12	

Source: Based on Appendixes 2 (column D), 13, and 14 (column F).

---

[6] On the "Cotton Famine" see Clapham, Economic History, II, 80, 220–225, 384, and 434. See also Henderson, Lancashire Cotton Famine. On the "Great Depression" see Rostow, British Economy, esp. pp. 58–59 and 145–146; H. L. Beales, "The 'Great Depression,'" pp. 406–415.

trial consumers' goods production. In 1780–1789, when the increase in the volume of cotton-yarn production in the United Kingdom was 227 per cent and the increase in volume of cotton consumption of England and Wales was 208 per cent, the increase in the volume of industrial consumers' goods production in the United Kingdom was only 34 per cent. These rates include the highest attained in the cotton industry, but not the highest achieved in industrial consumers' goods output. The 34 per cent increase in the output of consumers' goods was exceeded in 1790–1799, 1800–1809, 1820–1829 and 1830–1839. Thus, while the output of the cotton industry reached its highest rate of increase in the 1780's, the production of industrial consumers' goods did not reach this point until 1830–1839. Even in that decade, however, the rate of increase in the output of the cotton industry was twice as large as the one for total industrial consumers' goods production (see Table 17).

As can be seen in Tables 18 and 19, the extraordinary growth of the cotton industry's output was not merely part of a larger development of all the textile industries inspired by—let us say—the rapid growth of population. There was, rather, a substitution of cotton for other fibers, both at home and abroad.[7]

The remarkable thing about the percentage increases in the volumes of production of cotton, linen, and woollen and worsted yarns and cloths was the extent to which the increases in cotton yarn and cloth output exceeded the increases in that of the other yarns and cloths. Except for the decades 1860–1869 and 1890–1899, the increases in the volume of cotton yarn and cloth were larger, and usually much larger, than the corresponding increases for linen and woollen and worsted yarn and cloth production. Even in 1860–1869, the decade that includes the "Cotton Famine," the increase in the volume of cotton-yarn production almost paralleled the increase in linen-yarn production, although

---

[7] Alfred P. Wadsworth and Julia De Lacy Mann, *The Cotton Trade and Industrial Lancashire, 1600–1780* (Manchester, 1931), pp. 145–192.

the percentage increase in woollen-and-worsted–yarn production was much larger. In the other exceptional decade, 1890–1899, the percentage increase in cotton-yarn production exceeded the increase in the output of linen yarn, but was exceeded by the increase in woollen-and-worsted–yarn production.

Table 18. Growth of the volume of production of cotton, linen, and woollen and worsted yarns and of the volume of industrial consumers' goods output, United Kingdom, 1770–1899

| | % increases in average annual indexes of volume of production | | | |
| | A | B | C | D |
Years	Cotton yarn	Linen yarn	Woollen and worsted yarn	Industrial consumers' goods
1770–1779	38	15		14
1780–1789	227	17		34
1790–1799	64	26	7	38
1800–1809	125	22	10	39
1810–1819	53	12	11	23
1820–1829	89	21	17	37
1830–1839	92	25	25	45
1840–1849	64	23	14	28
1850–1859	51	1	20	30
1860–1869	2	2	30	16
1870–1879	49	16	36	30
1880–1889	21	−17	9	14
1890–1899	12	−4	18	17

Source: Based on Appendixes 2, 17, and 18.

A jump to a new sustained level of growth in the output of the linen and woollen and worsted industries comparable to the one in the cotton industry did not occur during the periods covered by the available production indexes. The 1780's have no special significance in the growth of the linen and woollen and worsted industries. In 1770–1779 and 1780–1789, the increases in the average annual volume of cotton-yarn production were 38 per cent and 227 per cent respectively. The comparable figures for both

188

linen yarn and cloth production were 15 per cent and 17 per cent respectively; for woollen and worsted cloth the figures were 12 per cent and 6 per cent respectively.

Table 19. Growth of the volume of production of cotton, linen, and woollen and worsted cloths and of the volume of industrial consumers' goods output, the United Kingdom, 1750–1899

| Years | % increases in average annual index of volume of production | | | |
	A Cotton cloth	B Linen cloth	C Woollen and worsted cloth	D Industrial consumers' goods
1750–1759			10	17
1760–1769			1	4
1770–1779		15	12	14
1780–1789		17	6	34
1790–1799		26	21	38
1800–1809	115	22	10	39
1810–1819	52	11	8	23
1820–1829	69	20	19	37
1830–1839	81	13	23	45
1840–1849	65	7	9	28
1850–1859	63	−2	13	30
1860–1869	7	−7	27	16
1870–1879	47	32	43	30
1880–1889	24	−7	10	14
1890–1899	16	5	15	17

Source: Based on Appendixes 2, 17, and 18.

The percentage increases in the production of cotton yarn were at least twice as large as the increases in the outputs of linen and woollen and worsted yarns from the beginning of each series through 1850–1859. The increases in the output of cotton cloth were also at least twice as large as the percentage increases in the production of linen and woollen and worsted cloth in the periods for which comparison is possible (see Tables 18 and 19).

The absence of a strong correlation between the secular growth of the output of the cotton industry and the secular movement of the prices of large categories of goods is not surprising and does not preclude the possibility of a short-term correlation.[8] What is surprising is the disparity between the increases in the *prices* of producers' goods and the increase in the volume of *output* in the cotton industry. This suggests the desirability of examining the secular course of the prices of the factors contributing to the costs of production in the industry. The movements in the prices of the items entering into the manufacturers' costs are suggested by Table 20.

Table 20. Indexes of the costs of production in the cotton industry, 1710–1799

	% increases			
Years	A Lancashire money wages	B English producers' goods prices	C Prices of raw cotton	D Yield on government 3% stock
1710–1719	9	−5	30	
1720–1729	15	−4	24	
1730–1739	8	−4	−15	
1740–1749	0	5	49	3.2
1750–1759	−2	−1	15	3.2
1760–1769	22	11	−5	3.6
1770–1779	26	0	−2	3.7
1780–1789	6	13	59	4.7
1790–1796	10			
1790–1799		10	−3	4.5

Source: Based on Appendixes 11, 19, 21, and 22.

The crucial decade 1780–1789, which saw the spectacular increases in total and per capita raw-cotton consumption, coincided with a 6 per cent rise in Lancashire money wages, a 13 per cent rise in producers' goods prices for the United Kingdom, a 59 per cent rise in raw-cotton prices, and the highest yield on government stock between 1740–1749 and 1790–1799.[9]

---

[8] See Tables 46 and 47 in Appendix 20 below for the comparison.

[9] The percentage increases in Lancashire wages are taken as an approximation to the percentage increases in cotton-industry wages.

The 6 per cent rise in Lancashire money wages was a small one by the standards of the eighteenth century. The period for which wage figures are available, 1700–1796, saw only one fall in money wages (2 per cent in 1750–1759) and only one decade in which wages neither fell nor rose; all the remaining periods saw money wages rise by 8 per cent to 26 per cent. On the other hand, the wage rise of 1780–1789 immediately follows the two largest increases in wages, 22 per cent in 1760–1769 and 26 per cent in 1770–1779.

The 13 per cent rise in producers' goods prices in 1780–1789 is the largest recorded in the century. It follows two decades in which these prices first rose by 11 per cent and then were stable. The trends tend to suggest, as those for the national aggregates do, the existence in 1780 of excess industrial capacity, which could be used in the decade of very rapid growth of output without straining the producers' goods sector of the economy (see Chapter I). In the absence of more specific data relating to the cotton industry, however, this hypothesis cannot be proved.

Raw-cotton prices show a 59 per cent rise in 1780–1789 and a fall of 3 per cent in 1790–1799. If the scattered figures for the years before 1770 are at all accurate, the average of 24.09 pence per pound in 1780–1789 is quite high.[10] None of these average annual prices is as high as 24.09 pence per pound. The highest prices before 1780 are three quotations of 21 pence in 1748, 1749, and 1751. Although the average price for the decade 1770–1779 is only 15.14 per pound, the decade really fell into two different halves. The average for 1770–1774 is only 11.65 pence; the average for 1775–1779 rose to 18.63 pence, continued to rise through 1780–1789, and then fell slightly for the decade 1790–1799, although the years 1798 and 1799 saw the highest prices recorded in the eighteenth century.[11]

---

[10] For the annual figures, which are based on only fifty-two quotations for the eighteen years before 1770, see Table 45 in Appendix 19 below.

[11] For the annual averages and the sources of the figures see Appendix 19 below.

To the limited extent that the yield on government stock can be regarded as an indicator of "the" rate of interest (see Chapter I), the 4.7 per cent average yield in 1780–1789 is an indication of the high price of capital. The yield remained high throughout the Industrial Revolution.[12] The 1780–1889 yield was only 1 per cent greater than the one in the previous decade, but this constitutes the largest difference between any two successive decades from 1740–1749 through 1890–1899. This yield was exceeded only once (by 0.1 per cent in 1800–1809).

For the cotton manufacturer the high yield of 1780–1789 probably meant capital costs that were high compared to his costs a decade earlier, but this increase would not have been too significant if, as is possible, the price of capital had risen equally for the entrepreneur who was producing a competing product like linen goods. The importance of the relatively sharp rise lies in the absolute level reached. When "the" interest rate approached 5 per cent, there was a tendency, because of the operation of the usury laws, to divert capital from agriculture to industry.[13] With the yield on the funds averaging 4.7 per cent, a lender, particularly one lending in the provinces, was likely to need a personal, noneconomic reason to lend at 5 per cent, or he had to be willing and able to evade or break the law. Violation of the usury laws probably was most successful when personal ties moderated the interest rate and made repudiation unlikely.

The secular changes in the real prices of the items entering into the costs of production can only be approximately estimated. These price changes are summarized in Table 21.

---

[12] The yields, as given below, were calculated from the annual figures in Appendix 11. The difference between the average yields for 1760–1829 and 1780–1829 suggests, as other indicators did, that the proper decade with which to start the Industrial Revolution, if one is thinking in statistical terms, is 1780–1789.

Average annual yield on 3% government securities, by periods, 1740–1899: 1740–1759, 3.2%; 1740–1799, 3.4%; 1760–1829, 4.2%; 1780–1829, 4.5%; 1830–1899, 3.1%

[13] On the operation of the usury laws, see Chapter II above.

Real wages in Lancashire [14] fell during three periods (by 5 per cent in 1740–1749, 7 per cent in 1750–1759, and 4 per cent in 1790–1796), while money wages fell during one decade (by 2 per cent in 1750–1759). The decade of remarkable expansion of output, 1780–1789, saw the smallest increase in real wages (2 per cent, an increase that was exceeded by increases of 4 per cent to 19 per cent in five of the nine periods for which it has been possible

Table 21. Indexes of the relative movements of raw-cotton prices, producers' goods prices, and consumers' goods prices, 1700–1799

Years	Price indexes				Ratios			
			Consumers' goods					
	A Raw cotton	B Producers' goods	C Including cereals	D Excluding cereals	E A/B	F A/C	G A/D	H % increase in G
1700–1709	25	74	60	67	34	37	41	
1710–1719	32	70	64	70	46	46	50	21
1720–1729	39	67	60	65	58	60	66	34
1730–1739	33	64	54	60	50	55	62	−6
1740–1749	50	67	57	63	75	79	87	41
1750–1759	57	66	59	62	86	92	97	11
1760–1769	54	74	62	65	73	83	87	−10
1770–1779	53	74	68	69	72	76	78	−11
1780–1789	84	82	73	75	102	111	115	48
1790–1799	83	90	85	86	92	97	97	−16

Base: 1796–1800 = 100.
Source: Calculated from Appendixes 4, 5, and 19.

to calculate them). This increase, however, follows two decades with substantially larger increases (10 per cent in 1760–1769 and 11 per cent in 1770–1779). The largest increases in the century came much earlier (19 per cent in 1720–1729 and 18 per cent in 1730–1739), and are probably partly a reflection of population trends (see Appendix 10). The small size of the increase in

---

[14] For the index of real wages in Lancashire see Appendix 21 below.

1780–1789 suggests profit inflation in Lancashire. Although it was a small increase, it was nevertheless an increase. It would be more reasonable to find profit inflation in the decades 1740–1759, before the Industrial Revolution. In the first of these decades, real wages fell by 5 per cent, and in the second, by 7 per cent.

In the absence of a single index of the general level of eighteenth-century prices, the best indicators of the relative levels of real cotton prices are the ratios between the index of cotton prices and the indexes of producers' and consumers' goods prices that are to be found in Table 21. The boom decade 1780–1789 saw the century's highest ratios.

An analogy to real wages would be the ratio between the index of the price of cotton and the index of the price of consumers' goods (including cereals). The 1780's saw not only the highest ratio but also the largest percentage increase in the ratio. This 48 per cent increase was not quite as large as the 59 per cent increase in the price of cotton, but it was nevertheless quite substantial. It followed two decades in which the ratio had fallen, however, and preceded one in which it once again fell.

The closest analogy to an index of the real price of producers' goods would be the ratio between the indexes of producers' goods prices and consumers' goods prices in Table 22. The ratios suggest a moderate level of real producers' goods prices.

Taken together, the various indexes of the real prices of the factors entering into the costs of production in the cotton industry suggest that a relatively high level of costs prevailed during the decade of the industry's most rapid expansion. However, the importance of the contribution of each of the factors was different.

Rising money and real prices of the items entering into the cost of producing cotton yarn could have been compensated for by a rise in the price of the product or by an increase in productivity that could reduce cost per unit of output. Each is difficult to measure for the eighteenth century. The product was not uniform, and differences in quality were reflected in enormous differences in price and substantial differences in productivity. In addition,

Table 22. Ratios of producers' goods price index to consumers' goods price indexes, 1700–1799

Years	Price indexes			Ratios	
		Consumers' goods			
	A	*B*	*C*	*D*	*E*
	Producers' goods	Including cereals	Excluding cereals	*A/B*	*A/C*
1700–1709	74	60	67	123	110
1710–1719	70	63	70	109	100
1720–1729	67	60	65	112	103
1730–1739	64	54	60	118	107
1740–1749	67	57	63	118	106
1750–1759	66	59	62	112	106
1760–1769	74	62	65	119	114
1770–1779	74	68	69	108	107
1780–1789	82	73	75	112	109
1790–1799	90	85	86	106	105

Base: 1796–1800 = 100.
Source: Calculated from Appendixes 4 and 5.

only scattered yarn prices are available for the years before 1790.

On the basis of these scattered prices, which are summarized in Table 23, it seems that yarn prices rose between 1743 and some time in or before the early 1780's, when they turned down in the face of rising prices of the factors of production.[15]

The downward movement in the 1780's was gradual when compared with what was to come, and the lower numbers led the way.[16] The index of the price of No. 30 yarn went from 142 in 1781 to 110 in 1785, 100 in 1790, and 82 in 1795; No. 50 went

---

[15] It is possible that yarn prices turned down before the eighties, but with only one usable price quotation available for 1744 to 1781, there is no basis for judgment. Raw-cotton prices rose in the seventies and continued to rise in the eighties.

[16] The numbers referred to give the number of hanks required to make up one pound of yarn. The higher the number, the finer the yarn and, as a rule, the lower the ratio of its raw-cotton content to its selling price.

195

from 161 in 1781 to 135 in 1785, 100 in 1790, and 81 in 1795. On the other hand, No. 100 went from 113 in 1789 to 100 in 1790 and then dropped precipitously to 30 in 1795.

Table 23. Indexes of consumers' goods prices, raw-cotton prices, and yarn prices, England, 1743–1823

Years	A Con- sumers' goods prices	B Raw cotton prices	C No. 30 yarn prices	D No. 40 yarn prices	E No. 50 yarn prices	F No. 60 yarn prices	G No. 100 yarn prices
1743	76	70		73	87	82	
1779	90	112		204			
1781	93		142	146	161	158	
1784	102	112		147			
1785	97	127	110	120	135	150	
1789	94	103				89	113
1790	100	100	100	100	100	100	100
1795	119	127	83	83	81		30
1799	129	230		101			30
1800	171	158				41	28
1812	191	101		34			16
1815	154	125		42			22
1816	139	111		36			21
1817	152	122		34			17
1818	156	121	58	34			23
1819	155	82	40	26			19
1820	131	70	37	21			16
1821	121	50	31	19			14
1822	101	42	29	19			13
1820–1823	112	52	32	20			14
1823	103	44	31	19			13

Base: 1790 = 100.
Source: Based on Appendixes 19, 20, and 23.

The pattern of price movements suggests that the prices of the lower counts fell first and relatively slowly and were soon followed by the higher counts, which fell much more rapidly. The course of yarn prices suggests that prices broke soon after factory production became feasible, that it was first feasible in the lower counts, and that investment proceeded in the face of falling prices. Much effort and capital must have gone into attempting to produce the higher counts—those whose prices tended to fall later. This may be one reason why producers' goods prices did not rise more rapidly in the eighties. Factories were no doubt needed and were built, but there was also some pressure on the entrepreneur to train or hire a labor force that could produce the higher counts and to build, or have built for him, machinery of advanced design, so that he could keep pace with the demand for these relatively high counts.

Each sharp fall in the prices of the higher counts probably set off new attempts to adapt, improve on, or replace slightly older machinery until the point was reached at which improvements in spinning technology ceased to be urgent. The limit was determined, perhaps, by the natural failure of the effective demand for finer and finer yarns to continue to expand indefinitely. The date at which the limit was reached is uncertain.[17]

A similar picture emerges from a consideration of the real prices of yarn, which appear in Table 24. In contrast to a 100 per cent increase in price between 1743 and about 1781, there is one of about 50 per cent in the real prices of the lower numbers. Real

---

[17] John Kennedy, who was probably very well informed, made a series of calculations between 1812 and 1830 in which he evidently assumed that the composition of yarn output had been stabilized at an average count of about 40. (Greg seemed to accept the same average figure for 1833, and it formed the basis of some official calculations in that year.) Kennedy apparently made estimates in, or for, 1812, 1817, 1819, and 1830 on this assumption. They can be found in John Kennedy, "Observations on the Rise and Progress of the Cotton Trade in Great Britain: Particularly in Lancashire and the Adjoining Counties," *Memoirs and Proceedings of the Literary and Philosophical Society of Manchester*, 2nd ser., III (1819), 115–137; M'Connel and Co., *A Century of Fine Cotton-Spinning* (Manchester, 1913), p. 50; Arthur D. Gayer, W. W. Rostow, and Anna Jacobson Schwartz, *The Growth and Fluctuation of the British Economy, 1790–1850* (Oxford, 1953), I, 223; G. R. Porter, *The Progress of the Nation*, ed. F. W. Hirst (London, 1912), p. 301; Henry Smithers, *Liverpool, Its Commerce: With a History of the Cotton Trade* (Liverpool, 1825), pp. 125–126.

prices, however, fell rather more steeply between 1781 and 1795 than money prices for the same counts. The fall in the real price of the higher numbers, was, if anything, slightly sharper between 1789 and 1799 than the drop in the money price. Hence, the movement of the general price level relative to the movement of

Table 24. Indexes of the real prices of raw cotton and yarn, England, 1743–1823

Years	Index of real price					
	A Raw cotton	B No. 30 yarn	C No. 40 yarn	D No. 50 yarn	E No. 60 yarn	F No. 100 yarn
1743	92		96	114	108	
1779	124		227			
1781		153	157	173	170	
1784	110		144			
1785	131	113	124	139	155	
1789	109				95	120
1790	100	100	100	100	100	100
1795	107	69	70	68		25
1799	178		78			23
1800	92				24	16
1812	53		18			8
1815	81		27			14
1816	80		26			15
1817	80		22			11
1818	78	34	22			15
1819	53	26	17			12
1820–1823	46	29	18			13

Base: 1790 = 100.
Source: Based on Appendixes 19 and 23 and on Table 23.

yarn prices probably tended to accentuate the need for the early adoption of new techniques for the production of higher counts. Clearly, the adoption of advanced techniques, in turn, tended to push down the prices of the higher counts.

The long-term tendency in the nineteenth century for cotton prices to fall more rapidly than yarn prices and the general price level did not set in until the adoption of the cotton gin in the

1790's. This invention substantially reduced the costs of production and facilitated the widespread use of cotton from the United States.[18] This reduction of the upward pressure on yarn prices was a matter of great importance, as the contribution of the cost of raw cotton to the total cost of producing yarn rose from at least 1779 to 1812 and thereafter remained considerably higher than it had been in the 1770's or 1780's (see Appendix 23).

The key factor in determining the size of profits was probably an increase in productivity, but this increase is impossible to measure. There are only two sets of figures for the eighteenth century from which it is possible to calculate productivity. Both are for individual mills, not for national aggregates. One is a series of estimates of output in 1743 for Edward Cave's power-driven spinning mill; the other is a series of estimates for Samuel Oldknow's Mellor mill in 1798 and 1799.[19] By torturing the figures, it is possible to extract two sets of productivity figures for different counts of yarn, including an indication of a somewhat higher average annual output of yarn per worker in Cave's mill in 1743 than in Oldknow's in 1797.[20] The usefulness of the figures is limited, however, by the probably optimism of the estimators, the lack of comparability between the yarns produced, and the important assumptions that must be made to obtain the results.

There are many more estimates for the early nineteenth century, but while each of these is interesting and perhaps some are even accurate, they all lack comparability with the estimates for

---

[18] T. S. Ashton, "Some Statistics of the Industrial Revolution," *Essays in Economic History: Reprints Edited for the Economic History Society*, ed. E. M. Carus-Wilson, III (London, 1962), 249, table 3; Gayer, Rostow, and Schwartz, *Growth and Fluctuation*, II, 837–842.

[19] The Cave estimates can be found in Wadsworth and Mann, *Cotton Trade*, pp. 433–438. The Oldknow estimates can be found in George Unwin, Arthur Hulme, and George Taylor, *Samuel Oldknow and the Arkwrights* (Manchester, 1924), pp. 194–196.

[20] The yarn counts are no. 15 in Cave's mill and no. 20 in Oldknow's mill. The average annual output per worker were 36 lbs. in Cave's mill and 34 lbs. in Oldknow's mill.

Cave's and Oldknow's mills and most of them lack comparability with each other.[21] In most cases, the usefulness of the estimates is destroyed by differences in the counts produced, by assumptions about the composition of the national output of yarn,[22] or by an ambiguity about the number of workers covered by the estimate. All the estimates, except the first two, indicate a considerable increase in productivity.

Tables 25 and 26 are suggestive of the rate of increase in

Table 25. Yarn production and wages in Thomas Houldsworth's Glasgow mill, 1823 and 1833

Years	A No. 120 yarn production (lbs./week) *	B Number of spindles on mule used *	C Number of hours worked per week *	D Net spinners wages (d./week) *
1823	46.0	336	74.5	319
1833	52.5	336	69.0	358

* Output is the average for several different workers.

Source: The figures are from G. R. Porter, *The Progress of the Nation,* ed. F. W. Hirst (London, 1912), pp. 298–302.

productivity which could be attained. Output per spindle per week of No. 120 yarn rose by 14 per cent between 1823 and 1833. The output of No. 180 yarn per pound sterling of operator's wages rose 25 per cent between 1804 and 1814 and 65 per cent between 1814 and 1833; for No. 200 yarn the comparable increases are 13 per cent and 94 per cent. The overall increase for No. 180 yarn was 106 per cent between 1804 and 1833 and 119 per

---

[21] Chief among the early nineteenth-century estimates are the Kennedy estimates referred to above and several estimates of the output of Thomas Houldsworth's Manchester and Glasgow mills for the years 1804, 1814, 1823, and 1833 in Porter, *Progress,* pp. 298–302.

[22] Later estimates have foundered on the same reef. Blaug's estimates for the years 1834–1892 are probably much weakened by his assumptions about the insignificance of the (probably) changing composition of yarn output ("Productivity of Capital," pp. 358–381).

Table 26. Yarn production and wages in Thomas Houldsworth's Manchester mill, 1804–1833

| Years | No. 180 yarn * | | | | | No. 200 yarn * | | | | |
| | A | B | C | D | E | F | G | H | I | J |
	Production (lbs./week)	Gross wages (d./week)	Piecers wages (d./week)	Net (i.e. spinners) wages (d./week)	Hours worked per week	Production (lbs./week)	Gross wages (d./week)	Piecers wages (d./week)	Net (i.e. spinners) wages (d./week)	Hours worked per week
1804	12.0	720	330	390	74	9.0	810	372	438	74
1814	18.0	864	330	534	74	13.5	1080	360	720	74
1833	22.5	656	252	404	69	19.0	783	270	513	69

* Output is the average for several workers.

Source: The figures are from G. R. Porter, *The Progress of the Nation*, ed. F. W. Hirst (London, 1912), pp. 298–302.

cent for No. 200 yarn. While the output per pound sterling approximately doubled, the value of the pound rose by about one-third, so that the fall in Houldsworth's real wage cost per pound of yarn must have been about 60 per cent. Because these are comparatively high counts and because developments affecting high counts tended to first affect low counts, these productivity figures are probably suggestive, but no more than suggestive, of what happened in the eighteenth century.

The other factor affecting the size of profits was the growth of output combined with the growth of exports.[23] Throughout the eighteenth century, textiles had accounted for between 50 per cent and 60 per cent of the total volume of exports.[24] By 1829, textiles constituted over 80 per cent of the volume of exports and accounted for almost 68 per cent of the value of exports.[25]

In 1700, woollens had accounted for 57 per cent and cotton for 0.5 per cent of the total volume of exports. Britain started to export domestically manufactured goods made entirely of cotton about 1750. By 1772, woollens constituted 42 per cent and cottons somewhat more than 2 per cent of the volume of exports. In 1800, woollens were down to 29 per cent of the total, and cottons, including yarn, had risen to 24 per cent of the total volume of exports. By 1802, cottons had surpassed wool textiles as Britain's most important export.[26]

In 1815, the declared value of cottons was three times as large as

---

[23] T. S. Ashton, introduction to Elizabeth Boody Schumpeter, *English Overseas Trade Statistics, 1697–1808* (Oxford, 1960); Albert H. Imlah, *Economic Elements in the Pax Britannica: Studies in British Foreign Trade in the Nineteenth Century* (Cambridge, Mass., 1958); and S. B. Saul, *Studies in British Overseas Trade, 1870–1914* (Liverpool, 1960), pp. 3–16, contain the best discussions of the role of the cotton industry in British foreign trade.

[24] Ashton's introduction to Schumpeter, *English Overseas Trade Statistics,* p. 12.

[25] Calculated from B. R. Mitchell and P. Deane, *Abstract of British Historical Statistics* (Cambridge, 1962), pp. 282, 295, and 302.

[26] Ashton's introduction to Schumpeter, *English Overseas Trade Statistics,* p. 12.

the average had been for 1801 to 1805 and accounted for 40 per cent of total exports of domestic produce. From 1820 to 1850, the volume of cotton exports increased fivefold, while their value rose by only 50 per cent.[27] The Industrial Revolution had come of age, and cotton was king.

---

[27] Saul, *Studies,* pp. 9 and 14.

Chapter VII

Conclusion

DURING the late eighteenth and early nineteenth centuries, agricultural prices rose more steeply than industrial prices. This phenomenon seems to have been due to an increase in population that, by increasing the demand for food, brought into cultivation marginal land with high costs of production, while the supply and demand price-elasticities of agricultural products remained lower than those for industrial goods. This analysis, in turn, suggests the possibility that in the late eighteenth century the industrial sector of the economy was subject to cost pressures as a result of the increasing price of its agricultural inputs.

It seems fairly clear, however, that the cotton industry, using, as it did, an imported agricultural raw material, was not subject to price pressure from this source. Nevertheless, the cotton industry, like other industries, was subject to cost pressures from other directions. In industrial areas, money wages (and possibly real wages) rose relatively rapidly in the latter part of the eighteenth century, as did the prices of industrial producers' goods. The relatively rapid introduction of the factory system in the cotton industry may have been due to the advantage that the industry enjoyed with regard to its principal raw material and to the desirability of preventing increases in the prices of the factors of production from being transmitted into proportionately large real cost increases.

Another characteristic feature of the British economy in the late eighteenth and early nineteenth centuries was the transition to a new high rate of output of consumers' and producers' goods, a rate which was sustained for at least three generations and was not undone by the concurrent increases in population. In this transition, consumers' goods led producers' goods by about a decade, probably because of the existence of excess industrial capacity in the 1780's.

The spectacular secular growth in industrial output implied an increase in the demand for industrial capital. The usury laws, however, limited the inducements that could be offered for capital, particularly when interest rates were high, as they indeed were in the late eighteenth and early nineteenth centuries.

The effect of the usury laws varied from sector to sector of the economy. The government was immune. The laws were most easily enforced in agriculture and probably produced a diversion of landowners' capital out of agriculture. The partial effectiveness of the usury laws and the limited extent to which investors responded to interest rates and to yields on capital impeded the flow of capital. By limiting the attractiveness of alternative investments, however, the laws probably encouraged the reinvestment of industrial profits.

In order to carry on his enterprise, the cotton manufacturer needed about twice as much long-term as short-term capital; little, if any, of either was obtained from foreign sources. He found it relatively easy to obtain short-term capital. In his search for short-term capital his first resort was likely to be the developing loose network of formal and quasi-formal banking institutions.

Most of the burden of distributing short-term capital to the cotton industry fell on the growing number of country banks. They served as the terminal points of the mechanism that made it possible to transfer large temporary capital surpluses from predominantly agricultural to predominantly industrial areas by way of London. In this task, the country banks were aided by the London banks, the bill brokers, and bill dealers. The operation of this transfer mechanism depended on the highly periodic nature of the demand for short-term capital in both agriculture and industry and on the existence of differentials between the London and provincial interest rates.

The supply of short-term capital made available through the country banks was supplemented from a large number of other sources; the cotton broker, shopkeeper, and even the laborer were all laid under contribution, as indeed the government was, on a few rare occasions, and the Bank of England, on one occasion.

The cotton broker supplied the cotton manufacturer with short-term capital because he found it profitable to finance his customer.

The worker was an involuntary supplier of short-term capital. This was not a novel development. The long-pay, which was carried over from the putting-out system, was characteristic of both domestic industrial production and factory production. The persistence of the long-pay was probably due to the appalling lack of an adequate supply of a means of payment suitable for the frequent payment of wages. This shortage of the means of payment frequently turned the cotton manufacturer into a quasi-banker in the sense that he was an issuer of acknowledgments of indebtedness that passed current; it also turned the local shopkeeper into a quasi-banker in the sense that he became a dealer in debts. Quasi-banking probably was more important before 1800, when the isolated "colonial" water-powered mill was the dominant type of factory, than after 1800, when the urban steam-powered mill was establishing its supremacy.

The entrepreneur's issue of private money, which often circulated at a discount, placed the shopkeeper, and to some extent the entire community, in the position of financing the consumption of the mill hand and thereby indirectly helped the manufacturer to finance his production.

The relative backwardness of the long-term capital market, with the concomitant emphasis on personal contact as a prerequisite for much long-term industrial investment, made personal savings an important element in the capital supply of the entrepreneur. This was, of course, in perfect accord with England's stratified and localized social organization. The structure and functioning of British banks relegated most of them to a role of relative insignificance in the long-term capital market. These considerations limited the available supply of long-term loans as well as the supply of participating capital. Personal savings were mobilized by the partnership, the most personal of business organizations.

The cotton manufacturers, drawn from a very large portion of the British social spectrum, were able to tap many different pools of long-term capital, and this, in conjunction with the wide variety of sources from which the industry drew its short-term capital, helps to account for the sustained growth of the industry. The supply of capital was not dependent on the fortunes of any single group or type of institution outside of the industry.

The plowing back of profits was crucial. The size of the profits from which reinvestment came was probably a product of rising productivity and large-scale manufacture for a large, expanding national and international market.

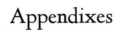

Appendixes

Introduction

THE growing volume of British economic statistics still verges on being inadequate for the study of some important aspects of eighteenth- and nineteenth-century economic history. Several controversies feed upon the quantitative and qualitative shortcomings of eighteenth-century statistics. The persistent disagreement about the standard of living during the Industrial Revolution and about the related, recently revived dispute about the magnitude, timing, causes, and consequences of population growth are among the most important of these.[1] The vigor with which the conflicting arguments are pressed probably stems from the implications they hold for political, economic, and social theory and policy.[2]

---

[1] The history of the standard-of-living controversy can be found in R. M. Hartwell, "Interpretations of the Industrial Revolution in England: A Methodological Inquiry," *Journal of Economic History,* XIX (1959), 229–49, and A. J. Taylor, "Progress and Poverty in Britain, 1780–1850," *History,* XLV (1960). Taylor's belief that the area of disagreement has narrowed seems to be wishful thinking. His article was shortly followed by a contribution to the debate: R. M. Hartwell, "The Rising Standard of Living in England, 1800–1850," *Economic History Review,* 2nd ser., XIII (1961), 397–416.

The controversy about population growth forms part of the dispute about the standard of living. See the works of Hartwell and Taylor referred to above and the following articles by H. J. Habakkuk: "English Population in the Eighteenth Century," *Economic History Review,* 2nd ser., VI (1953), 117–33; "Essays in Bibliography and Criticism, XXXII: The Eighteenth Century," *Economic History Review,* 2nd ser., VIII (1956), 438; "New Viewpoints on the Economic History of Europe: The Economic History of Modern Britain," *Journal of Economic History,* XVIII (1958), 486–501.

[2] Hartwell, "Interpretations," pp. 229–49.

There are statistical difficulties peculiar to any attempt to construct indexes bridging the eighteenth and nineteenth centuries. Even before the eighteenth century, officials charged with keeping some statistics tended to combine figures relating to England and Wales and, in common with later writers, to refer to them as if they only covered England.[3] The converse error appeared still later when the same figures were sometimes treated as if they pertained to Great Britain or the United Kingdom. The resulting difficulties have been compounded by some students of nineteenth-century economic history who have published their statistical results without subtotals for the components of the United Kingdom. In the absence of subtotals, it is impossible to construct continuous statistical series for England or for England and Wales during the eighteenth and nineteenth centuries without, at best, repeating a large number of time-consuming calculations.[4]

Under these circumstances, the relative scarcity of statistical series relating to Ireland and Scotland in the eighteenth century is a serious obstacle to the study of the Industrial Revolution. In a few important instances, however, it has been possible to determine that a particular index that purports to cover the United Kingdom in the eighteenth and nineteenth centuries is actually composed of two consecutive indexes, one relating to England and Wales in the eighteenth century and the other to the United Kingdom in the nineteenth century.[5]

Finally, there is the general unavoidable difficulty inherent in

---

[3] T. S. Ashton, in his introduction to Elizabeth Boody Schumpeter, *English Overseas Trade Statistics, 1697–1808* (Oxford, 1960), discusses this general problem.

[4] *Ibid.* This probably would not have been at all possible for foreign trade. From the last decade of the eighteenth century onward, changes were made in the methods of recording trade figures so that for a few series Mrs. Schumpeter was not able to extract the figures for England and Wales from those for Great Britain.

[5] This is particularly true of some of the output series constructed by Walther G. Hoffmann in *British Industry, 1700–1950* (Oxford, 1955). See Appendix 2 below.

interpreting time series that extend over long periods. Any attempt to assign dates to the Industrial Revolution results in limiting its first impact to a period of fifty to one hundred years. Ideally this period should be compared and contrasted to preceding and succeeding periods of comparable duration. The time series would therefore have to cover one hundred fifty to three hundred years. Even if the comparison was only made between the first and last years or decades of the Industrial Revolution, the time series would have to span fifty to one hundred years of enormous change. This difficulty can only be dealt with by stating the need for caution and by supporting statistical data with other evidence whenever feasible.

The statistical methods used have been kept as simple as possible; the use of sophisticated statistical methods is not warranted by the basic data. Because of the shortcomings of some of the data, "average" always refers here to the arithmetic mean and "interpolation" and "extrapolation" to linear interpolation and extrapolation.[6]

In order to avoid repeated qualification, "Great Britain" and the "United Kingdom" are used as geographic rather than political designations.

---

[6] As a test of the assumption that the simpler procedures make little difference, the population index was constructed in two ways. It was first constructed by using the geometric mean and exponential interpolation and extrapolation; then by the simpler method used throughout this work. The difference between the two results for the size of the average population in 1800–1809 was 0.1%. Since the U. S. census of 1940 may have missed 1% to 2% of the population (J. T. Krause, "Changes in English Fertility and Mortality, 1781–1850," *Economic History Review,* 2nd ser., XI [1958], 60) , it is safe to assume that a 0.1% error introduced by this choice of method is insignificant. It is likely that analagous situations can be found with regard to all the series used here. The basic data in each case probably contains errors much larger than any likely to be introduced by this choice of statistical method.

Appendix 1

Profit Inflation Theory
and the Industrial Revolution

THE recognition of the importance of retained profits as a source of capital in the Industrial Revolution poses a significant question.[1] Were there any market forces at work that generated abnormally large profits and thereby facilitated exceptionally heavy industrial investment? Earl J. Hamilton has offered a plausible answer to this question: "Profit inflation through a lag of wages behind prices, a factor hitherto overlooked by economists and historians, facilitated the Industrial Revolution during the second half of the eighteenth century, the critical incipient stage."[2]

This theory demands careful consideration. If it has been or can be verified, it marks a long step toward the goal of explaining the nature and causes of the Industrial Revolution. Verification could provide one of the building blocks for the construction of a historical generalization about the relationship between prices and economic progress.

Verification or refutation of the profit inflation theory could also be significant for economic theory and policy. There is, for example, an

---

[1] George Unwin, "Introduction," in G. W. Daniels, *The Early English Cotton Industry* (Manchester, 1920), pp. xxix-xxx; T. S. Ashton, *Iron and Steel in the Industrial Revolution* (Manchester, 1924), pp. 46–48 and 266; T. S. Ashton and J. Sykes, *The Coal Industry of the Eighteenth Century* (Manchester, 1929), p. 6; Leland Hamilton Jenks, *The Migration of British Capital to 1875* (New York, 1927), p. 15.

[2] "Profit Inflation and the Industrial Revolution, 1751–1800," *Quarterly Journal of Economics*, LVI (1942), 257. The claim to priority may be literally valid, since it is restricted to the role of profit inflation in the Industrial Revolution. The effects of something like profit inflation and price inflation in economic growth have been discussed by economic writers since about 1800 as one form of "forced-saving." Alfred Marshall, for one, recognized this lag of wages behind prices before Hamilton wrote, but was much more cautious in interpreting it. (*Principles of Economics: An Introductory Volume* [8th ed.; New York, 1949], pp. 620–621).

almost symbiotic relationship between Hamilton's theory and some aspects of Keynesian economics. The theory has also had an impact on the study of the development of underdeveloped areas. In addition, since the profit inflation theory is demonstrably a theory of economic progress through the exploitation of labor, verification or refutation could have implications in the realms of social and political theory.

In proposing the theory, Hamilton not only designated divergent secular rises in prices and wages as the strategic factor, but also attempted to account for the divergence. He attributed the price rise to an upswing in Mexican silver production and to the monetary effects of the French Revolutionary and Napoleonic Wars, while "the chief factor in the failure of wages to keep pace with soaring prices in the second half of the eighteenth century was the natural inertia of wage movements in both directions." Hamilton distinguished between the effect of inventory appreciation on profits and that of a divergence in wage and price trends. He concluded that "in a period of rising prices such as England experienced in the last half of the eighteenth century, inventory appreciation raised normal business profits, but this gain was insignificant in comparison with the windfalls accruing from a lag of wages behind prices." [3]

The role of profit inflation in economic development was not limited to the industrial Revolution in England. In his 1952 presidential address to the Economic History Association, Hamilton restated the theory as a historical generalization. After discussing the economic development of several countries, including England, France, and Spain, for several eras, including the sixteenth century and the second half of the eighteenth century, he concluded that price inflation at a "creeping rate of less than two per cent cumulatively in the most extreme case and less than one per cent in all other cases . . . [had been] beneficial." He estimated that the divergent movements in prices and wages should have resulted in something like a quadrupling of profits between 1500 and 1600 and a further quadrupling between 1741–1750 and 1791–1800. [4] From these quadrupled profits came the savings and investments required for economic progress.

---

[3] Hamilton, "Profit Inflation," pp. 273 and n. 3, 259, and 262–263.

[4] "Prices and Progress," *Journal of Economic History*, XII (1952), 346, 335, and 339–340.

It is necessary to distinguish clearly between profit inflation and what can be called profit expansion. Profit expansion can be defined as any abnormal increase in profits. Profit inflation is a special case of profit expansion. Profit inflation can be defined as an abnormal increase in profits due to a lag of wages behind rising prices. The profit inflation theory states that the wage lag is due to the natural inertia of wages, that the price rise is due to an increase in the money supply, and that the abnormal profits generated by the wage lag are the critical source of unusually heavy capital investment required for rapid economic growth. As applied to the problem of the Industrial Revolution, the profit inflation theory identifies an influx of bullion as the cause of the price rise. Profit expansion could take place in a number of ways, of which the most obvious, in this context, would be a decrease in labor costs through innovation.

On the basis of his generalization, Hamilton made a foray into the theory of economic development of underdeveloped countries. He voiced a doubt that "any backward area . . . [could develop] to a significant degree in the next quarter or half century without the stimulus of rising prices and lagging wages." [5] The policy implicit in this point of view is quite clear.

At first, Hamilton had argued that the wage lag of the second half of the eighteenth century implied a fall in real wages.[6] He later qualified his position and conceded that "it is possible that the annual consumption of goods and services by working class families fell very little . . . [but] leisure was certainly sacrificed." [7]

Both forms of the argument imply that capital formation in the Industrial Revolution involved an exploitation of the industrial worker. The first assumes an exploitation of labor that was reflected in a fall in real wages; the second an exploitation that was reflected in a decrease in economic welfare.[8] This implication accounts for his refer-

----

[5] *Ibid.,* p. 348.   [6] Hamilton, "Profit Inflation," pp. 260 and 272–273.

[7] Hamilton, "Prices and Progress," pp. 343–344.

[8] I here generally follow A. C. Pigou in restricting "economic welfare" to "that part of social welfare that can be brought directly into relation with the measuring-rod of money" (*The Economics of Welfare* [London, 1952], p. 11) . However, since Hamilton includes leisure in his discussion of welfare, I have

ences to "the sacrifices imposed on workers by rising prices and lagging wages" and to "price-wage ratios that forced four generations of workers to forego leisure which was precious to them or portions of their low real incomes for the immediate benefit of the well to do." [9] He offered little evidence, however, to support his conjecture that the English worker's standard of economic welfare deteriorated in the second half of the eighteenth century.[10]

---

also done so, although Pigou classified it as a "quasi-commodity" and excluded it from his analysis (*ibid.,* pp. 87–88, n. 1). For a theoretical discussion of exploitation see *ibid.,* pp. 466–467, 556–571, and 676–680.

[9] Hamilton, "Prices and Progress," pp. 342 and 347.

[10] The literature generated by the dispute over the course of real wages, real income, the standard of living, the standard of comfort, economic welfare, and social welfare in the era of the Industrial Revolution continues to grow. A thoughtful history of the dispute can be found in R. M. Hartwell, "Interpretations of the Industrial Revolution in England: A Methodological Inquiry," *Journal of Economic History,* XIX (1959), 229–249. He attributes the disagreement about whether or not the condition of the people was improving or deteriorating in the late eighteenth century in large measure to a disagreement among historians and observers stemming "from passionately held views about values and how they are affected by social change" (*ibid.,* p. 241). He recognizes three main phases in the development of political bias: "In the first and contemporary phase the argument was between Whig and Tory, a reflection of the shift in economic and political power that was occurring between 1800 and 1850, with Whig praising economic and political change and Tory decrying it. In the second phase the conflict was between progressives—and by this time both Liberal and Conservative viewed the nineteenth century as one of massive and continuous progress—and distributionists, especially the Fabians, who condemned the organization and ethos of capitalism and who wished to change it. In the third and modern phase the Fabian attack had been reinforced by the Marxists, . . . who argue that capitalism both in its evolution and present form must be evil" (*ibid.*[1] p. 240). However, there is implicit in the entire dispute a question that is never explicitly asked: Who paid for industrialization? Even those who argue the case for deterioration would not claim that the populace was worse off in 1900 or 1950 than it had been in 1750, 1790, or 1800, indicating that the above question is the one being asked rather than a question about the general desirability of industrialization. For some, the answer is "the workers were exploited and thus were made to pay for the Industrial Revolution." For others the answer is either "nobody in particular paid" or "somebody paid but it wasn't the working classes." The answer in each case is a reflection of

The undocumented statement that workers were forced to sacrifice leisure is followed by the assertion that "we know from the long and determined resistance of workers to factory discipline and to the regular hours essential in group employment that loss of leisure was a genuine hardship." [11] The logic of the argument is not very compelling. To assume that the problem of factory discipline was due to a reduction of leisure is to misunderstand the problem. The resistance of the factory worker to factory discipline is only a special case of the resistance of the industrial worker to industrial discipline. There was some similarity between discipline problems faced by the factory master and those faced by the merchant engaged in putting-out raw materials to domestic workers. Some of these common problems had common causes.

The theft or embezzlement by workers of raw materials, partly finished goods, or finished goods, a rather extreme form of indiscipline, illustrates this point. These crimes caused the employer of domestic workers a great deal of concern. In 1703, the penalty had been a fine equal to twice the value of the materials; in 1740, the cost of prosecution was added to the fine; in 1749, it became a criminal offense punishable by two weeks in jail; in 1777, the penalty was raised to three months for a first offense and six months for a second.[12] As the

---

the social sympathies of the disputants. For a fairly recent example of the arguments for deterioration see E. J. Hobsbawm, "The British Standard of Living, 1790–1850," *Economic History Review*, 2nd ser., X (1957), 46–68; for a recent and convincing statement of the case for a rising standard of living, see R. M. Hartwell, "The Rising Standard of Living in England, 1800–1850," *Economic History Review*, 2nd ser., XIII (1961), 397–416. Also see E. P. Thompson, *The Making of the English Working Class* (New York, 1964), and E. J. Hobsbawm and R. M. Hartwell, "The Standard of Living during the Industrial Revolution: A Discussion," *Economic History Review*, 2nd ser., XVI (1963), 119–146.

[11] Hamilton, "Prices and Progress," p. 344.

[12] Neil J. Smelser, *Social Change in the Industrial Revolution: An Application of Theory to the Lancashire Cotton Industry, 1770–1840* (London, 1959), pp. 65–66. These activities of the workers cannot simply be regarded as theft. "The line of demarcation between extention of established rights and barefaced robbery is difficult to draw" (T. S. Ashton, *An Economic History of England: The 18th Century* [London, 1955], p. 210).

penalties were made more severe, enforcement was pressed for and financed by associations of employers.[13]

The same problem arose in the factories and brought forth similar responses. The Strutts, for example, had to deal with theft and embezzlement in their stocking-knitting and cotton mills, and they contributed to an association for the enforcement of the laws dealing with the crimes. Although the centralization of workers in a factory and the resulting possibility of closer supervision and surveillance of employees probably tended to produce a lower incidence of theft and embezzlement, the fact remains that these crimes were a problem in the factories.

One of the probable causes of the crimes throws a great deal of light on the discipline problem. Some of the causes, perhaps even the most important ones, are unrelated to this problem. The "normal" impulse to commit these crimes was probably magnified by one aspect of the wage system, the "long-pay." The long-pay, common to domestic and factory production, coupled relatively large, infrequent wage payments with smaller and more frequent subsistance advances against earnings. It involved the workers in a complex network of credit relationships that probably encouraged resistance to discipline in general and embezzlement or theft in particular. It also provided the employer with a means of disciplining his hands.[14] The Strutts, for example, withheld about one-sixth of the wages due their employees and paid it to them every three months if they did not leave the mill without notice. The money could be forfeited for misconduct; more often, however, small fines were levied against it for infractions of discipline inside or outside the factory.[15]

Although the long-pay may have served to enforce discipline and to

---

[13] Ashton, *18th Century*, pp. 210–211. Enforcement was not easy. "The weaver continued to take his almost traditional cut from the woven piece, and the spinner to relinquish her weft to a hawker for a bribe" (Smelser, *Social Change*, p. 66).

[14] R. S. Fitton and A. P. Wadsworth, *The Strutts and the Arkwrights, 1758–1830: A Study of the Early Factory System* (Manchester, 1958), pp. 54 and 234; Ashton, *18th Century*, pp. 206–212.

[15] Fitton and Wadsworth, *The Strutts*, pp. 232–240.

keep the high rate of labor turnover from rising,[16] the system was probably largely the result of the chronic shortage of the means of payment in the eighteenth century. The entrepreneurs could alleviate the shortage by ingenuity and exertion, but the solution to the problem was beyond their means and had to await the development of the economy (see Chapter III). In addition to helping to ease the shortage of the means of payment by making it possible to occasionally substitute less-scarce for scarce means of payment, the long-pay allowed the firm to economize on short-term capital and formed the basis for some forced short-term financing of industry by the workers.[17]

If the factory hand had a stronger impulse to resist discipline than the employee of a domestic-industry firm, the reasons should be sought for in the nature of factory discipline itself and, perhaps, in the age structure of the factory work force rather than in a hypothetical reduction in leisure that is supposed to serve as evidence of a hypothetical exploitation of labor.[18]

Centralized production made possible a high degree of supervision of employees inside and outside the factory. However benevolent the employer and however beneficial the outside supervision may have been, its beneficiaries may well have found it irksome. Concentration of employees may have made factory discipline more necessary and more burdensome. The problems raised by concentration were probably intensified when a large part of the working force was very young, but this condition only existed in some industries and only at some stages of their development.[19]

Because the profit inflation theory is a theory of economic progress

---

[16] At the Strutts' Belper and Milford mills, the rate was about 16 per cent a year between 1805 and 1812 (*ibid.*, p. 240).

[17] See Chapter IV above. By their very nature, domestic-industry firms must have contributed heavily to the demand for short-term financing that made these uses of long-pay attractive to the entrepreneur.

[18] Judging by a list of the fines imposed in the Strutts' mills, discipline was likely to be more exacting in a factory than outside it (Fitton and Wadsworth, *The Strutts*, pp. 234–237).

[19] The impressions of factory discipline practices of essentially benevolent manufacturers come from the operation of cotton mills by the Strutts and Owen (Fitton and Wadsworth, *The Strutts, passim;* Robert Owen, *The Life of Robert Owen by Himself* (1st pub. 1857; New York, 1920), *passim;* Robert Dale Owen, *Threading My Way* [London, 1874]).

through the exploitation of labor, it can be compared with the Marxist theory of capitalist accumulation. The two theories differ on most fundamentals. Unlike Marx, Hamilton does not foresee any revolutionary end of the process of capitalist accumulation, does not subscribe to a labor theory of value, and does not regard "the general movements of wages . . . as exclusively regulated by the expansion and contraction of the industrial reserve army." [20]

Marx and Hamilton analyze economic development over periods which are of different orders of magnitude. Marx was concerned with very long periods, like the capitalist and precapitalist eras, and with shorter periods, like business cycles.[21] Hamilton, on the other hand, is concerned with periods of intermediate duration, like the Price Revolution and the second half of the eighteenth century.

For Marx, value was created only by the expenditure of labor. Part of the value created was returned to the workers as wages. Capitalist accumulation originated in the surplus value that was not returned to the workers.[22] The capitalist expended part of the surplus value as rent, interest, and commercial profit. The remainder, which could be regarded as industrial profit, was divided between consumption and investment after "a Faustian conflict between the passion for accumulation, and the desire for enjoyment." [23]

------

[20] Karl Marx, *The Process of Capitalist Production* (*Capital: A Critique of Political Economy*, Vol. I), ed. Frederick Engels, rev. Ernest Untermann, trans. Samuel Moore and Edward Aveling (New York, 1906), p. 699. A very good concise summary of the central argument of *Capital* can be found in the article "Marx" in the *Encyclopaedia Britannica* (11th ed.; New York, 1911). It was written by Eduard Bernstein, the great German revisionist, and includes his critique of Marx's thought.

[21] Examples of Marx's long period analysis can be found in *Capital*, I, 784–837. For examples of Marx's discussions of cycles see *Capital*, I, 671–681, and Karl Marx, *The Process of Capitalist Production as a Whole* (*Capital: A Critique of Political Economy*, Vol. III), ed. Frederick Engels, trans. Ernest Untermann (Chicago, 1909), pp. 125–167 and 559–580. Short summaries of Marxist cycle theory can be found in Wesley C. Mitchell, *Business Cycles The Problem and Its Setting* (New York, 1927), pp. 8–9, and W. Arthur Lewis, *The Theory of Economic Growth* (Homewood, Ill., 1955), pp. 288–289. Lewis also discusses various misinterpretations of Marx's cycle theory.

[22] Marx, *Capital*, Vol. I, pp. 656–677.   [23] *Ibid.,* p. 651.

Marx regarded the ratio between capitalist consumption and investment as variable;[24] Hamilton overlooks this possibility. Hamilton, concerned with shorter periods than Marx, may have regarded such changes as negligible over periods of fifty or one hundred years. This is in marked contrast, however, to Hamilton's attitude toward changes in workers' consumption (and economic welfare) during the same periods. It seems at least plausible that the pattern of consumption and investment by capitalists and the pattern of workers' consumption both changed during the course of periods of fifty to one hundred years.

In his discussion of trade cycles, Marx produced a relatively short-term analysis. He argued that capital accumulated and the demand for labor increased during a boom. The increasing competition for labor raised wages faster than prices and thereby reduced profits. As profits fell, investment slowed down and a slump started. Wages then fell faster than prices until investment once again became profitable.[25] It is by no means surprising, therefore, that Soviet economic doctrine rejects inflation and, like some types of much more conservative economic theory, favors a secularly falling price level.[26]

Marx's short-term analysis highlights important specific differences between the two labor-exploitation theories of economic development. Marx, like Hamilton, postulates a divergence in the movements of

---

[24] *Ibid.,* pp. 648–656.

[25] This is Marx's description of the mechanism of business cycles. According to Marx, crises have a more fundamental cause. "The last cause of all real crises always remains the poverty and restricted consumption of the masses as compared to the tendency of capitalist production to develop the productive forces in such a way, that only the absolute power of consumption of the entire society would be their limit" (*Capital,* III, 568) .

[26] David Felix, "Profit Inflation and Industrial Growth: The Historical Record and Contemporary Analogies," *Quarterly Journal of Economics,* LXX (1956) , 462, n. 2. Von Mises, von Hayek, and Schumpeter, for example, also favor a secularly falling price level for economic growth; their reasons for doing so are, of course, different from those of the Soviet economists. According to Felix: "In the Soviet countries . . . profit inflation is a superfluous addition to the State's potent arsenal of economic techniques. The inflation which has paralleled their efforts from time to time has been cost inflation, the result of planning miscalculations, bad harvests, and war destruction" (*ibid*) .

prices and wages and a relationship between this divergence and the rates of profit and investment. Hamilton regards wages as naturally sticky and therefore likely to lag behind prices; Marx regards prices as naturally sticky and therefore likely to lag behind wages. Because Marx postulated wage movements that would always be steeper than price movements and a secular trend in wages that was not upward, it is possible to ignore the difference in time periods in making this comparison. It is evident that Marx and Hamilton postulate completely different relationships between prices and wages and arrive at the same conclusion with regard to the importance of the exploitation of labor in capital formation.

Looked at in another way, the profit inflation theory can be regarded as a special application of the "forced-saving" doctrine.[27] The doctrine holds that an increase in the quantity of money will produce an increase in the prices of goods without a corresponding increase in the prices of the factors of production. This procedure "forced-saving"

---

[27] The history of the doctrine is discussed in the following works: Jacob Viner, *Studies in the Theory of International Trade* (New York, 1937), pp. 187–197; F. A. von Hayek, "A Note on the Development of the Doctrine of 'Forced Saving,'" *Quarterly Journal of Economics*, XLVII (1932), 123–133; Karl H. Niebyl, *Studies in Classical Theories of Money* (New York, 1946), pp. 59–79. In England the doctrine was first stated about 1800 by Bentham in the *Manual of Political Economy*, which was not published until 1843 (in Sir John Bowring, ed., *The Works of Jeremy Bentham*, Vol. III [Edinburgh, 1843], pp. 33–84) and first found its way into print in Henry Thornton, *An Enquiry into the Nature and Effects of the Paper Credit of Great Britain* (London, 1802). During the next two decades, the doctrine was taken up by a number of distinguished economic writers, including Malthus, Ricardo, Dugald Stewart, Lauderdale, Torrens, Tooke, and Joplin. See von Hayek, "Note," *passim*, for the relevant works of all these writers except Tooke and Joplin. On Tooke and Joplin see Viner, *Studies*, pp. 189, n. 12, and 190–191. The doctrine was evidently a product of the inflation that followed the suspension of specie payments by the Bank of England in 1797 and formed a part of the Bullionist Controversy, which is of such great importance in the history of the theory of international trade (*ibid.*, pp. 119–120). The doctrine had previously been stated in France in G. de Saint Peravy, *Principes du commerce opposé au trafic*, pt. 1 (Paris, 1786), pp. 80–83 (Viner, *Studies*, p. 188, n. 4). Viner points out that an abstract of the doctrine appeared in 1825 in Bentham's *The Rationale of Reward* (London, 1825), pp. 312–313 (*Studies*, p. 188, n. 8).

on the part of the receivers of fixed incomes, "not in the monetary sense of an increase in the amount of unspent funds, but in the opposite sense of a decrease in the amount of real consumption while money expenditures are maintained."[28] The entrepreneur is a beneficiary of this process. As Malthus put it, "All those who sell as well as buy, are, during the progressive rise of prices, making unusual profits."[29]

The profit inflation theory differs from the doctrine of forced-saving in ignoring all the receivers of fixed or flexible incomes except the workers. It also ignores the prices of all the factors of production except labor.

The profit inflation theory has received support and a broad theoretical rationale from Lord Keynes. In *A Treatise on Money*, his most mature work, Keynes stated that "it is the teaching of this treatise that the wealth of nations is enriched, not during Income Inflations, but during Profit Inflations—at times, that is to say, when prices are running away from costs."[30] His views on wages are also similar to Hamilton's: "A relatively low level of real wages is necessarily a characteristic of a period of Profit Inflation because it is partly at the expense of current consumption that the abnormal growth of capital-wealth which accompanies a Profit Inflation is derived."[31]

---

[28] Viner, *Studies*, pp. 187–188.

[29] "Depreciation of Paper Currency," *Edinburgh Review*, XVII (Feb. 1811), pp. 364–365, as quoted in Niebyl, *Studies*, p. 76.

[30] *A Treatise on Money* (New York, 1930), II, 154. According to R. F. Harrod, the author of an excellent biography of Keynes, the *Treatise on Money* "was the work of a lifetime, not of five years only. It is his most mature work. . . . There is . . . something to be said for the view that the student of the future, if he had to choose among Keynes' works, would get the best picture of his total contribution of economics in the Treatise" (*The Life of John Maynard Keynes* [New York, 1951], p. 403).

[31] Keynes, *Treatise on Money*, p. 162. It should be pointed out that in the very next sentence Keynes goes on to state that "it does not follow therefore that a Profit Inflation is to be desired; it is a much safer conclusion that a Profit Deflation is to be avoided." In this sentence he seems to be opting for either profit inflation or profit stability. However, this qualification seems to be pointless since profit inflation or profit deflation seem much more likely to occur than profit stability. In any case, this qualification runs counter to the general tenor of the work.

Drawing heavily on Hamilton's work on the Price Revolution, Keynes concludes that "never in the annals of the modern world has there existed so prolonged and so rich an opportunity for the business man, the speculator and the profiteer. In these golden years modern capitalism was born." [32]

The profit inflation theory has also found its way into the field of modern economic development theory. W. A. Lewis in his *Theory of Economic Growth* stated that

the fundamental explanation of any "industrial revolution," that is to say of any sudden acceleration of the rate of capital formation, is a sudden increase in the opportunities for making money. . . . The British, the Japanese, the Russian industrial revolutions all fit into this pattern. In each case the immediate result is that the benefits of rising producivity go not to the classes who would increase their consumption—peasants, wage earners—but into private profits or public taxation, where the proceeds are used for further capital formation. More and more labor is taken into wage employment, but real wages are not allowed to rise as fast as productivity.

This increase in capitalist profits is also accelerated by the inflations which occur regularly in all capitalist economies either in the mild form associated with the expansionary phase of the trade cycle or in the more virulent form associated with wars and with the extravagance of governments. Inflation raises profits relative to other incomes, and also stimulates a flight out of money into bricks and steel. . . . Most of the historical periods which are associated with rapidly increasing production and with investment rising rapidly relatively to national income and also associated with rising prices and profits—for example, the British Industrial Revolution after 1780.[33]

Although such inflation is desirable, it is neither necessary nor sufficient for Lewis. "Inflation is not an essential explanation of economic growth. Profits could grow and investment would occur even if there were no inflations. On the other hand, a little inflation from time to time increases profits and speeds up the rate of capital formation." [34]

Persuasive as the profit inflation theory seems to be, it does not hold up under close scrutiny. The theory's claim to be a historical generali-

---

[32] *Ibid.*, p. 159.

[33] Page 235. This book is a good standard advanced textbook. One of Hamilton's articles on profit inflation appears in Lewis' bibliography.

[34] *Ibid.*, p. 236.

zation is based largely on the supposed similarity between investment during the Price Revolution and investment during the second half of the eighteenth century. Numerous weaknesses in Hamilton's analysis of the Price Revolution make the generalization untenable.

One of Hamilton's chief analytical tools is the quantity theory of money, which has been subjected to extensive criticism.[35] No attempt is made to meet this criticism. Even if the quantity theory is valid, his application of it is questionable. The quantity theory could under certain circumstances explain a correlation between changes in the price level and changes in the total amount of bullion or money in circulation. Hamilton misuses it to explain a correlation between bullion imports and changes in the price level.[36] Although such a correlation may exist, the quantity theory does not purport to explain it. In addition, the theory states that the velocity of the circulation of money and the volume of money transactions in an economy must be considered in explaining changes in the level of prices or in the volume of money or bullion. Although it is conceivable that the velocity of circulation and the volume of money transactions may not change much in the short run, it seems likely that institutional and dynamic changes over a period of a century would affect them.[37] These considerations make Hamilton's explanation of the nature of price movements during the Price Revolution suspect.

Hamilton's explanation of the relationship between prices and investment during the Price Revolution is also suspect, undermined by John U. Nef's comparative studies of the development of French and English industry in the sixteenth and seventeenth centuries, which led him to conclude that "industry was responding in different ways in the various European countries to the strains and stimuli provided by the inflow of American Treasure and the debasement of the coinage.

---

[35] For examples and references see William Howard Steiner and Eli Shapiro, *Money and Banking* (rev. ed.; New York, 1947), pp. 636–654.

[36] Ingrid Hammarström, "The 'Price Revolution' of the Sixteenth Century: Some Swedish Evidence," *Scandinavian Economic History Review*, V (1957), 121–125.

[37] *Ibid.*, pp. 123–125. The principal criticism here concerns Hamilton's *American Treasure and the Price Revolution in Spain, 1501–1560* (Cambridge, Mass., 1934) on which much of the argument in his "Profit Inflation" and "Prices and Progress" is based.

Whether or not the response took the form of greatly increased activity in sinking mining shafts and setting up new manufacturing enterprises, depended mainly on conditions independent of the Price Revolution." [38] Nef's careful use of comparisons lends authority to his conclusions, since it allows him to consider the effects of institutional differences and changes and helps to prevent all the evidence from being dominated by the strong secular trend in prices.

Ingrid Hammarström has advanced an explanation of the Price Revolution which fits the evidence better and suggests an alternative to the profit inflation theory.[39] She argues that the central fact in the Price Revolution is a greater rise in the prices of agricultural than industrial products, as a result of pressures generated by population growth. During the sixteenth and seventeenth centuries, population and agricultural price changes moved together because population growth increased the demand for food and brought into production marginal land with higher costs of production. Industrial prices rose more slowly than those of agricultural products because the supply and demand elasticities of agricultural products were lower than those of industrial goods. Profit inflation, if it occurred at all, occurred in agriculture rather than industry, since rising agricultural prices meant rising costs of production in industry.[40]

The evidence that industrial investment in the sixteenth century was independent of price movement does not mean that the bullion influx was without economic effect. For Europe as a whole, the new specie probably helped to cover a trade deficit with the East; [41] for

---

[38] "Prices and Industrial Capitalism in France and England, 1540–1640," *Essays in Economic History: Reprints Edited for the Economic History Society*, ed. E. M. Carus-Wilson, I (London, 1954), 134. This article is an attack on the profit inflation theory as stated by Hamilton in his article "American Treasure and the Rise of Capitalism," *Economica*, XXVII (1929), 338–357, and his book *American Treasure*. Nef also takes issue with Keynes's interpretation of the theory in the latter's *Treatise on Money* II, 152–163. See John U. Nef, *Industry and Government in France and England, 1540–1640* (Ithaca, N. Y., 1957) and "A Comparison of Industrial Growth in France and England from 1540 to 1640," *Journal of Political Economy*, XLIV (1936), 289–317, 505–533, and 643–666.

[39] " 'Price Revolution' of the Sixteenth Century."   [40] *Ibid.*, pp. 136–141.

[41] Charles H. Wilson, "Treasure and Trade Balances: The Mercantilist Problem," *Economic History Review*, 2nd ser., II (1949), 152–161; Charles H.

England in particular, it probably helped to cover an adverse balance with northern Europe.[42] The influx of bullion may have facilitated an expansion of international trade, making possible economies of scale and thereby increasing profits. This is not, however, the mechanism postulated in Hamilton's theory.

The profit inflation theory's failure to explain industrial investment during the Price Revolution destroys its validity as a historical generalization and calls into question the theory's claim to provide the basis for economic development policy in modern underdeveloped countries. As presented by Hamilton, the claim is a logical deduction from the mistaken belief in the validity of the generalization.

W. A. Lewis also favors a mild inflation resulting from a price level that rises faster than the wage level; unlike Keynes or Hamilton, however, he regards the inflation as desirable rather than necessary. He bases his concurrence on Hamilton's evidence and his own theoretical argument. His conclusion about profit inflation is contradicted by the

---

Wilson, "Treasure and Trade Balances: Further Evidence," *Economic History Review,* 2nd ser., IV (1951) , 231–242. The drain of bullion was usually to India, Turkey, the Levant, and the Baltic, and it seems possible that there was a further flow of bullion from the Baltic to the East (Wilson, "Treasure and Trade Balances: Further Evidence," pp. 235–236) .

[42] Wilson, "Treasure and Trade Balances: Further Evidence," pp. 152–161. Wilson concurs in J. M. Keynes' defense of mercantilist theory (J. M. Keynes, *The General Theory of Employment, Interest and Money* [London, 1936], pp. 333–371) and suggests thet "there were indispensable practical uses to which precious metals were put in international trade in the mercantilist period." (Wilson, "Treasure and Trade Balances: The Mercantilist Problem," pp. 152–153) . Eli Heckscher took exception to Wilson's defense of mercantilist theories in "Multilateralism, Baltic Trade, and the Mercantilists," *Economic History Review,* 2nd ser., III (1950) , 219–228. Heckscher argues that the Baltic trade was of little importance to Britain and that the loss of bullion to the Baltic as a result of an unfavorable balance of trade must have been much smaller than the gain in bullion due to the favorable balance with Holland. In his rebuttal ("Treasure and Trade Balances: Further Evidence," pp. 231–242) , Wilson argued convincingly that, small as the unfavorable balances with the Baltic were, they were of a kind that could only be settled by bullion shipments, given the conditions of the Baltic trade in the first three quarters of the eighteenth century.

actual course of relatively recent economic development in some backward countries.[43]

The profit inflation theory's failure to provide an explanation of industrial growth during the Price Revolution and its probable failure as a key to economic development policy for backward nations makes the theory suspect.

---

[43] In a number of South American countries, inflation after World War II tended to be cost rather than price inflation in the industrial sectors of their economies (Felix, "Profit Inflation," pp. 459–462). Inflationary pressure in these countries can be attributed to rising agricultural prices brought about by population growth that increases the demand for food more rapidly than agricultural output can be expanded. Rising agricultural prices result in rising wages and, at the same time, raise the costs of the agricultural inputs required by industry. Rising costs tend to depress rather than inflate profits (*ibid.*, pp. 459–460). In these countries it is necessary not to attribute gains due to foreign exchange earnings (the modern equivalent of an influx of bullion) to the inflation that may or may not accompany the acquisition of the foreign exchange (*ibid.*, p. 459). Some Latin-American countries displayed relatively high rates of export expansion and domestic investment accompanied by a low rate of inflation, while others had a low rate of export expansion and a high rate of inflation (*ibid.*, p. 461 and n. 1). Felix announced his intention of amplifying these points, but the amplification has not been found.

Appendix 2

The Total Industrial Production
of the United Kingdom, 1700-1899

TABLE 27 is based on Walther G. Hoffmann's pioneer work, *British Industry, 1700–1950*, which is still the most ambituous attempt ever made to analyze the volume of British industrial output from 1700 to 1950.[1] Because of the general difficulties inherent in any attempt to measure the volume of building in the eighteenth and nineteenth centuries and the special difficulties for the years before 1785, Hoffmann's index of the total annual industrial production (including building) is probably less accurate than the index of the total annual industrial production (excluding building) in the United Kingdom.

An examination of Hoffmann's methods and sources indicate that, because of the relative scarcity of eighteenth-century production statistics for Ireland and Scotland, for the eighteenth century the indexes are probably better measures of the growth of industrial output in

---

[1] *British Industry, 1700–1950.* For a criticism of Hoffmann's methods see Arthur D. Gayer, W. W. Rostow, and Anna Jacobson Schwartz, *The Growth and Fluctuation of the British Economy, 1790–1850* (Oxford, 1953), II, 689–692 and 714. The criticisms do not seem to be devastating. The statement that the indexes are too heavily weighted with textiles carries some weight, perhaps, but there are no alternative indexes with which to compare Hoffmann's for most of the eighteenth century. An examination of the role played by textiles in the imports and exports of England and Wales in the eighteenth century suggests that Hoffmann's weighting of textiles may not be excessive (see T. S. Ashton, "Introduction," in Elizabeth Boody Schumpeter, *English Overseas Trade Statistics, 1697–1808* [Oxford, 1960], pp. 11–12). The criticism that there is too low a conformity between the movement of Hoffmann's figures and the 1790–1850 cyclical peaks and troughs identified by Gayer, Rostow, and Schwartz does not affect the value of Hoffmann's indexes as indicators of *secular* trends.

Table 27. Average annual physical volume of industrial production,
United Kingdom, 1700–1899

Years	A Index of total industrial production (including building)	B % increase of A	C Index of total industrial production (excluding building)	D % increase of C
1700–1709	26.1		26.1	
1710–1719	29.7	13.9	29.5	12.7
1720–1729	33.3	12.2	33.4	13.4
1730–1739	34.2	2.5	34.9	4.3
1740–1749	37.0	8.2	36.1	3.6
1750–1759	40.9	10.7	41.5	14.9
1760–1769	43.9	7.3	43.6	5.0
1770–1779	50.7	14.3	49.8	14.3
1780–1789	64.5	28.6	64.3	29.2
1790–1799	90.4	40.2	89.4	39.0
1800–1809	120.8	33.6	122.0	36.4
1810–1819	148.8	23.2	150.0	23.0
1820–1829	202.6	36.1	208.1	38.7
1830–1839	281.7	39.0	304.6	46.4
1840–1849	386.8	37.3	420.0	37.9
1850–1859	537.1	38.9	584.4	39.2
1860–1869	729.9	35.9	748.8	28.1
1870–1879	955.1	30.9	986.3	37.1
1880–1889	1124.4	17.7	1205.8	22.3
1890–1899	1351.0	20.1	1413.3	17.2

Base: 1796–1800 = 100.

Source: Column A was obtained from Walther G. Hoffmann's index of the total annual industrial production (including building) of the United Kingdom (*British Industry, 1700–1950,* trans. W. O. Henderson and W. H. Chaloner [rev. ed.; Oxford, 1955] tables 54A and B, facing p. 330) by calculating the arithmetic mean for each decade and changing the base from 1913 = 100 to the arithmetic mean for 1796–1800 = 100. *Column B* was actually computed from the arithmetic means of Hoffmann's series before conversion of the base from 1913 to 1796–1800 in order to reduce the possibility of introducing an additional mechanical or human error. *Column C* was obtained from Hoffmann's index of the annual total industrial production (excluding building) for the United Kingdom (Hoffmann, *British Industry,* p. 291) by the same methods used in calculating column *A. Column D* was calculated by the same method used in obtaining column *B.*

England and Wales than in the United Kingdom.[2] This statement is not intended to convey the impression that Hoffmann's aggregate indexes are without value for the measurement of output in the United Kingdom during the eighteenth century. A perfect index of industrial production in the United Kingdom in the eighteenth century would be heavily weighted with English or English and Welsh output. All that is claimed here is that Hoffmann's indexes are better indicators for England or for England and Wales than they are for the United Kingdom.

About 1800, economic statistics in general and production data in particular began to be collected and organized on a basis that made it possible to obtain figures for the United Kingdom. For this reason Hoffmann was able to construct indexes that are, in fact, indicators of the growth of output in the United Kingdom during the nineteenth century.[3]

---

[2] For the methods see *ibid.*, pp. 1–28; for the discussion of sources see pp. 228–304. The weighting of the individual industries in the aggregate indexes can be found in *ibid.*, pp. 18–19, table 2. The weights for the period 1700–1760 are determined by the weights as calculated for 1740. For 1740, Hoffmann has eight indexes covering 47.2% of total industrial production. At least 80% of the output covered by these indexes can be clearly traced to England or England and Wales in the sense that the data used to construct the individual indexes refer to these areas rather than Great Britain or the United Kingdom. The 80% figure is the minimum; a further examination of the other indexes might raise this percentage. None of the indexes of the remaining 20% of the output is an indicator of output in Scotland or Ireland alone; all of them pertain to Great Britain or the United Kingdom. The contribution of England or of England and Wales to the industrial output of Great Britain or the United Kingdom must have been very large. Hence, 90 or 95% of that part of the output that determines the movement of the indexes can be attributed directly to England or to England and Wales.

[3] This is clearly indicated by a comparison between the areas covered by Hoffmann's indexes for 1740, which serves as his weighting year for the period 1700–1760, and those covered by his indexes for 1812, which serves as his weighting year for 1801–1830 (*ibid.*, pp. 18–19 and 227–304). See also Ashton's introduction to Schumpeter, *English Overseas Trade Statistics.*

Appendix 3

Production of Consumers' and Producers'

Goods in the United Kingdom, 1700-1899

Table 28. Average annual physical volume of consumers' and producers' goods production, United Kingdom, 1700–1899

Years	A Index of consumers' goods production	B % increase of A	C Index of producers' goods production	D % increase of C
1700–1709	26.1		27.3	
1710–1719	28.9	10.8	31.1	13.9
1720–1729	32.2	11.2	36.7	18.3
1730–1739	33.5	4.2	38.3	4.1
1740–1749	35.1	4.8	38.3	0.0
1750–1759	41.0	16.9	47.0	22.8
1760–1769	42.7	3.9	54.6	16.1
1770–1779	48.5	13.6	62.5	14.6
1780–1789	64.7	33.6	68.6	9.7
1790–1799	89.5	38.3	89.0	29.8
1800–1809	124.0	38.5	117.4	31.9
1810–1819	152.9	23.3	143.2	21.9
1820–1829	209.6	37.1	203.8	42.3
1830–1839	304.7	45.4	304.9	49.6
1840–1849	389.2	27.7	487.9	60.0
1850–1859	506.7	30.2	762.9	56.4
1860–1869	588.6	16.1	1126.1	47.6
1870–1879	767.4	30.4	1547.4	37.4
1880–1889	870.8	13.5	2018.6	30.5
1890–1899	1019.4	17.1	2381.8	18.0

Base: 1796–1800 = 100.

Source: Based on Walther G. Hoffman, *British Industry, 1700–1950*, trans. W. O. Henderson and W. H. Chaloner (rev. ed.; Oxford, 1955). The comments on Hoffmann's work made in Appendix 2 apply equally to this

Appendix. *Column A* was obtained from Hoffmann's index of the annual industrial consumers' goods production of the United Kingdom by calculating the arithmetic mean for each decade and changing the base from 1913 = 100 to the arithmetic mean for 1796–1800 = 100. *Column B* was actually computed from the arithmetic means of Hoffmann's series before conversion of the base from 1913 to 1796–1800 in order to reduce the possibility of introducing an additional mechanical or human error. *Column C* was obtained from Hoffmann's index of the annual industrial production of producers' goods in the United Kingdom by the same methods used in calculating column *A*. *Column D* was calculated by the same methods used in calculating column *B*.

Appendix 4

The Prices of Industrial Consumers' Goods in England, 1700-1823

TABLE 29 is based on Elizabeth Boody Schumpeter's "English Prices and Public Finance, 1660–1822." She obtained her price data from the

Table 29. Prices of industrial consumers' goods, England, 1700–1823

Years	A Index of prices of consumers' goods (including cereals)	B % increase of A	C Index of prices of consumers' goods (excluding cereals)	D % increase of C
1700–1709	60		67	
1710–1719	64	7.1	70	5.2
1720–1729	60	−6.7	65	−6.9
1730–1739	54	−9.2	60	−7.5
1740–1749	57	5.6	63	4.6
1750–1759	59	2.1	62	−2.2
1760–1769	62	6.3	65	4.5
1770–1779	68	9.8	69	7.5
1780–1789	73	6.3	75	8.0
1790–1799	85	16.8	86	14.8
1800–1809	116	36.7	110	28.2
1810–1819	124	7.4	122	10.7
1820–1823	85	−31.9	92	−24.4

Base: October 1795–October 1800 = 100.

Source: Column A was obtained from Elizabeth Boody Schumpeter's annual index of the prices of English consumers' goods (including cereals) ("English Prices and Public Finance, 1660–1822," *Review of Economic Statistics*, XX [1938], 35) by calculating the arithmetic mean for each decade and converting the base of the series from October 1700 to October 1701 = 100 to the arithmetic mean of October 1795 to October 1800

then unpublished work of Sir William Beveridge *et al.*[1] Because the Beveridge statistics cover harvest years running from October to October, Mrs. Schumpeter's annual figures and her base year cover the last three months in one year and the first nine months in the following year. I have designated October 1699 to October 1709, for example, as 1700–1709 in order to keep the price data as nearly comparable to other data as is possible. Since decennial averages are used, the error thus introduced is probably quite small. Decennial averages also reduce the possible error due to the use of wholesale contract prices by Beveridge and Mrs. Schumpeter.

= 100. *Column B* was actually computed from the decennial arithmetic means of Mrs. Schumpeter's figures (before the base was changed) in order to reduce the possibility of introducing an additional error. *Column C* was calculated from Mrs. Schumpeter's annual index of the English prices of consumers' goods (exclusive of cereals) by the same methods used to obtain the figures in column *A*. *Column D* was obtained by the same methods used in calculating the figures in column *B*.

---

[1] *Prices and Wages in England from the Twelfth to the Nineteenth Century,* Vol. I (London, 1939) .

Appendix 5

The Prices of Industrial Producers' Goods

in England, 1700-1801

Table 30. Prices of industrial
producers' goods, England, 1700–1801

Years	A Index of prices o producers' goods	B % increase of A
1700–1709	74	
1710–1719	70	−5.0
1720–1729	67	−4.2
1730–1739	64	−4.4
1740–1749	67	4.6
1750–1759	66	−1.1
1760–1769	74	11.1
1770–1779	74	0.0
1780–1789	82	13.0
1790–1799	90	9.8
1800–1801	112	24.4

Base: October 1795–October 1800 = 100.

Source: Based on Elizabeth Boody (Schumpeter), "English Prices and Public Finance, 1660–1822," *Review of Economic Statistics,* XX (1938), p. 35. The remarks made in Appendix 4 apply here also. *Column A* is based on Mrs. Schumpeter's annual index of the English prices of producers' goods and was obtained by calculating the arithmetic mean for each decade and converting the resulting figures from the base October 1700 to October 1901 = 100 to the arithmetic mean October 1795 to October 1800 = 100. *Column B* was calculated from the arithmetic mean for each decade (before changing the base) in order to reduce the possibility of introducing an additional error.

Appendix 6

The Level of General Prices in the United Kingdom, 1790-1899

TABLE 31 is based on S. S. Kuznets' *Secular Movements in Production and Prices,* which used the series prepared by W. S. Jevons and A. Sauerbeck.[1]

It is necessary to account for a discrepancy in the movements of the eighteenth- and nineteenth-century indexes in those decades in the early nineteenth century for which they overlap. The indexes of average annual English consumers' goods prices (including and excluding cereals) show an increase in 1810–1819 (see Appendixes 3 and 4), while the index of the general level of average annual prices in the United Kingdom shows a decrease (see Table 31). The discrepancy is an illustration of the general disagreement about the course of prices in the early nineteenth century. Price indexes covering this period have been constructed by Kuznets, Jevons, Kondratieff, Rousseaux, Silberling, and Gayer, Rostow, and Schwartz.[2] All these indexes show prices secularly rising to some time between 1809 and 1814 and secu-

---

[1] W. S. Jevons, "On the Variation of Prices and the Value of Currency since 1782," *Investigations in Currency and Finance,* ed. H. S. Foxwell (London, 1884), pp. 119–150; A. Sauerbeck, "Prices of Commodities and the Precious Metals," *Journal of the Statistical Society,* XLIX (1886), 648–649.

[2] Kuznets, *Secular movements,* pp. 429–432; Jevons, "On the Variation of Prices," pp. 119–150; N. D. Kondratieff, "Die Preisdynamik der industriellen und landwirtschaftlichen Waren" *Archiv für Sozialwissenschaft und Sozialpolitik,* LX (1928), 1–85 (figures on p. 72); P. Rousseaux, *Les Mouvements de fond de l'économie anglaise, 1800–1913* (Louvain, 1938), pp. 72–79 and 262–267; Norman J. Silberling, "British Prices and Business Cycles, 1779–1850," *Review of Economic Statistics,* V (1923), 232–233; Arthur D. Gayer, W. W. Rostow, and Anna Jacobson Schwartz, *The Growth and Fluctuation of the British Economy, 1790–1850* (Oxford, 1953), I, 459–528 (indexes on pp. 468–470).

Table 31. Level of general prices,
United Kingdom, 1790–1899

Years	A Index of the general level of prices	B % increase of A
1790–1799	85.6	
1800–1809	106.4	24.3
1810–1819	95.2	−10.5
1820–1829	72.8	−23.4
1830–1839	65.6	−9.9
1840–1849	60.0	−8.5
1850–1859	60.0	0.0
1860–1869	64.0	6.7
1870–1879	63.2	−1.3
1880–1889	49.6	−21.5
1890–1899	43.2	−12.9

Base: 1796–1800 = 100.

Source: Column A was obtained from Kuznets'
annual index of the general level of prices in the
United Kingdom (*Secular Movements in Production
and Prices: Their Nature and Their Bearing upon
Cyclical Fluctuations* [New York, 1930], pp. 427–
432) by calculating the arithmetic mean for each
decade and changing the base of the series from
1782 = 100 to the arithmetic mean of 1796–
1800 = 100. *Column B* was actually calculated
from the arithmetic means (before changing the
base) in order to reduce the possibility of introducing an additional error.

larly falling for the rest of the first half of the nineteenth century.
Whether or not the decade 1810–1819 shows a fall or a rise in prices
depends on when the peak is reached and how the index is constructed. The Kuznets, Jevons, Kondratieff, and Rousseaux indexes
reach their peaks in 1809; the Gayer, Rostow, and Schwartz index
reaches its peak in 1813; and the Silberling index, in 1814.

Mrs. Schumpeter's indexes, on which the eighteenth-century indexes
used here are based, reach their peak in the harvest years of 1812–1813

and 1814–1815.[3] On the other hand, the peaks of the individual price series on which the various indexes are based are scattered over the comparatively long period 1799 to 1825.[4] Hence the selection of the component series for each of these indexes has a considerable effect on whether or not the average of the annual figures for 1810–1819 will show a decrease over the average for the previous decade. The choice of components for each of the indexes was a function of the availability of data, the purpose for which the index was to be used, and the period the index was intended to cover. Given the need for an index covering the entire nineteenth century, the discrepancy could not be eliminated by choosing another index for the nineteenth century. The only other index covering the entire century is Rousseaux's and it behaves in the same way as Kuznets' index.[5]

---

[3] The annual figures appear in Elizabeth Boody (Schumpeter), "English Prices and Public Finance, 1660–1822," *Review of Economic Statistics,* XX (1938), 35.

[4] Gayer, Rostow, and Schwartz, *Growth and Fluctuation,* I, 817–18. Raw cotton reached its secular peak in 1799; pig iron reached its secular peak in 1825.

[5] The argument in *ibid.,* pp. 509–528, is generally followed here.

Appendix 7

The Estimated Value of the Production

of Industrial Consumers' Goods

in England and Wales, 1700-1819

THE multiplication of a price index that pertains to England by a volume of output index that purports to refer to the United Kingdom to get a value index for England and Wales in Table 32 is justified.

Table 32. Estimated value of average annual production of industrial consumers' goods, England and Wales, 1700–1819

Years	A Index of volume of production of consumers' goods	B Index of consumers' goods prices, England	C Index of the value of consumers' goods production ([A × B]/100)	D % increase of C
1700–1709	26	60	15.6	
1710–1719	29	64	18.6	12.8
1720–1729	32	60	19.2	3.2
1730–1739	34	54	18.4	−4.2
1740–1749	35	57	20.0	8.7
1750–1759	41	59	24.2	21.0
1760–1769	43	62	26.7	10.3
1770–1779	49	68	33.3	24.7
1780–1789	65	73	47.5	42.6
1790–1799	90	85	76.5	61.1
1800–1809	124	116	143.8	88.0
1810–1819	153	124	189.7	31.9

Base: A—1796–1800 = 100; *B*—October 1795–October 1800 = 100.
Source: Column A is based on Appendix 3 and refers to the United Kingdom. *Column B* is based on Appendix 4 and refers to England. The index of the English prices of consumers' goods (including cereals) is used instead of the index of the English prices of consumers' goods (excluding cereals) because Hoffmann's index of the volume of industrial consumers'

The volume index actually is a better indicator for eighteenth-century England and Wales than for the United Kingdom (see Appendix 2). The index of English prices can serve as an index of prices in England and Wales. The relative isolation of Wales might have tended to produce a different price level there from the one prevailing in England. On the other hand, this tendency may have been largely counteracted by political integration and by the inclusion of England and Wales in the same customs systems.[1] In addition, English prices would heavily outweigh Welsh prices in a weighted index of the level prices in England and Wales. This consideration reduces the importance of a possible difference between prices in Wales and in England.

---

goods production includes processed foodstuffs. *Column C* is obtained by multiplying the figures in *A* by the figures in *B* for each decade and deflating the product by dividing by 100 in order to keep the base at 1796–1800 = 100. The deflated products are an index of the value of the average annual output of consumers' goods at English prices. *Column D* was calculated from column *C*.

---

[1] T. S. Ashton, "Introduction," in Elizabeth Boody Schumpeter, *English Overseas Trade Statistics, 1697–1808* (Oxford, 1960).

Appendix 8

The Estimated Value of the Production of Industrial Producers' Goods in England and Wales, 1700-1799

Table 33. Estimated value of average annual production of industrial producers' goods, England and Wales, 1700–1799

Years	A Index of physical volume of production of producers' goods	B Index of producers' goods prices	C Index of value of producers' goods production ($[A \times B]/100$)	D % increase of C
1700–1709	27	74	20.0	
1710–1719	31	70	21.7	8.5
1720–1729	37	67	24.8	14.3
1730–1739	38	64	24.3	−2.0
1740–1749	38	67	25.5	4.9
1750–1759	47	66	31.0	21.6
1760–1769	55	74	40.7	31.3
1770–1779	63	74	46.6	14.5
1780–1789	69	82	56.6	21.5
1790–1799	89	90	80.1	41.5

Base: A—1796–1800 = 100; *B*—October 1795–October 1800 = 100.

Source: Column A is based on Appendix 3 and refers to the United Kingdom. *Column B* is based on Appendix 5 and refers to England. *Column C* is obtained by multiplying the figure in *A* by the figure in *B* for each decade and deflating the result by dividing by 100. *Column D* was calculated from column *C*. The justification for multiplying the price-index figures for England by the volume of output-index figures for the United Kingdom to get a value of output index for England and Wales is given in Appendix 7.

Appendix 9

The Population of England
and Wales, 1700-1901

THE first census in the British Isles was taken in 1801 and covered Great Britain. The first census for the United Kingdom was taken in 1821. A population series for Britain in the eighteenth century must,

Table 34. Population of England and Wales in selected years, 1700–1901

Year		Population (in millions)	Year		Population (in millions)
1700		5.835	1801	*c*	9.193
1710		6.013	1801	*d*	9.677
1720		6.048	1801	*e*	9.29
1730		6.008	1811		10.468
1740		6.013	1821		12.190
1750		6.253	1831		14.701
1760		6.665	1841		16.050
1770		7.124	1851		17.928
1780		7.581	1861		20.066
1790		8.216	1871		22.712
1795		8.656	1881		25.974
1801	*a*	8.893	1891		29.003
1801	*b*	9.168	1901		32.528

therefore, be based upon estimates. The estimates should cover the entire country, and, if possible, they should be compatable with the nineteenth-century census figures.

There are no continuous series of accurate population estimates for the United Kingdom, Great Britain, or Scotland in the eighteenth century. There is a continuous series of estimates for Ireland, but it is not of much use here.[1] It might be possible to construct a population

---

[1] K. H. Connell, *The Population of Ireland, 1750–1845* (Oxford, 1950), p. 25, table 4. The estimates were constructed with great ingenuity.

series for England, Wales, and Ireland, but since there seem to be very few other economic series for England, Wales, and Ireland, such a population series would serve little purpose. In addition, the Irish estimates are for unevenly spaced years and were constructed by methods substantially different from those used in making the best estimates for England and Wales. Although Connell's estimates may well be the best that can be made for Ireland, they are probably a good deal less accurate than those for England and Wales. Hence there is a likelihood that a series of estimates for England, Wales, and Ireland would be less accurate than the existing estimates for England and Wales.

The best available continuous series of estimates covering England and Wales during the entire eighteenth century still seems to be the one constructed by G. Talbot Griffith.[2] The above estimates for 1770–1795 and figure *b* for 1801 are his. Since the publication of these estimates, several attempts have been made to partly or wholly replace them. Notable among these revisions are the ones made by T. H. Marshall,[3] J. T. Krause,[4] and G. Ohlin;[5] of these, only Ohlin's un-

---

[2] *Population Problems of the Age of Malthus* (Cambridge, 1926), p. 18, table 3.

[3] "The Population of England and Wales from the Industrial Revolution to the World War," *Essays in Economic History: Reprints Edited for the Economic History Society*, ed. E. M. Carus-Wilson, I (London, 1954), 331–343. His figures for the nineteeth century appear in *ibid*, p. 343. His suggestions for revision of the figures for the latter part of the eighteenth century are to be found in *ibid.*, and in his "The Population Problem during the Industrial Revolution: A Note on the Present State of the Controversy," *Essays*, ed. Carus-Wilson, I, 306–330. Marshall did not actually construct a new series, but he criticized and explained existing ones.

[4] "Changes in English Fertility and Mortality, 1781–1850," *Economic History Review*, 2nd ser., XI (1958), 52–70. His estimates for the census years 1801–1841 are in *ibid.*, p. 60, table 2. His suggestions for revision of the estimates for the last part of the eighteenth century are scattered through the article.

[5] I wish to thank Professor Ohlin for lending me the results of his calculations. They will be published shortly. His estimates are based on D. V. Glass's revision of Gregory King's estimate for the end of the seventeenth century and on upward revision of the census figures for 1801–1841 to allow for inevitable omissions. Between 1701 and 1801, Ohlin's figures are based on the same parish-register abstracts used by Griffith (and others before him). Ohlin, however, uses a new method to fix the corrections necessary to take account of the deficiencies of the baptism and burials in the registers.

published figures cover the entire eighteenth century and practical considerations make it impossible to use his estimates at present.[6] This consideration makes it necessary to use Griffith's series for the eighteenth century.

Table 35. Various population series for England and Wales, 1801–1841

Year	a Marshall (Census Report of 1851) *	b Griffith (Rickman) *	c Final official figure *	d Krause *	e Ohlin*
1801	8.89(L) †	9.17	9.19	9.68(H) †	9.29
1811	10.16(L) †	10.49	10.47	10.79(H) †	10.57
1821	12.00(L) †	12.22	12.19	12.31(H) †	12.31(H) †
1831	13.90(L) †	13.90(L) †	14.70(H) †	14.21	14.21
1841	15.91(L) †	15.91(L) †	16.05	16.21(H) †	16.21(H) †

* In millions.
† H = high for the year; L = low for the year.
Source: See the sources given for figures 1801 a, b, c, d, and e in Table 34.

The census figures for 1851–1901 have not been subjected to criticism and are accepted here without discussion.

The census figures for 1801–1841 have been questioned, and a number of alternative estimates have been constructed for these years. The results of these estimates depend in part on the correction made in the first census.

The sources of the five estimates of the population of England and Wales in 1801 are as follows:

1801 a: Adopted by Marshall from the Census Report of 1851.[7]

---

[6] The use of the figures would require a detailed study of the way in which they were obtained. Such a study will not be possible until the figures are published.

[7] Great Britain, Parliamentary Papers, Census Report of 1851 (Accounts and Papers of 1851), LXXXV (1852–1853), p. xxxiii. Marshall does not give this report as his source, but it is the place where his figures for 1801–1841 first appeared; he evidently got the figures from a later reprint of the figures.

1801 *b:* Adopted by Griffith from Rickman's correction of the Enumeration Abstracts.[8]

1801 *c:* The final official correction.[9]

1801 *d:* Krause's correction of *c*.[10]

1801 *e:* Ohlin's unpublished estimate.[11]

Each of these figures is the first of a series of estimates covering the census years 1801–1841. Each of the series tends to converge toward the final revised official figure for 1851 with Marshall's and Griffith's series approaching it from below and the others from above.

There are a number of reasons for using the final corrected official figures for the years 1801 through 1841 in constructing a population index. Because the difference between 1801 *b* and 1801 *c* is negligible, it is possible to link Griffith's eighteenth-century estimates to the final official figures without much risk of a large error. This is particularly important because the base of the index is to be 1796–1800. The use of the final official estimates is also suggested by the relative sizes of the various estimates. As a rule Marshall's and Griffith's figures are below and Ohlin and Krause's above the final official figures. In view of the widely different methods used in arriving at or defending the various series, the selection of the official figures as a sort of compromise seems justified. The weakest figure in the series is likely to be the one for 1831.

The figures selected for calculating the population index are those shown above except for 1801 *a, d,* and *e.* Those for 1700–1795 and 1801 *b* are Griffith's; 1801 *c* and 1811–1901 are the final corrected official census figures. The methods of computing the index and the results of the calculations appear below as Appendix 10.

---

[8] John Rickman was a civil servant working for the House of Commons. He devised the methods by which the first four censuses were taken and prepared the Census Reports (Griffith, *Population Problems,* p. 4). Rickman corrected the figures in the Enumeration Abstracts for 1801 and 1811 by adding one-thirtieth for absentees. For 1821, he added one-fiftieth. The difference between the first two additions and the third was the result of peace and a decrease in the armed forces. No additions were made for 1831 and 1841. Griffith accepts the changes made by Rickman and the unchanged figures for 1831 and 1841 (*ibid.,* p. 21).

[9] In Krause, "Changes in English Fertility," p. 60, table 2.

[10] *Ibid.*

[11] For sources see notes 2 to 5 above.

Appendix 10

The Population of England
and Wales, 1700-1899

Table 36. Population of England and Wales, 1700–1899

Years	A Average Population (estimated in millions)	B Index of A*	C % increase of B
1700–1709	5.915	66.4	
1710–1719	6.029	67.7	2.0
1720–1729	6.030	67.7	0.0
1730–1739	6.010	67.4	−0.4
1740–1749	6.121	68.7	1.9
1750–1759	6.438	72.2	5.1
1760–1769	6.872	77.1	6.8
1770–1779	7.330	82.3	6.7
1780–1789	7.867	88.3	7.3
1790–1799	8.605	96.6	9.4
1800–1809	9.639	108.2	12.0
1810–1819	11.071	124.2	14.8
1820–1829	13.069	146.7	18.1
1830–1839	14.734	165.3	12.7
1840–1849	16.707	187.5	13.4
1850–1859	18.676	209.6	11.8
1860–1869	20.992	235.6	12.4
1870–1879	23.854	267.7	13.6
1880–1889	27.034	303.4	13.3
1890–1899	30.237	339.3	11.8

* Base: 1796–1800 = 100.

Source: The methods of calculation used are dictated by the need to obtain percentage increases in population that are comparable to percentage increases in various types of production. Column A was calculated from selected figures in Appendix 9 above. The figures for 1700–1709 through 1780–1789 were calculated by linear interpolation of the figures for each year and obtaining the arithmetic mean for each decade. The percentage increases for 1790–1799 were calculated in the same way, except that annual figures were interpolated between 1790 and 1795 and 1795 and 1801 *b*. The arithmetic mean was then taken for 1790–1799. The base 1796–1800 = 100 was calculated by interpolating between 1795 and 1801 *b* and taking the arithmetic mean for 1796–1800. The figure for 1800–1809 was obtained by extrapolating from 1801 *c* to get 1800, after interpolating between 1801 *c* and 1811 to get the annual figures for 1801–1809. The arithmetic mean of 1800–1809 was then taken. The figures for 1810–1819 through 1890–1899 were obtained by interpolation and taking the arithmetic mean. *Column B* was obtained by dividing *A* by the base. *Column C* was calculated as the percentage increase of the average for one decade over the preceding decade.

Appendix 11

Yield on 3 Per Cent Government Securities, 1731-1900

Table 37. Average annual yield on 3% government securities, 1731–1900

Year	% yield	Year	% yield	Year	% yield	Year	% yield
1731	3.1	1761	3.9	1791	3.6	1821	4.1
1732	3.0	1762	4.3	1792	3.3	1822	3.8
1733	3.1	1763	3.4	1793	4.0	1823	3.8
1734	3.2	1764	3.6	1794	4.4	1824	3.3
1735	3.2	1765	3.4	1795	4.5	1825	3.5
1736	2.9	1766	3.4	1796	4.8	1826	3.8
1737	2.8	1767	3.4	1797	5.9	1827	3.6
1738	2.9	1768	3.3	1798	5.9	1828	3.5
1739	3.1	1769	3.5	1799	5.1	1829	3.3
1740	3.0	1770	3.6	1800	4.7	1830	3.5
1741	3.0	1771	3.5	1801	4.9	1831	3.8
1742	3.0	1772	3.3	1802	4.2	1832	3.6
1743	3.0	1773	3.5	1803	5.0	1833	3.4
1744	3.2	1774	3.4	1804	5.3	1834	3.3
1745	3.5	1775	3.4	1805	5.0	1835	3.3
1746	3.5	1776	3.5	1806	4.9	1836	3.4
1747	3.7	1777	3.8	1807	4.9	1837	3.3
1748	3.5	1778	4.5	1808	4.6	1838	3.2
1749	3.0	1779	4.9	1809	4.6	1839	3.3
1750	3.0	1780	4.9	1810	4.5	1840	3.4
1751	3.0	1781	5.2	1811	4.7	1841	3.4
1752	2.9	1782	5.3	1812	5.1	1842	3.3
1753	2.9	1783	4.8	1813	4.9	1843	3.2
1754	2.9	1784	5.4	1814	4.9	1844	3.0
1755	3.3	1785	4.8	1815	4.5	1845	3.1
1756	3.5	1786	4.1	1816	5.0	1846	3.1
1757	3.3	1787	4.1	1817	4.1	1847	3.4
1758	3.2	1788	4.0	1818	3.9	1848	3.5
1759	3.6	1789	3.9	1819	4.2	1849	3.2
1760	3.8	1790	3.9	1820	4.4	1850	3.1

Table 37 (continued)

Year	% yield	Year	% yield	Year	% yield	Year	% yield
1851	3.1	1861	3.3	1871	3.2	1881	3.0
1852	3.0	1862	3.2	1872	3.2	1882	3.0
1853	3.1	1863	3.2	1873	3.2	1883	3.0
1854	3.3	1864	3.3	1874	3.2	1884	3.0
1855	3.3	1865	3.4	1875	3.2	1885	3.0
1856	3.2	1866	3.4	1876	3.2	1886	3.0
1857	3.3	1867	3.2	1877	3.2	1887	3.0
1858	3.1	1868	3.2	1878	3.2	1888	3.0
1859	3.2	1869	3.2	1879	3.1	1889	2.8
1860	3.2	1870	3.2	1880	3.1	1890	2.9
1891	2.9						
1892	2.8						
1893	2.8						
1894	2.7						
1895	2.6						
1896	2.5						
1897	2.5						
1898	2.5						
1899	2.6						
1900	2.8						

Source: The yields for 1731–1800 are from T. S. Ashton, *An Economic History of England: The 18th Century* (London, 1955), p. 251; those for 1801–1900 are from G. R. Warren and F. A. Pearson, *Gold and Prices* (London, 1935), p. 403. For the years 1731–1757, the prices used were prices for the 3% annuities; for the years 1758–1800 the prices used were the prices for the 3% consolidated stock. The yields for the years 1801–1900 are also for the consolidated stock.

Appendix 12

McConnel and Kennedy's Net Worth, Drawings, and Profits

Table 38. Increases in McConnel and Kennedy's net worth, drawings, and profits

Year ending Dec. 31	A Net worth (£)	B Increase of A over previous year (£)	C % increase	D Kennedy's drawings (£)	E McConnel's drawings (£)	F Total drawings (£)	G Profits (B + F) (£)	H % rate of profit
1796 *	7,026	5,257 *	297 *					
1797	9,312	2,286	33					
1798	10,964	1,642	18					
1799	15,274	4,320	39					
1800	21,763	6,489	42					
1801	29,733	7,770	36					
1802	40,477	10,744	36					
1803	47,389	6,912	18	916	441	1,357	8,269	20
1804	62,363	14,974	32	642	1,694	2,336	17,310	37
1805	67,207	4,884	8	2,356	3,097	5,453	10,297	17
1806	68,207	1,704	3	1,039	3,622	4,661	6,365	9
1807	75,038	6,127	9	1,719	2,319	4,038	10,165	15
1808	79,637	4,599	6	1,905	1,454	3,359	7,958	11
1809	78,632	−1,005	−1					
1810	88,374	9,742	12					
Totals				8,577	12,627	21,204	60,364	

* Covers 22 months: March 1, 1795–December 31, 1796.

Source: McConnel and Kennedy MSS, Ledgers, Lewis Library of Congress, University of M

Appendix 13

The Physical Volume of Production

of Cotton Yarn and Piece Goods

in the United Kingdom, 1700-1899

Table 39. Average annual physical volume of production of cotton yarn and piece goods, United Kingdom, 1700–1899

Year	A Index of cotton yarn production *	B % increase of A	C Index of cotton piece goods production *	D % increase of C
1700–1709	2.9			
1710–1719	3.5	20.0		
1720–1729	4.1	16.7		
1730–1739	4.7	14.3		
1740–1749	5.9	25.0		
1750–1759	7.6	30.0		
1760–1769	9.4	23.1		
1770–1779	12.9	37.5		
1780–1789	42.4	227.3		
1790–1799	69.4	63.9		
1800–1809	156.5	125.4	149.4	115.3
1810–1819	238.8	52.6	226.5	51.6
1820–1829	450.6	88.7	382.4	68.8
1830–1839	866.5	92.3	690.6	80.6
1840–1849	1422.4	64.2	1142.4	65.4
1850–1859	2150.0	51.2	1863.5	63.1
1860–1869	2189.4	1.8	1988.8	6.7
1870–1879	3260.0	48.9	2920.6	46.9
1880–1889	3941.0	20.9	3591.8	24.1
1890–1899	4418.8	12.1	4154.1	15.7

* Base: 1796–1800 = 100.

Source: Column A is based on Walther G. Hoffmann's index of the volume of output of cotton yarn (*British Industry, 1700–1950,* trans. W. O. Henderson and W. H

Chaloner [Oxford, 1955], tables 54A and B, facing p. 330). It was calculated by taking the arithmetic mean of Hoffmann's annual index and changing the base from 1913 = 100 to 100 = the average for 1796–1800. (For the sources on which Hoffmann's index is based and a discussion of method, see *ibid.*, pp. 254–255.) *Column B* was calculated from the decennial averages of Hoffmann's figures before the base was changed in order to reduce the possibility of human or mechanical error. *Column C* is based on Hoffmann's index of the output of cotton cloth (*ibid.*, tables 54A and B) by the same method as that used to calculate column *A*. The figures for 1700–1709 through 1790–1799 were omitted. They are identical to column *A* and assume yarn production is an index of cloth production. This assumption is inaccurate, since it ignores mixing of yarns in the production of "Cotton" cloth—a practice which was prevalent up to the 1780's. (For Hoffmann's discussion of sources and methods, see *ibid.*, pp. 255–257.) *Column D* was calculated by the same method used in calculating column *B*.

Appendix 14

Raw-Cotton Imports, Re-exports, and Consumption in England and Wales, 1700-1799

Table 40. Average annual raw-cotton imports, re-exports, and consumption, England and Wales, 1700–1799

Years	A Raw cotton imports (millions of lbs.)	B % increase of A	C Raw cotton re-exports (millions of lbs.)	D % increase of C	E Con-sump-tion of Raw cotton (A-C)	F % increase of E
1700–1709	1.33		.08		1.23	
1710–1719	1.63	22.6	.15	87.5	1.54	25.2
1720–1729	1.66	1.8	.05	−66.7	1.61	4.5
1730–1739	1.86	12.0	.12	140.0	1.75	8.7
1740–1749	2.26	21.5	.13	8.3	2.16	23.4
1750–1759	3.04	34.5	.19	46.2	2.85	31.9
1760–1769	3.78	24.3	.30	57.9	3.48	22.1
1770–1779	5.20	37.6	.42	40.0	4.78	37.4
1780–1789	15.15	191.3	.41	−2.4	14.74	208.4
1790–1799	28.78	90.0	.92	124.4	27.92	89.4

Source: Column A was calculated from the annual figures compiled by Elizabeth Boody Schumpeter (English Overseas Trade Statistics, 1697–1808 [Oxford, 1960], pp. 61–62, table 18) by taking the arithmetic mean for each decade. (For the sources from which Mrs. Schumpeter's table was compiled, see T. S. Ashton's introduction.) Column B was calculated from column A. Column C was calculated from Mrs. Schumpeter's annual figures in the same way as column A. Column D was calculated from column C. Column E was calculated from Mrs. Schumpeter's annual figures in the same way as column A. Column F was calculated from column E.

Appendix 15

Per Capita Raw-Cotton Consumption in England and Wales, 1700-1799

Table 41. Per capita raw-cotton consumption, England and Wales, 1700–1799

Years	*A* Average annual consumption (millions of lbs.)	*B* Average population (millions)	*C* Average annual per capita consumption (lbs.) (*A/B*)	*D* % increase of *C*
1700–1709	1.23	5.92	0.21	
1710–1719	1.54	6.03	0.26	23.8
1720–1729	1.61	6.03	0.27	3.8
1730–1739	1.75	6.01	0.29	7.4
1740–1749	2.16	6.12	0.35	20.7
1750–1759	2.85	6.44	0.44	25.7
1760–1769	3.48	6.87	0.51	15.9
1770–1779	4.78	7.33	0.65	27.5
1780–1789	14.74	7.87	1.87	187.7
1790–1799	27.92	8.61	3.24	73.3

Source: Column A was taken from Appendix 14, Table 40, column *E. Column B* was taken from Appendix 10, Table 36, column *A. Column C* was calculated by dividing *A* by *B. Column D* was calculated from *C*.

Appendix 16

Imports of Raw Cotton into the

United Kingdom, 1781-1899

Table 42. Raw-cotton imports, United Kingdom, 1781–1899

Years	A Imports of raw cotton (millions of lbs.)	B Index of A	C % Increase in B
1781–1789	16.9	45.9	
1790–1799	29.6	79.1	75.1
1800–1809	61.7	165.0	108.4
1810–1819	105.0	441.2	70.2
1820–1829	189.6	507.0	80.6
1830–1839	354.5	947.9	87.0
1840–1849	606.5	1621.7	71.1
1850–1859	927.9	2481.0	53.0
1860–1869	1090.3	2915.2	17.5
1870–1879	1476.6	3948.1	35.4
1880–1889	1717.7	4592.8	16.3
1890–1899	1774.9	4745.7	3.3

Base: 1796–1800 = 100.

Source: Column A was calculated for each period by taking the arithmetic mean of the annual figures compiled by S. S. Kuznets (*Secular Movements in Production and Prices: Their Nature and Their Bearing upon Cyclical Fluctuations* [New York, 1930], pp. 433–436, table 27, col. 1), from E. Baines, *History of the Cotton Manufactures in Great Britain* (London, 1835), and W. Page, ed., *Commerce and Industry* (London, 1919). *Column B* was calculated from column A. *Column C* was calculated from column A to reduce the chance of introducing a mechanical or human error.

Appendix 17

The Physical Volume of Production of Linen Yarn and Linens in the United Kingdom, 1760-1899

Table 43. Physical volume of production of linen yarn and linens, United Kingdom, 1760–1899

Years	A Index of linen-yarn production	B % increase of A	C Index of linen production	D % increase of C
1760–1769	55.8		55.9	
1770–1779	64.1	14.8	64.2	14.9
1780–1789	75.2	17.4	75.2	17.2
1790–1799	94.9	26.1	94.9	26.1
1800–1809	115.3	21.5	115.4	21.7
1810–1819	128.6	11.6	128.4	11.3
1820–1829	155.6	20.9	153.4	19.5
1830–1839	195.1	25.4	174.0	13.4
1840–1849	240.0	23.0	186.3	7.0
1850–1859	242.7	1.1	183.6	−1.5
1860–1869	247.1	1.8	170.6	−7.1
1870–1879	287.4	16.3	225.0	31.9
1880–1889	239.8	−16.6	209.3	−7.0
1890–1899	231.3	−3.6	219.4	4.8

Base: 1796–1800 = 100.

Source: Column A was calculated from Walther G. Hoffmann's index of average annual linen yarn output (*British Industry, 1700–1950* [Oxford, 1955], tables 54A and B, facing p. 330) by taking the arithmetic mean for each decade after changing the base from 1913 = 100 to 100 = average for 1700–1800. (For a discussion of Hoffmann's sources and methods, see *ibid.*, pp. 265–267.) *Column B* was calculated from column A. *Column C* was calculated from Hoffmann's index of average annual linen output (*ibid.*, tables 54A and B) by the same method used in obtaining column A. (On the sources used by Hoffmann, see *ibid.*, pp. 267–269.) *Column D* was calculated from column C.

Appendix 18

The Physical Volume of Production of Woollen and Worsted Yarn and Cloth in the United Kingdom, 1740–1899

Table 44. Average annual physical volume of production of woollen and worsted yarn and cloth, United Kingdom, 1740–1899

Years	A Index of woollen and worsted yarn production	B % increase of A	C Index of woollen and worsted cloth production	D % increase of C
1740–1749			58.8	
1750–1759			64.7	10.0
1760–1769			65.4	1.0
1770–1779			73.2	12.0
1780–1789	89.0		77.8	6.3
1790–1799	96.4	7.2	94.1	21.0
1800–1809	105.8	9.7	103.2	10.4
1810–1819	117.3	10.9	112.4	8.2
1820–1829	137.4	17.2	133.3	18.6
1830–1839	171.2	24.6	163.4	22.5
1840–1849	195.7	14.3	178.4	9.2
1850–1859	235.3	20.2	200.7	12.5
1860–1869	305.8	30.0	255.6	27.4
1870–1879	414.4	35.5	365.4	43.0
1880–1889	451.8	9.0	400.7	9.7
1890–1899	533.1	18.0	460.8	15.0

Base: 1796–1800 = 100.

Source: Column A was calculated from Walther G. Hoffmann's index of the average annual woollen and worsted yarn output (*British Industry, 1700–1950* [Oxford, 1955], tables 54A and B, facing p. 330) by taking the arithmetic mean for each decade after changing the base from 1913 = 100 and to 100 = average of 1796–1800. (For Hoffmann's discussion of sources, see *ibid.*, pp. 257–259.) *Column B* was calculated from column A. *Column C* was calculated from Hoffmann's index of the average annual output of woollen and worsted cloth (*ibid.*, tables 54A and B) by the same method used in calculating column A. (For Hoffmann's discussion of sources, see *ibid.*, pp. 259–262.) *Column D* was calculated from column C.

Appendix 19

Price of Raw Cotton, 1700-1799

Table 45. Average price of raw cotton, 1700–1799

Years	A Price of raw cotton (d./lb.)	B Index of A	C % increase of A
1700–1709	7.00	24.5	
1710–1719	9.08	31.7	30
1720–1729	11.25	39.3	24
1730–1739	9.56	33.4	−15
1740–1749	14.23	49.8	49
1750–1759	16.38	57.3	15
1760–1769	15.50	54.2	−5
1770–1779	15.14	52.9	−2
1780–1789	24.09	84.2	59
1790–1799	23.35	82.7	−3

Base: 1796–1800 = 100.

Source: Based on Table 46 below. *Column A* was calculated from the scattered annual figures in Table 46 by taking the arithmetic mean. *Columns B* and *C* were calculated from column *A*.

Only scattered raw-cotton prices are available for the years before 1770 and even those are for varying grades and qualities of cotton from different sources. It has been possible to calculate raw-cotton prices in eighteen years falling between 1770–1779 on the basis of fifty-one price quotations. More, and perhaps better, price quotations are available from 1770 onward. Therefore, the decennial average before 1770–1779 is highly suspect and makes any calculation of a percentage increase in raw-cotton prices suspect; however, the figures for the percentage increase in average prices in 1780–1789 and 1790–1799 are much better.

Table 46. Average annual raw-cotton prices, 1703–1799

Year	Raw-cotton prices (d./lb.)	Year	Raw-cotton prices (d./lb.)
1703	7.00	1776	18.50
1716	9.08	1777	18.50
1723	6.25	1778	18.50
1724	17.50	1779	18.50
1729	10.00	1780	22.80
1732	12.00	1781	
1735	8.25	1782	31.00
1736	8.25	1783	24.50
1738	10.16	1784	18.50
1739	9.15	1785	21.00
1740	8.76	1786	32.00
1742	8.88	1787	26.50
1743	11.50	1788	23.50
1748	21.00	1789	17.00
1749	21.00	1790	16.50
1751	21.00	1791	21.50
1755	11.75	1792	25.00
1766	15.50	1793	17.55
1770	12.25	1794	15.00
1771	11.50	1795	21.00
1772	11.50	1796	20.50
1773	11.50	1797	24.50
1774	11.50	1798	33.50
1775	19.17	1799	38.50

Source: The prices used in Table 46 can be found in Alfred P. Wadsworth and Julia de Lacy Mann, *The Cotton Trade and Industrial Lancashire, 1600–1780* (Manchester, 1931); E. Baines, *A History of Cotton Manufacture in Great Britain* (London, 1835); Thomas Ellison, *The Cotton Trade of Great Britain: Including a History of the Liverpool Cotton Market and of the Liverpool Cotton Broker's Association* (London, 1886); and T. S. Ashton, "Some Statistics of the Industrial Revolution," *Essays in Economic History: Reprints Edited for the Economic History Society*, ed. E. M. Carus-Wilson, Vol. III (London, 1962). They are for various grades of cotton. Some price quotations were discarded because they were for exceptionally good or exceptionally bad or damaged cotton.

Appendix 20

Prices and Production in the

Cotton Industry, 1700-1899

Table 47. Percentage increases in the index of consumers' and producers' goods prices and production in the cotton industry, 1700–1799

Years	A Con- sumers' goods (including cereals), England	B Con- sumers' goods (excluding cereals), England	C Producers' goods, England	D Raw cotton con- sumption England and Wales	E Per capita raw cotton con- sumption England and Wales
1710–1719	7	5	−5	25	24
1720–1729	−7	−7	−4	5	4
1730–1739	−9	−8	−4	9	7
1740–1749	6	5	5	23	21
1750–1759	2	−2	−1	32	26
1760–1769	6	5	11	22	16
1770–1779	10	8	0	37	28
1780–1789	6	8	13	208	188
1790–1799	17	15	10	89	73

Source: Taken from Appendixes 4, 5, 14, and 15.

Table 48. Percentage increases in the index of the general level of prices and production in the cotton industry, United Kingdom, 1800–1899

Years	A General level of prices	B Cotton-yarn production	C Cotton-cloth production
1800–1809	24	125	115
1810–1819	−11	53	52
1820–1829	−24	89	69
1830–1839	−10	92	81
1840–1849	−9	64	65
1850–1859	0	51	63
1860–1869	7	2	7
1870–1879	−1	49	47
1880–1889	−22	21	24
1890–1899	−13	12	16

Source: Taken from Appendixes 6 and 13.

Appendix 21

Wages in England, 1700-1796

Table 49. Indexes of average annual wages, England, 1700–1796

	A	B	C	D	E	F	G	H
Years	London money wages	% change of A	London real wages	% change of C	Lanca-shire money wages	% change of E	Lanca-shire real wages	% change of G
1700–1709	107		108		97		99	
1710–1719	109	1.9	106	−1.9	106	9.3	103	4.0
1720–1729	110	0.9	110	3.8	122	15.1	123	19.4
1730–1739	115	4.5	129	17.3	132	8.2	145	17.9
1740–1749	117	1.7	123	−4.7	132	0	138	−4.8
1750–1759	118	0.9	117	−4.9	129	−2.3	128	−7.2
1760–1769	120	1.7	109	−6.8	157	21.7	141	10.2
1770–1779	120	0	95	−12.8	198	26.1	157	11.3
1780–1787	123	2.5	94	2.5	204	3.0	156	−0.6
1780–1789					210	6.1	160	1.9
1790–1796					231	10.0	154	−3.7

Base: 1700 = 100.

Source: Calculated from E. W. Gilboy, "Cost of Living and Real Wages in 18th Century England," *Review of Economic Statistics,* XVIII (1936), 140, table 2. She uses money-wage figures from her own *Wages in 18th Century England* (Cambridge, Mass., 1834) and gets her prices from Elizabeth Boody (Schumpeter), "English Prices and Public Finance, 1660–1822," *Review of Economic Statistics,* XX (1938), 35, table 5. The Lancashire wages are for building and road-mending laborers.

Appendix 22

Real Prices of Raw Cotton, 1700-1799

Table 50. Average real prices of raw cotton, 1700–1799

Years	A Index of price of raw cotton	B Index of consumers' goods prices	C Index of real raw- cotton prices (*A/B*)	D % increase in *C*
1700–1709	24.5	60	40.8	
1710–1719	31.7	64	49.5	21
1720–1729	39.3	60	65.5	34
1730–1739	33.4	54	61.9	−6
1740–1749	49.8	57	87.4	41
1750–1759	57.3	59	97.1	11
1760–1769	54.2	62	87.4	−10
1770–1779	52.9	68	77.8	−11
1780–1789	84.2	73	115.3	48
1790–1799	82.7	85	97.3	−16

Base: 1796–1800 = 100.

Source: Column A was taken from Appendix 19. *Column B* was taken from Appendix 4. *Column C* was obtained by dividing the figures in column *A* by those in column *B. Column D* is the percentage change of the figure in *C* for one decade over the figure for the previous decade.

The Contribution of the Cost of Raw Cotton and Waste to the Cost of Producing Yarn, 1779-1882

Table 51. Contribution of the cost of raw cotton and waste to the cost of producing yarn in various years, 1779–1882

	No. 40 yarn					No. 100 yarn				
	A	B	C	D	E	F	G	H	I	J
Years	Selling price of yarn (d./lb.)	Cost of cotton and waste (d./18 oz.)	Other costs of producing yarn (d./lb.)	B as % of A	C as % of A	Selling price of yarn (d./lb.)	Cost of cotton and waste (d./18 oz.)	Other costs of producing yarn (d./lb.)	G as % of F	H as % of F
1779	182.00	24.00	158.00	13.2	86.8					
1784	131.00	24.00	107.00	18.3	81.7					
1786						456.00	48.00	408.00	10.5	89.5
1796						228.00	42.00	186.00	18.4	81.6
1799	90.00	40.00	50.00	44.4	55.6					
1806						86.00	36.00	50.00	41.9	58.1
1812	30.00	18.00	12.00	60.0	40.0	62.00	28.00	34.00	45.2	54.8
1830	14.50	7.75	6.75	53.8	49.2	40.50	13.75	26.75	34.1	65.9
1860	11.50	6.88	4.63	60.0	40.0	28.00	11.00	17.00	39.3	60.7
1882	10.50	7.13	3.38	67.6	32.4	22.00	9.63	12.38	43.6	56.4

Source: Computed from Thomas Ellison, *The Cotton Trade of Great Britain: Including a History of the Liverpool Cotton Market and of the Liverpool Cotton Broker's Association* (London, 1886), p. 61.

Bibliography and Index

Bibliography

MANUSCRIPTS AND MANUSCRIPT COLLECTIONS

Abstract of Sir Richard Arkwright's Title to the Manor of Cromford, 1789. Additional MSS, no. 6689, f. 378, British Museum.

Arkwright Deed. Manchester Central Library.

Bentham Papers. Additional MSS, British Museum.

Burton Deeds. Manchester Central Library.

Correspondence of Samuel Crompton, 1801–1812. Egerton MSS, British Museum.

Farrer MSS. Manchester Central Library.

Graham, J. "The Chemistry of Calico Printing from 1790 to 1835 and the History of Printworks in the Manchester District from 1760 to 1846." MS book, n.d. [1847–1848], Manchester Central Library.

Huskisson Papers. Additional MSS, British Museum.

Liverpool Papers. Additional MSS, British Museum.

Lund Papers. Lewis Library of Commerce, University of Manchester.

McConnel and Kennedy MSS. Lewis Library of Commerce, University of Manchester.

Owen MSS. Manchester Central Library.

Peel Papers. Additional MSS, British Museum.

J. B. Smith MSS. Manchester Central Library.

J. B. Smith Papers. Manchester Central Library.

OFFICIAL PUBLICATIONS AND REPRINTS

Great Britain. *Hansard's Parliamentary Debates.*

Great Britain, House of Commons. *Journal of the House of Commons.*

——. *Parliamentary Papers, Report from the Select Committee on the Usury Laws, 1818.* 1845 (376/611).

——. *Report from the Select Committee on Manufactures, Commerce and Shipping.* (*Reports,* 1833 [690].) Vol. VI, pt. 1.

——. *The Report of the Committee of 1804 on the Condition of the Irish Currency.* Printed in Frank Whitson Fetter, ed., *The Irish Pound, 1797–1826* (Evanston, Ill., 1955). With selections from the minutes of evidence presented to the committee and an introduction by the editor.

Great Britain, House of Lords. *House of Lords Papers.* N.S.

Great Britain, Parliament, Select Committee on the High Price of Gold Bullion. *The Paper Pound of 1791–1821: A Reprint of the Bullion Report.* London, 1919.

Great Britain, Parliamentary Papers. *Census Report of 1851* (*Accounts and Papers of 1851*), LXXXV (1852–1853).

BOOKS AND PAMPHLETS

Published in or before 1860

Baines, E. *A History of the Cotton Manufacture in Great Britain.* London, 1835.

Baynes, A. *The Cotton Trade: Two Lectures.* London, 1857.

Bentham, Jeremy. *Manual of Political Economy,* in *The Works of Jeremy Bentham,* ed. Sir John Bowring (Edinburgh, 1843), III, 33–84.

——. *The Rationale of Reward.* London, 1825.

Brayley, Edward Wedlake, and John Britton. *The Beauties of England and Wales.* 18 vols. London, 1801–1816.

Calico Printers' Committee. *Report of the Calico Printers' Committee on Wages: Resolutions of the Meeting and List of Prices.* Manchester, 1831.

Collins, Walsingham. *Address to . . . the Representatives in Parliament for the City of London, with Proposals for the Better Regulation of Bankers and Brokers. . . . Also a Scheme for Establishing a Loan Bank.* London, 1778.

Engels, Friedrich. *Die Lage der arbeitenden Klasse in England.* Trans. and ed. W. O. Henderson and W. H. Chaloner. New York, 1958. (First printed in Leipzig, 1845.)

——. *Socialism, Utopian and Scientific.* New York, 1928.

Forbes, Sir William. *The Memoirs of a Banking House.* London, 1860.

Forsyth, R. *The Beauties of Scotland.* 5 vols. Edinburgh, 1805–1808.

Foster, Thomas Campbell. *Letters on the Condition of the People of Ireland.* 2nd ed. 8 vols. London, 1847.

Galt, John. *The Annals of the Parish,* Vol. I and part of Vol. II of *The Works of John Galt,* ed. D. S. Meldrum and William Roughead (10 vols.; Edinburgh, 1936). (First printed in 1821.)

Gaskell, P. *Artisans and Machinery: The Moral and Physical Condition of the Manufacturing Population Considered with Reference to Mechanical Substitutes for Human Labour.* London, 1836.

Henry, W. C. *A Biographical Notice of the Late Peter Ewart, Esq.* Manchester, 1844.

Hibbert-Ware, S. *Remarks on the Facility of Obtaining Commercial Credit.* Manchester, 1806.

Liverpool and Manchester Railway Company. *A Synopsis of the Proceedings Necessary in Soliciting the Bill, with Observations.* Liverpool, 1824.

Macgregor, J. *Commercial Statistics.* London, 1850.

A Manufacturer in the North of England. *A Letter to the Earl of Liverpool . . . Regarding Country Banks and the Currency in the Manufacturing Districts.* London, 1826.

McCulloch, J. R. *A Descriptive and Statistical Account of the British Empire.* 4th ed. London, 1854.

——, ed. *Early English Tracts on Commerce.* Cambridge, Eng., 1952. (First published in 1856 by the Political Economy Club, London.)

McPherson, David. *Annals of Commerce, Manufactures, Fisheries and Navigation.* 4 vols. London, 1805.

Mercator. *A Letter to the Inhabitants, of Manchester on the Exportation of Cotton Twist.* Manchester, April 28, 1800.

Munn, Thomas. *Englands' Treasure by Forraign Trade or, The Ballance of our Forraign Trade is the Rule of our Treasure.* London: J. G. for Thomas Clark, 1664. Reprinted in J. R. McCulloch, ed., *Early English Tracts on Commerce* (Cambridge, Eng., 1952).

O'Brien, Charles. *The British Manufacturer's Companion and Calico Printer's Assistant*. . . . N. pub., 1795.

Owen, Robert. *The Life of Robert Owen by Himself*. New York, 1920. (First published in 1857.)

Radcliffe, W. *Letters on the Evils of the Exportation of Cotton Yarns*. Stockport, 1811.

Rogers, J. W. *The Potato Truck System of Ireland*. . . . 2nd ed. 1847.

[Saint Peravy, G. de.] *Principes du commerce opposé au trafic*, pt. 1. Paris, 1786.

A Shareholder. *A Letter to the Trading Community of Manchester in Reference to the Principles and Practices of Joint Stock Banks*. Manchester, 1834.

Smith, Adam. *An Inquiry into the Nature and Causes of the Wealth of Nations*. Ed. E. R. A. Seligman. 1910 ed.; Everymans' Library. 2 vols. London, 1947. (First published in 1778.)

Smithers, Henry. *Liverpool, Its Commerce: With a History of the Cotton Trade*. Liverpool, 1825.

Thornton, Henry. *An Enquiry into the Nature and Effects of the Paper Credit of Great Britain*. London, 1802.

The Trial of a Cause . . . to Repeal a Patent Granted . . . in 1775 to Mr. Richard Arkwright . . . at Westminster-hall, on Saturday the 25th of June, 1785. London, 1785.

Walker, George. *Observations . . . upon . . . Exporting of Cotton Twist*. London, May 5, 1803.

Wright, John. *An Address to . . . Parliament on the late Tax . . . on Fustian and other Cotton Goods*. Warrington, 1785.

Published after 1860

Allen, R. D. G. *Statistics for Economists*. 2nd ed. London, 1951.

Ashton, T. S. *Economic Fluctuations in England, 1700–1800*. Oxford, 1959.

——. *An Economic History of England, The 18th Century*. London, 1955.

——. *Iron and Steel in the Industrial Revolution*. Manchester, 1924.

—— and R. S. Sayers, eds. *Papers in English Monetary History*. Oxford, 1953.

—— and J. Sykes. *The Coal Industry of the Eighteenth Century*.

("Victoria University of Manchester Economic History Series," no. 5.) Manchester, 1929.

Axon, William E. A. *The Annals of Manchester.* London, 1886.

Bagehot, Walter. *Lombard Street: A Description of the Money Market.* Ed. Hartley Withers. London, 1915. (First published in Leipzig, 1874.)

Beveridge, William Henry, *et al. Prices and Wages in England from the Twelfth to the Nineteenth Century.* London, 1939. Vol. I.

Bowley, Arthur Lyon. *Wages in the United Kingdom in the Nineteenth Century.* Cambridge, Eng., 1899.

Cameron, Hector Charles. *Samuel Crompton.* London, 1951.

Carus-Wilson, E. M., ed. *Essays in Economic History: Reprints Edited for the Economic History Society.* 3 vols. London, 1954 (Vol. I) and 1962 (Vols. II and III).

Chaloner, William Henry. *The History of the Cotton Manufacture in Nantwich, 1785–1874.* Nantwich, n.d. [*ca.* 1930]. Excerpt from *Johnson's Almanac.*

Chambers, J. D. *The Vale of Trent 1670–1806: A Regional Study of Economic Change.* (*Economic History Review,* supp. no. 3.) London, n.d.

Chapman, S. J. *The Lancashire Cotton Industry.* Manchester, 1904.

Cipolla, Carlo M. *The Economic History of World Population.* London, 1962.

———. *Money Prices and Civilization in the Mediterranean World: Fifth to Seventeenth Century.* Princeton, 1956.

Clapham, Sir John Harold. *The Bank of England: A History, 1694–1914.* 2 vols. Cambridge, Eng., 1944.

———. *An Economic History of Modern Britain.* Cambridge, Eng., 1939 (Vol. I), 1932 (Vol. II), 1938 (Vol. III).

Clark, G. N. *Guide to English Commercial Statistics, 1696–1782.* ("Royal Historical Society Guides and Handbooks," no. 1.) London, 1938.

———. *The Idea of the Industrial Revolution: David Murray Foundation Lecture.* ("Glasgow University Publications," no. 95.) Glasgow, 1953.

Cole, Margaret Isabel. *Robert Owen of New Lanark.* New York, 1953.

Connell, K. H. *The Population of Ireland, 1750–1845.* Oxford, 1950.

Court, W. H. B. *A Concise Economic History of Britain: From 1750 to Recent Times.* Cambridge, Eng., 1954.

Craig, Sir John. *The Mint: A History of the London Mint from A.D. 287 to 1948.* Cambridge, Eng., 1953.

Daniels, G. W. *The Early English Cotton Industry.* Manchester, 1920.

Davies, David Jeffrey. *The Economic History of South Wales Prior to 1800.* Cardiff, 1933.

Dodd, Arthur Herbert. *The Industrial Revolution in North Wales.* Cardiff, 1933.

Dubois, Armand Budington. *The English Business Company after the Bubble Act, 1720–1800.* New York, 1938.

Ellison, Thomas. *The Cotton Trade of Great Britain: Including a History of the Liverpool Cotton Market and of the Liverpool Cotton Broker's Association.* London, 1886.

Evans, George Heberton. *British Corporation Finance, 1775–1850: A Study of Preference Shares.* ("The Johns Hopkins University Studies in Historical and Political Science," extra vols., N.S., no. 23.) Baltimore, 1936.

Fay, C. R. *English Economic History: Mainly since 1700.* 2nd ed. Cambridge, Eng., 1948.

Feavearyear, A. E. *The Pound Sterling: A History of English Money.* Oxford, 1931.

Ferguson, Thomas. *The Dawn of Scottish Social Welfare: A Survey from Medieval Times to 1863.* London, 1948.

Fitton, R. S., and A. P. Wadsworth. *The Strutts and the Arkwrights, 1758–1830: A Study of the Early Factory System.* Manchester, 1958.

Gayer, Arthur D., W. W. Rostow, and Anna Jacobson Schwartz. *The Growth and Fluctuation of the British Economy, 1790–1850.* 2 vols. Oxford, 1953.

Gilboy, Elizabeth W. *Wages in 18th Century England.* Cambridge, Mass., 1934.

Goodwin, A., ed. *The European Nobility in the Eighteenth Century: Studies of the Nobilities of the Major European States in the Pre-Reform Era.* London, 1953.

Griffith, G. Talbot. *Population Problems of the Age of Malthus.* Cambridge, Eng., 1926.

Grindon, Leo H. *Manchester Banks and Bankers.* Manchester, 1877.

Grubb, Isabel. *Quakerism and Industry before 1800.* London, 1930.

Halévy, Elie. *A History of the English People in the Nineteenth Century.* 2nd ed. rev. 7 vols. London, 1949–1952.

Hamilton, Earl J. *American Treasure and the Price Revolution in Spain, 1501–1560.* Cambridge, Mass., 1934.

Hamilton, Henry. *The Industrial Revolution in Scotland.* Oxford, 1932.

Harrod, R. F. *The Life of John Maynard Keynes.* New York, 1951.

Hawtrey, R. G. *A Century of Bank Rate.* London, 1938.

——. *Currency and Credit.* 4th ed. London, 1950.

——. *The Gold Standard: In Theory and Practice.* 5th ed. London, 1947. (First published in 1927.)

Henderson, William Otto. *Britain and Industrial Europe 1750–1870; Studies in British Influence on the Industrial Revolution in Western Europe.* Liverpool, 1954.

——. *The Lancashire Cotton Famine, 1861–1865.* ("Publications of the University of Manchester Economic History Series," no. 9.) Manchester, 1934.

Hoffmann, Walther G. *British Industry, 1700–1950.* Trans. from 1939 German ed. by W. O. Henderson and W. H. Chaloner, with notes by translators and additions by author. Oxford, 1955.

Holden, J. Milnes. *The History of Negotiable Instruments in English Law.* London, 1955.

Holdsworth, Sir William Searle. *A History of English Law.* 7th ed. rev. 16 vols. Ed. A. L. Goodhart and H. G. Hanbury. London, 1938–1966.

Hope-Jones, Arthur. *Income Tax in the Napoleonic Wars.* Cambridge, Eng., 1939.

Horne, H. Oliver. *A History of Savings Banks.* London, 1947.

Hoselitz, B. *The Progress of Under-Developed Areas.* Chicago, 1953.

Imlah, Albert H. *Economic Elements in the Pax Britannica: Studies in British Foreign Trade in the Nineteenth Century.* Cambridge, Mass., 1958.

James Finlay and Company Limited: Manufacturers and East India Merchants, 1750–1950. Glasgow, 1951.

Jenks, Leland Hamilton. *The Migration of British Capital to 1875.* New York, 1927.

Jevons, William Stanley. *Investigations in Currency and Finance.* Introduction by H. S. Foxwell. London, 1884.

Keynes, John Maynard. *The General Theory of Employment, Interest and Money.* London, 1936.

——. *A Treatise on Money.* 2 vols. London, 1930.

King, W. T. C. *History of the London Discount Market.* London, 1936.

Knox, John. *A View of the British Empire, More Especially Scotland.* 3rd ed. London, 1875.

Kuznets, Simon. *Economic Change: Selected Essays in Business Cycles, National Income, and Economic Growth.* New York, 1953.

——. *Secular Movements in Production and Prices: Their Bearing upon Cyclical Fluctuations.* Boston, 1930.

Layton, Sir Walter, and Geoffrey Crowther. *An Introduction to the Study of Prices.* 3rd ed. London, 1938.

Leavens, Dickson. *Silver Money.* ("Cowles Commission for Research in Economics Monographs," no. 4.) Bloomington, Ind., 1939.

Lewis, W. Arthur. *The Theory of Economic Growth.* Homewood, Ill., 1955.

Maitland, F. W. *Maitland: Selected Essays.* Ed. Hazelton, Lapsley, and Winfield. Cambridge, Eng., 1936.

Mann, F. A. *The Legal Aspect of Money: With Special Reference to Comparative, Private, and Public International Law.* 2nd ed. Oxford, 1953.

Mantoux, Paul. *The Industrial Revolution in the Eighteenth Century: An Outline of the Beginnings of the Modern Factory System in England.* 2nd ed. rev. Trans. Marjorie Vernon. London, 1928.

Marshall, Alfred. *Principles of Economics: An Introductory Volume.* 8th ed., reprint of 1920 ed. New York, 1949.

Marwick, William Hutton. *Economic Developments in Victorian Scotland.* London, 1936.

Marx, Karl. *Capital: A Critique of Political Economy.* Ed. Frederick Engels. Vol. I: *The Process of Capitalist Production,* rev. and amplified according to 4th German ed. by Ernest Untermann and trans. from 3rd German ed. by Samuel Moore and Edward Aveling (New York, 1906). Vol. II: *The Process of Circulation of Capital,* trans. from 2nd German ed. by Ernest Untermann (Chicago, 1908). Vol. III: *The Process of Capitalist Production as a Whole,* trans. from 1st German ed. by Ernest Untermann (Chicago, 1909).

Matthews, R. C. O. *A Study in Trade-Cycle History: Economic Fluctuations in Great Britain, 1833–1842.* Cambridge, Eng., 1954.

McConnel, J. W. *A Century of Fine Cotton Spinning.* Manchester, 1906.

M'Connel and Co. *A Century of Fine Cotton Spinning.* Manchester, 1913.

Mingay, G. E. *English Landed Society in the Eighteenth Century.* London, 1963.

Mitchell, Wesley C. *Business Cycles: The Problem and Its Setting.* New York, 1927.

Morgan, E. Victor. *The Study of Prices and the Value of Money.* ("Historical Association Pamphlets," no. 53.) London, 1950.

Namier, Sir Lewis. *The Structure of Politics at the Accession of George III.* 2nd ed. London, 1957.

Nef, J. U. *Industry and Government in France and England, 1540–1640.* Ithaca, 1957.

Niebyl, Karl H. *Studies in Classical Theories of Money.* New York, 1946.

Owen, Robert Dale. *Threading My Way.* New York, 1874.

Pigou, A. C. *The Economics of Welfare.* Reprint of 4th ed. (1932) London, 1952.

Pressnell, L. S. *Country Banking in the Industrial Revolution.* Oxford, 1956.

——, ed. *Studies in the Industrial Revolution: Essays Presented to T. S. Ashton.* London, 1960.

Prothero, R. E. *English Farming Past and Present.* London, 1912.

Robertson, D. H. *Lectures on Economic Principles.* 3 vols. London, 1957–1959.

——. *Money.* Ed. C. W. Guillebaud and Milton Friedman. Chicago, 1962. (First published in 1929.)

Rosseaux, P. *Les Mouvements de fond de l'economie Anglaise, 1800–1913.* Louvain, 1938.

Rostow, W. W. *The British Economy of the Nineteenth Century.* Oxford, 1948.

Saul, S. B. *Studies in British Overseas Trade, 1870–1914.* Liverpool, 1960.

Saunders, Laurence James. *Scottish Democracy, 1815–1840: The Social and Intellectual Background.* Edinburgh, 1950.

Schumpeter, Elizabeth Boody. *English Overseas Trade Statistics, 1697–1808.* Oxford, 1960.

Scott, W. R. *The Constitution and Finance of English, Scottish, and Irish Joint-Stock Companies to 1720.* Cambridge, Eng., 1911.

Shaw, Wm. A. *Select Tracts and Documents Illustrative of English Monetary History, 1626–1730.* ("Wheeler Economic and Historical Reprints," no. 1.) London, 1935. (First printed in London in 1896.)

Smelser, Neil J. *Social Change in the Industrial Revolution: An Application of Theory to the Lancashire Cotton Industry, 1770–1840.* Chicago, 1959.

Sraffa, Piero, and M. H. Dobb, eds. *The Works and Correspondence of David Ricardo.* 10 vols. Cambridge, Eng., 1951–1955.

Steiner, William Howard, and Eli Shapiro. *Money and Banking.* rev. ed. New York, 1941.

Thomas, Samuel Evelyn. *The Rise and Growth of Joint Stock Banking.* Vol. I (only vol. published). London, 1934.

Toynbee, Mrs. Paget, ed. *Letters of Horace Walpole.* London, 1903–1905.

Tucker, G. S. L. *Progress and Profits in British Economic Thought, 1650–1850.* ("Cambridge Studies in Economic History.") Cambridge, Eng., 1960.

Unwin, George, Arthur Hulme, and George Taylor. *Samuel Oldknow and the Arkwrights.* Manchester, 1924.

Usher, A. P. *A History of Mechanical Inventions.* 1954 ed. rev. Boston, 1959.

Viner, Jacob. *International Trade and Economic Development.* Glencoe, Ill., 1952.

——. *The Long View and the Short: Studies in Economic Theory and Policy.* Glencoe, Ill., 1958.

——. *Studies in the Theory of International Trade.* New York, 1937.

Wadsworth, Alfred P., and Julia De Lacy Mann. *The Cotton Trade and Industrial Lancashire, 1600–1780.* Manchester, 1931.

Warren, George Frederick, and Frank Ashmore Pearson. *Gold and Prices*. London, 1935.

Webb, S. and B. *English Poor Law History*. Pt. 2, Vol. I. London, 1929.

Wood, George Henry. *The History of Wages in the Cotton Trade*. London, 1910.

Young, G. M., ed. *Early Victorian England, 1830–1865*. 2 vols. London, 1934.

Youngson, A. J. *Possibilities of Economic Progress*. Cambridge, Eng., 1959.

ARTICLES

Published before 1860

Kennedy, John. "Brief Notice of My Early Recollections," *Miscellaneous Papers on Subjects Connected with the Manufactures of Lancashire* (Manchester, 1849).

——. "Observations on the Rise and Progress of the Cotton Trade in Great Britain: Particularly in Lancashire and the Adjoining Counties," *Memoirs and Proceedings of the Literary and Philosophical Society of Manchester*, 2nd ser., III (1819), 115–137. Read Nov. 3, 1815.

Malthus, T. "Depreciation of Paper Currency," *Edinburgh Review*, XVII (Feb., 1811), 340–372.

The Manchester Magazine. 2 vols. (no others published); Manchester, 1815–1816.

Published after 1860

The following abbreviations will be used in this section:
Ec.H.R. Economic History Review
J.Ec.H. Journal of Economic History
Q.J.Ec. Quarterly Journal of Economics

Ashton, T. S. "The Bill of Exchange and Private Banks in Lancashire, 1790–1830," *Papers in English Monetary History*, ed. T. S. Ashton and R. S. Sayers (Oxford, 1953), pp. 37–49.

——. "Changes in the Standards of Comfort in Eighteenth Century

England" ("Raleigh Lecture on History"), *The Proceedings of the British Academy,* XLI (1955), 171–187.

——. "Essays in Bibliography and Criticism, XXX: Economic Fluctuations, 1790–1850," *Ec.H.R.,* 2nd ser., VII (1955), 377–381.

Ashworth, W. "British Industrial Villages in the Nineteenth Century," *Ec.H.R.,* 2nd ser., III (1951), 378–387.

Beales, H. L. "The 'Great Depression' in Industry and Trade," *Essays in Economic History: Reprints Edited for the Economic History Society,* ed. E. M. Carus-Wilson, I (London, 1954), 406–415.

Bennett, M. K. "British Wheat Yield per Acre for Seven Centuries," *Economic History,* III (1935), 12–29.

Berrill, K. E. "Essays in Bibliography and Criticism, XXXIV: Economic Growth," *Ec.H.R.,* 2nd ser., IX (1956), 359–363.

——. "International Trade and the Rate of Economic Growth," *Ec.H.R.,* 2nd ser., XII (1960), 351–359.

Blaug, M. "The Productivity of Capital in the Lancashire Cotton Industry during the Nineteenth Century," *Ec.H.R.,* 2nd ser., XIII (1961), 358–381.

Bowley, A. L. "Statistics of Wages in the United Kingdom during the Last Hundred Years," *Journal of the Royal Statistical Society,* LXII (1899), 140–151.

Broadbridge, S. A. "The Early Capital Market: The Lancashire and Yorkshire Railway," *Ec.H.R.,* 2nd ser., VIII (1955), 200–212.

Buckatzsch, E. J. "The Geographical Distribution of Wealth in England, 1086–1843," *Ec.H.R.,* 2nd ser., III (1950), 180–201.

Cairncross, A. K. "Essays in Bibliography and Criticism, XLV: The Stages of Economic Growth," *Ec.H.R.,* 2nd ser., XIII (1961), 450–458.

Carter, A. "Dutch Foreign Investment, 1738–1800," *Economica,* N.S., XX (1953), 322–340.

——. "Note on a 'Note on Yardsticks,'" *Ec.H.R.,* 2nd ser., XII (1960), 440–444.

Chambers, J. D. "Enclosure and Labour Supply in the Industrial Revolution," *Ec.H.R.,* 2nd ser., V (1953), 319–343.

Checkland, S. G. "Growth and Progress: The Nineteenth Century View in Britain," *Ec.H.R.,* 2nd ser., XII (1959), 49–62.

——. "John Gladstone as Trader and Planter," *Ec.H.R.,* 2nd ser., VII (1954), 216–229.

Coleman, D. C. "Industrial Growth and Industrial Revolutions," *Essays in Economic History: Reprints Edited for the Economic History Society,* ed. E. M. Carus-Wilson, III (London, 1962), 334–352.

Collier, F. "Samuel Greg and the Styal Mill," *Memoirs and Proceedings of the Manchester Literary and Philosophical Society,* LXXXV (1941–1943), 139–156.

Connell, K. H. "Land and Population in Ireland, 1780–1845," *Ec.H.R.,* 2nd ser., II (1950), 278–289.

——. "The Population of Ireland in the 18th Century," *Ec.H.R.,* 1st ser., XVI (1946), 111–124.

Daniels, G. W. "The Early Records of a Manchester Cotton-Spinning Firm," *Economic Journal,* XXV (1915), 175–188.

Davies, E. "Essays in Bibliography and Criticism, XLIV: Empire and Capital," *Ec.H.R.,* 2nd ser., XIII (1960), 105–110.

——. "The Small Landowner, 1780–1832, in the Light of the Land Tax Assessments," *Essays in Economic History: Reprints Edited for the Economic History Society,* ed. E. M. Carus-Wilson, I (London, 1954), 87–113.

Davis, Ralph. "English Foreign Trade, 1700–1774," *Ec.H.R.,* 2nd ser., XV (1962), 285–303.

Farnie, D. A. "The Commercial Empire of the Atlantic, 1607–1783," *Ec.H.R.,* 2nd ser., XV (1962), 205–218.

Felix, David. "Profit Inflation and Industrial Growth: The Historical Record and Contemporary Analogies," *Q.J.Ec.,* LXX (1956), 441–463.

Fitton, R. S. "Overseas Trade during the Napoleonic Wars, as Illustrated by the Records of W. G. and J. Strutt," *Economica,* N.S., XX (1953), 53–60.

Flinn, M. W. "The Poor Employment Act of 1817," *Ec.H.R.,* 2nd ser., XIV (1961), 82–92.

Fussell, G. E., and M. Compton. "Agricultural Adjustment after the Napoleonic Wars," *Economic History,* III (1939), 184–204.

Gilboy, Elizabeth W. "The Cost of Living and Real Wages in 18th Century England," *Review of Economic Statistics,* XVIII, no. 3 (Aug. 1936), 134–143.

——. "Wages in Eighteenth Century England," *Journal of Economic and Business History,* II (1929–1930), 603–629.

Gould, J. D. "Agricultural Fluctuations and the English Economy in the Eighteenth Century," *J.Ec.H.*, XXII (1962), 313–333.

Gray, Malcolm. "The Abolition of Runrig in the Highlands of Scotland," *Ec.H.R.*, 2nd ser., V (1952), 46–57.

Habakkuk, H. J. "English Population in the Eighteenth Century," *Ec.H.R.*, 2nd ser., VI (1953), 117–133.

——. "Essays in Bibliography and Criticism, XXXII: The Eighteenth Century," *Ec.H.R.*, 2nd ser., VIII (1956), 434–438.

——. "Family Structure and Economic Change in Nineteenth-Century Europe," *J.Ec.H.*, XV (1955), 1–12.

——. "New Viewpoints on the Economic History of Europe: The Economic History of Modern Britain," *J.Ec.H.*, XVIII (1958), 486–501.

Hamilton, Earl J. "American Treasure and the Rise of Capitalism," *Economica*, XXVII (1929), 338–357.

——. "Prices and Progress," *J.Ec.H.*, XII (1952), 325–349.

——. "Profit Inflation and the Industrial Revolution, 1751–1800," *Q.J.Ec.*, LVI (1942), 256–273.

Hammarström, Ingrid. "The 'Price Revolution' of the Sixteenth Century: Some Swedish Evidence," *Scandinavian Economic History Review*, V (1957), 118–155.

Hancock, W. K. "Essays in Bibliography and Criticism, XXVII: The Under-Developed Economies," *Ec.H.R.*, 2nd ser., VI (1954), 310–315.

Hartwell, R. M. "Interpretations of the Industrial Revolution in England: A Methodological Inquiry," *J.Ec.H.*, XIX (1959), 229–249.

——. "The Rising Standard of Living in England, 1800–1850," *Ec.H.R.*, 2nd ser., XIII (1961), 397–416.

Hayek, F. A. von. "A Note on the Development of the Doctrine of 'Forced Saving,'" *Q.J.Ec.*, XLVII (1932), 123–133.

Heaton, Herbert. "Criteria of Periodization in Economic History," *J.Ec.H.*, XV (1955), 267–272.

Heckscher, Eli. "Multilateralism, Baltic Trade, and the Mercantilists," *Ec.H.R.*, 2nd ser., III (1950), 219–228.

Hilton, G. W. "The Truck Act of 1831," *Ec.H.R.*, 2nd ser., X (1958), 470–479.

Hobsbawm, E. J. "The British Standard of Living, 1790–1850," *Ec.H.R.*, 2nd ser., X (1957), 46–68.

Horsefield, J. K. "The Duties of a Banker: II," *Papers in English Monetary History*, ed. T. S. Ashton and R. S. Sayers (Oxford, 1953), pp. 16–36.

Hunt, H. G. "The Chronology of Parliamentary Enclosure in Leicestershire," *Ec.H.R.*, 2nd ser., X (1957), 265–72.

Hyde, F. E., B. B. Parkinson, and Sheila Marriner. "The Cotton Broker and the Rise of the Liverpool Cotton Market," *Ec.H.R.*, 2nd ser., VIII (1955), 75–83.

Imlah, Albert H. "British Balance of Payments and the Export of Capital, 1816–1913," *Ec.H.R.*, 2nd ser., V (1952), 208–239.

Jevons, W. Stanley. "On the Variation of Prices and the Value of Currency since 1782," *Investigations in Currency and Finance*, ed. H. S. Foxwell (London, 1884), pp. 119–150.

John, A. H. "Insurance Investment and the London Money Market of the 18th Century," *Economica*, N.S., XX (1953), 137–158.

Joslin, D. M. "London Bankers in Wartime, 1739–1784," *Studies in the Industrial Revolution: Essays Presented to T. S. Ashton*, ed. L. S. Pressnell (London, 1960), pp. 156–177.

——. "London Private Bankers, 1720–1785," *Ec.H.R.*, 2nd ser., VII (1954), 167–186.

Koebner, R. "Adam Smith and the Industrial Revolution," *Ec.H.R.*, 2nd ser., XI (1959), 381–391.

Kondratieff, N. D. "Die Preisdynamik der industriellen und landwirtschaftlichen Waren," *Archiv für Sozialwissenschaft und Sozialpolitik*, LX (1928–1929), 1–85.

Krause, J. T. "Changes in English Fertility and Mortality, 1781–1850," *Ec.H.R.*, 2nd ser., XI (1958), 52–70.

——. "Some Neglected Factors in the English Industrial Revolution," *J.Ec.H.*, XIX (1959), 528–540.

Leuilliot, Paul. "The Industrial Revolution in France," *J.Ec.H.*, XVII (1957), 245–254.

Maitland, F. W. "Trust and Corporation" (1904), *Maitland: Selected Essays*, ed. H. D. Hazeltine, G. Lapsley, and P. H. Winfield (Cambridge, 1936), pp. 141–222.

Marshall, T. H. "The Population in England and Wales from the Industrial Revolution to the World War," *Ec.H.R.*, V (1935), 65–78.

——. "The Population Problem during the Industrial Revolution: A Note on the Present State of the Controversy," *Economic History*, I (1929), 429–456.

Marwick, W. H. "A Bibliography of Works on Scottish Economic History Published during the Last Twenty Years," *Ec.H.R.*, 2nd ser., IV (1952), 376–382.

——. "The Cotton Industry and the Industrial Revolution in Scotland," *Scottish Historical Review*, XXI, no. 83 (April 1924), 207–218.

Mauro, F. "Towards an Intercontinental Model: European Overseas Expansion between 1500 and 1800," *Ec.H.R.*, 2nd ser., XIV (1961), 1–17.

Mitchell, G. M. "The English and Scottish Cotton Industries: A Study in Interrelation," *Scottish Historical Review*, XXII, no. 86 (Jan. 1925), 104–114.

Musgrove, C. F. "Middle Class Education and Employment in the Nineteenth Century," *Ec.H.R.*, 2nd ser., XII (1959), 99–111.

Musson, A. E., and E. Robinson. "The Early Growth of Steam Power," *Ec.H.R.*, 2nd ser., XI (1959), 418–439.

Nef, John U. "A Comparison of Industrial Growth in France and England from 1540 to 1640," *Journal of Political Economy*, XLIV (1936), 289–317, 505–533, and 643–666.

——. "Prices and Industrial Capitalism in France and England, 1540–1640," *Ec.H.R.*, VII (1937), 155–185. Reprinted in *Essays in Economic History: Reprints Edited for the Economic History Society*, ed. E. M. Carus-Wilson, I (London, 1954), 108–134.

North, Douglass. "Ocean Freight Rates and Economic Development, 1750–1913," *J.Ec.H.*, XVIII (1958), 537–555.

Pares, Richard. "Economic Factors in the History of Empire," *Essays in Economic History: Reprints Edited for the Economic History Society*, ed. E. M. Carus-Wilson, I (London, 1954), 416–438.

Parker, R. A. C. "Coke of Norfolk and the Agrarian Revolution," *Ec.H.R.*, 2nd ser., VIII (1955), 156–166.

284

Perkin, H. J. "Middle-Class Education and Employment in the Nineteenth Century: A Critical Note," *Ec.H.R.*, 2nd ser., XIV (1961), 122–130.

Pollard, S. "Investment, Consumption and the Industrial Revolution," *Ec.H.R.*, 2nd ser., XI (1958), 215–226.

Pollins, Harold. "The Finances of the Liverpool and Manchester Railway," *Ec.H.R.*, 2nd ser., V (1952), 90–97.

——. "The Marketing of Shares in the First Half of the Nineteenth Century," *Ec.H.R.*, 2nd ser., VII (1954), 230–239.

Postan, M. M. "Essays in Bibliography and Criticism, XXIII: Economic Growth," *Ec.H.R.*, 2nd ser., VI (1953), 78–83.

——. "Recent Trends in the Accumulation of Capital," *Ec.H.R.*, 1st ser., VI (1935), 1–12.

Pressnell, L. S. "Public Monies and the Development of English Banking," *Ec.H.R.*, 2nd ser., V (1953), 378–397.

——. "The Rate of Interest in the Eighteenth Century," *Studies in the Industrial Revolution,* ed. L. S. Pressnell (London, 1960), 178–214.

Robertson, M. L. "Scottish Commerce and the American War of Independence," *Ec.H.R.*, 2nd ser., IX (1956), 123–131.

Rostow, W. W. "The Interrelation of Theory and Economic History," *J.Ec. H.*, XVII (1957), 509–523.

——. "The Stages of Economic Growth," *Ec.H.R.*, 2nd ser., XII (1959), 1–16.

——. "The Terms of Trade in Theory and Practice," *Ec.H.R.*, 2nd ser., III (1950), 1–20.

Sauerbeck, Augustus. "Prices of Commodities and the Precious Metals," *Journal of the Royal Statistical Society,* XLIX (1886), 581–648.

Sayers, Richard Sidney. "Ricardo's Views on Monetary Questions," *Papers in English Monetary History,* ed. T. S. Ashton and R. S. Sayers (Oxford, 1953).

[Schumpeter], Elizabeth Boody. "English Prices and Public Finance, 1660–1822," *Review of Economic Statistics,* XX (1938), 21–37.

Seltzer, Lawrence. "The Mobility of Capital," *Q.J.Ec.,* XLVI (1931–1932), 496–507.

Shannon, H. A. "The Coming of General Limited Liability," *Essays in Economic History: Reprints Edited for the Economic History Society,* ed. E. M. Carus-Wilson, I (London, 1954), 359–379.

Silberling, Norman J. "British Prices and Business Cycles, 1780–1850," *Review of Economic Statistics,* V (1923), 219–262.

Solomon, Morton R. "The Structure of the Market in Undeveloped Economies," *Q.J.Ec.,* LXII (1948), 519–541.

Spring, David. "The English Landed Estate in the Age of Coal and Iron: 1830–1880," *J.Ec.H.,* XI (1951), 3–24.

——. "English Landownership in the Nineteenth Century: A Critical Note," *Ec.H.R.,* 2nd ser., IX (1957), 472–484.

Stern, Walter M. "The Isle of Dogs Canal: A Study in Early Public Investment," *Ec.H.R.,* 2nd ser., IV (1952), 472–484.

Tate, W. E. "The Cost of Parliamentary Enclosure in England (with Special Reference to the County of Oxford)," *Ec.H.R.,* 2nd ser., V (1952), 258–265.

Taylor, A. J. "Concentration and Specialization in the Lancashire Cotton Industry, 1825–1850," *Ec.H.R.,* 2nd ser., I (1948), 114–122.

——. "Progress and Poverty in Britain, 1780–1850," *History,* XLV (1960), 16–31.

Thompson, F. M. L. "The End of a Great Estate," *Ec.H.R.,* 2nd ser., VIII (1955), 36–52.

——. "English Landownership: The Ailesbury Trust, 1832–1856," *Ec.H.R.,* 2nd ser., XI (1958), 121–132.

Tucker, Rufus S. "Real Wages of Artisans in London, 1729–1935," *Journal of the American Statistical Society,* XXXI (1936), 73–84.

Unwin, George. "Indian Factories in the 18th Century," *Studies in Economic History: The Collected Papers of George Unwin,* ed. R. H. Tawney (London, 1927).

——. "Introduction," in G. W. Daniels, *The Early English Cotton Industry* (Manchester, 1920).

Viner, Jacob. "Clapham on the Bank of England," *The Long View and the Short: Studies in Economic Theory and Policy* (Glencoe, Ill., 1958).

Wilson, Charles H. "Mercantilism: Some Vicissitudes of an Idea," *Ec.H.R.,* X (1957), 181–188.

——. "Treasure and Trade Balances: Further Evidence," *Ec.H.R.,* 2nd ser., IV (1951), 231–242.

———. "Treasure and Trade Balances: The Mercantilist Problem," *Ec.H.R.*, 2nd ser., II (1949), 152–161.

Wood, George H. "Real Wages and the Standard of Comfort since 1850," *Journal of the Royal Statistical Society*, LXXIII (1909), 91–103.

Woodruff, W. "Capitalism and the Historians: A Contribution to the Discussion on the Industrial Revolution in England," *J.Ec.H.*, XVI (1956), 1–17.

Wrigley, E. A. "The Supply of Raw Materials in the Industrial Revolution," *Ec.H.R.*, 2nd ser., XV (1962), 1–16.

REFERENCE WORKS

Dictionary of National Biography. London, 1961. Founded in 1822 by George Smith.

Encyclopaedia Britannica. 11th ed. New York, 1911.

McCulloch, J. R. *Commercial Dictionary.* London, 1837.

Palgrave's Dictionary of Political Economy. Ed. H. Higgs. 3 vols. London, 1918–1926.

Index

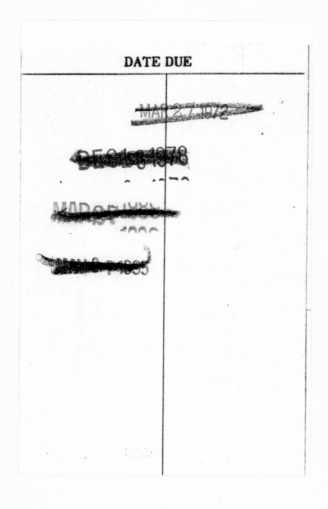